A Teacher's Guide To

multisensory
LEARNING

Improving Literacy by Engaging the Senses

A Teacher's Guide To

multisensory
LEARNING

Improving Literacy by Engaging the Senses

Lawrence Baines

Association for Supervision and Curriculum Development
Alexandria, Virginia USA

Association for Supervision and Curriculum Development
1703 N. Beauregard St. • Alexandria, VA 22311-1714 USA
Phone: 800-933-2723 or 703-578-9600 • Fax: 703-575-5400
Web site: www.ascd.org • E-mail: member@ascd.org
Author guidelines: www.ascd.org/write

Gene R. Carter, *Executive Director;* Nancy Modrak, *Publisher;* Julie Houtz, *Director of Book Editing & Production;* Leah Lakins, *Project Manager;* Cathy Guyer, *Senior Graphic Designer;* BMWW, *Typesetter;* Sarah Plumb, *Production Specialist;* Mike Kaylan, *Production Manager*

All Web links in this book are correct as of the publication date below but may have become inactive or otherwise modified since that time. If you notice a deactivated or changed link, please e-mail books@ascd.org with the words "Link Update" in the subject line. In your message, please specify the Web link, the book title, and the page number on which the link appears.

PAPERBACK ISBN: 978-1-4166-0713-7   •   ASCD product #108009   •   n10/08
Also available as an e-book through ebrary, netLibrary, and many online booksellers (see Books in Print for the ISBNs).

Quantity discounts for the paperback edition only: 10–49 copies, 10%; 50+ copies, 15%; for 1,000 or more copies, call 800-933-2723, ext. 5634, or 703-575-5634. For desk copies: member@ascd.org.

Library of Congress Cataloging-in-Publication Data

Baines, Lawrence.
   A teacher's guide to multisensory learning : improving literacy by engaging the senses / Lawrence Baines.
      p. cm.
   Includes bibliographical references and index.
      ISBN 978-1-4166-0713-7 (pbk. : alk. paper)   1. Language arts.   2. Perceptual learning.   3. Teaching—Aids and devices.   I. Title.

   LB1576.B245 2008
   371.3–dc22   2008021542

A Teacher's Guide to
Multisensory LEARNING

Improving Literacy by Engaging the Senses

■   ■   ■

To Judith Daso Herb,
a woman of vision and compassion

Acknowledgments ■ ■ ■

I extend my thanks to the many people whose contributions enriched this book: For their work in Chapter 3, David James Poissant of Tucson, Arizona; Mike Angelotti of Norman, Oklahoma; and Debra Winston of Carbondale, Colorado. For their work in Chapter 4, Chris Goering of the University of Arkansas; and Mark Rabbit and Rob Deckard of Toledo, Ohio. For their work in Chapter 6, Lesley Kahle of Tampa, Florida; Robert Masters III of Temperance, Michigan; and Matt Copeland of Topeka, Kansas. For their work in Chapter 7, Pamela Sissi Carroll of Tallahassee, Florida; and Michael W. Kibby, William J. Rapaport, Karen M. Wieland, and Debra A. Dechert of Buffalo, New York. I'm grateful to Berenice Felix-Diaz of Irving, Texas, for sharing a beautiful quotation from one of her young students.

Special thanks to David Pyles and Lori Keleman, who over a period of three-and-a-half years helped me gather enough books and articles to fill 16 filing cabinets; 34 cardboard boxes; all the drawers of my massive, clunky desk; and half the floor of my office. Thanks to Mom, Dad, and my wife Coleen for help with editing and for dispensing much-needed warm fuzzies.

Introduction ■ ■ ■

Yo puedo oler el perfume de las flores que planta cada año mi Tía Maria. Leyendo bajo los árboles un libro perfecto a mi primita, me siento mágica. Jugando y disfrutando con mi prima junto al aire fresco de otoño, yo pienso, "Que rico el aire que salpica en mi cara." Después de que me canso de jugar siento al misma vez paz y sueno.

I can smell the perfume of the flowers planted each year by Aunt Maria. Reading a perfect book to my little cousin under the arbor, I feel the magic. Playing together with my cousin in the outdoors, I think, "The rich air sprinkles in my face." In time, I tire of playing, but I feel the peace nevertheless.

—3rd grade student of Berenice Felix-Diaz, Irving, Texas

Two of the greatest challenges for teachers in the years ahead will be student engagement and achievement. Multisensory learning techniques provide an effective, highly adaptable method for addressing both. The premise of multisensory learning is simple. When students invoke more than one sense, simultaneously or over a period of time, they tend to interact with the material more intensely and thereby retain what they have learned for longer periods of time. In multisensory learning, a teacher engages students through hands-on, visual, auditory, and olfactory stimuli, then links the activity to relevant academic objectives. It is through the reciprocal relationship between sensory input and thinking that multisensory techniques gain their power.

Sensory input without thought yields only transitory sensations. If you notice a funny smell in the classroom one day but are too tired to bother identifying it, then a natural gas leak might go undetected for weeks. Without a reason to remember sensory input, the information communicated via the senses disappears. How many windows do you have in your classroom? How many floor tiles? Although you teach in your classroom every day, unless you have a reason to keep such information in your head, the sensory input is lost.

On the other hand, thought without sensory input is difficult to retain. Anyone who has tried to study for a mathematics exam by memorizing formulas or slogged through pages of abstruse musings in philosophy journals knows the difficulties of trying to learn through abstraction without the benefit of real, sensory experience.

For purposes of illustration, assume that an academic objective is for students to learn the definition of the word *mephitic* (which means offensive smelling or noxious). A traditional approach for teaching new vocabulary has been for students to copy a word three times, write its definition, then use it in a sentence. "It was mephitic" is the kind of sentence that students in my classes used to write when I made such a request.

Teaching the meaning of *mephitic* through multisensory stimuli would constitute a dramatic departure for both teacher and learner. Instead of having students flip through the pages of a dictionary to find and record a formalized definition they might not comprehend, a teacher would ask students to picture in their minds a foul-smelling odor. After students discussed the images in their minds that related to a foul-smelling odor, the teacher would show a photo of a chicken farm, an outhouse, and a smokestack emitting black puffs of industrial waste—all visual representations of *mephitic*. At the appearance of each image, the teacher would point to the word *mephitic*, perhaps written on the board in a large font, and pronounce it. Students would repeat "Mephitic!" after hearing the pronunciation by the teacher. Finally, the teacher would walk students outside to a safe area on the school grounds—perhaps a grassy patch of land or a piece of empty asphalt. After students gathered around, the teacher would spray a fetid scent into the air. As students pinched their noses and complained about the smell, the teacher would say, "Mephitic."

Learning the meaning and pronunciation of *mephitic* through such a process would take approximately the same amount of time as using the "write three times/define/use in a sentence" approach. Yet, students who participated in the multisensory experience of *mephitic* would likely retain the word's meaning for the next 60 years, whereas students participating in the quiet seatwork lesson likely would not retain the meaning until the end of the class period.

The tenets of multisensory learning are already familiar to the handful of specialized doctors, psychiatrists, and educators who routinely work with individuals with severely impaired mental capacities. The research base that affirms the power of using multisensory approaches with learning-disabled children and adults is vast and growing—I cite only a fraction of the available studies in this book.

In reading descriptions of the quantum leaps in motivation and achievement experienced by participants in multisensory studies, I have marveled that the techniques were not co-opted by teachers years ago. Because multisensory approaches have been used effectively with populations of profoundly disabled students, it seems logical that similar techniques would work in classrooms of the nondisabled. Yet multisensory techniques remain relatively obscure in nontherapeutic settings such as classrooms.

Instead of focusing on making learning more engaging, relevant, and enduring, the emphasis in some schools seems to be on assigning and assessing. Often, the specter of the state standardized exam is the rationale used to justify a seemingly intractable assign-and-assess approach to learning. However, assign and assess has proven time and again that it can deliver, at best, mediocre academic results of limited duration, even when the sole unit of measurement is the test score. Indeed, how unsatisfying it must be to teach expressly to a narrow, predetermined curriculum for the purpose of documenting tiny, ephemeral increments in test scores.

When a student is asked to read a story silently from a textbook and answer the questions at the end of the story in complete sentences, what is being learned? Basically, such an exercise evaluates a student's ability to perform two tasks:

1. To independently extract meaning from dark squiggles on a page (words).
2. To communicate a précis of the meaning of the squiggles to an audience of one—the teacher.

In this scenario, the teacher is not doing anything to influence the understanding of words or the formulation of a written response. The teacher has merely assigned a task, then assessed the extent to which students can independently perform the task. There has been no discovery, no interaction, no risk, no negotiation, no learning. Of course, silent reading is an essential practice, but the point is that an assign-and-assess approach teaches little. Assigning and assessing do not alter the behaviors in which students already engage; this approach merely involves recording them.

On the other hand, multisensory techniques have the power to be transformative—to change student behavior. In contrast to the somber routine of assign and assess, multisensory techniques can make learning enjoyable.

In this book, I offer an argument for the use of multisensory techniques as a foundational strategy for teaching. Chapter 1 describes the dramatic changes in the use of leisure time and the decline in reading among children and young adults in the recent past. Students who inhabit schools today truly possess different talents, skills, and weaknesses than students who preceded them. Chapter 1 explains how and why students are different and emphasizes the urgency of developing a more engaging and authentic approach to instruction, especially in light of the centrality of literacy to 21st century skills, as noted by a plethora of special commission reports and recommendations.

Chapter 2 offers a brief overview of the history, milestones, and seminal studies in fields related to multisensory learning. One major point of the chapter is that teaching through abstract representation is one of the least effective methods for cultivating learning. Unfortunately, because it is easy to implement, teaching through abstract representation continues to be among the most popular instructional methods in schools today.

Chapters 3 to 6 describe specific research relating to each sense— sight, sound, smell and taste, movement and touch—with commentary on a few studies that seem especially pertinent to teachers. Chapters 3 to 6 also feature proven multisensory lessons straight from the classroom, many replete with samples of student work.

Chapter 7 asserts the importance of making learning fun. Through ingenious simulations, these final activities demonstrate the effectiveness of learning through a sense of play.

To close the loop, samples of student work and grading criteria are included with most activities. To provide consistency, I adapted the 6-point scale commonly used by the National Assessment of Educational Progress (NAEP) to assess competence in writing. This 6-point scale is also widely used in various state assessments across the country. In the NAEP system, the basic evaluation system is as follows:

0	1	2	3	4	5	6
No response	Unsatisfactory	Insufficient	Uneven	Sufficient	Skillful	Excellent

Sometimes, when perusing the assessment criteria of state or other national tests, teachers can get confused over what would appear to be different evaluation instruments. For example, in some reports, a 5-point scale is used. In most cases, this 5-point scale is the same as the 6-point scale except that the categories of 0 (no response) and 1 (unsatisfactory response) are combined.

0 No response or unsatisfactory response	1 Insufficient	2 Uneven	3 Sufficient	4 Skillful	5 Excellent

Sometimes, even a 4-point scale is used. For example, in some reports, the NAEP will use the terms *advanced, proficient, basic*, and *below basic* as classifications to characterize student competence. Again, this is a 6-point scale in disguise, with 6 associated with advanced (or excellent), 5 with proficient (or skillful), 4 with basic (or sufficient), and all scores below 4 as below basic (uneven, insufficient, unsatisfactory, and no response).

0	1	2	3	4	5	6
No response	Unsatisfactory	Insufficient	Uneven	Sufficient	Skillful	Excellent
Below basic	Below basic	Below basic	Below basic	Basic	Proficient	Advanced

The general guidelines for placing student work in the 4-point scale categories are listed in Figure 1.

Figure 1   General Guidelines for Categories in 4-Point Scale

Grade 4

Basic/ Below Basic	• Is somewhat organized • Includes some supporting details • Has some mistakes in grammar, spelling, and capitalization that get in the way of meaning
Proficient	• Is organized • Includes supporting details • Demonstrates audience awareness through form, content, and language • Has some mistakes in grammar, spelling, and capitalization, but they do not interfere with meaning
Advanced	• Is clearly organized • Has a consistent topic or theme • Has a logical sequence • Includes details • Has a clearly marked beginning and ending • Shows evidence of precise and varied language • May show signs of analytical, evaluative, or creative thinking • Has grammar, spelling, and capitalization errors that are so few and so minor that a reader can easily skim over them

Grade 8

Basic/ Below Basic	• Demonstrates a general understanding of the task • Shows awareness of the audience • Provides some supporting details • Has some mistakes in grammar, spelling, and capitalization that get in the way of meaning
Proficient	• Is organized • Includes supporting details • Uses precise language • Uses varied sentence structure • Demonstrates audience awareness through form, content, and language • Shows analytical, evaluative, or creative thinking • Has some mistakes in grammar, spelling, and capitalization, but they do not interfere with meaning
Advanced	• Is clearly and consistently organized • Is logically sequenced • Is fully developed • Includes details and elaboration • Uses strategies such as analogies, illustrations, examples, anecdotes, or figurative language to clarify a point • Shows some analytical, evaluative, or creative thinking • Uses precise word choice • Uses varied sentence structure • May show signs of analytical, evaluative, or creative thinking • Has few errors in grammar, spelling, punctuation, capitalization, and sentence structure; demonstrates good control of these elements and may use them for stylistic effect

Figure 1 *(continued)*	

Grade 12

Basic/ Below Basic	• Demonstrates understanding of task and audience • Shows some analytical, evaluative, or creative thinking • Includes details that support and develop the central idea • Is clearly organized, making use of techniques such as a consistency in topic or theme, sequencing, and a clear introduction and conclusion • Demonstrates enough accuracy in grammar, spelling, punctuation, and capitalization to communicate to a reader; may have some errors, but these should not get in the way of meaning
Proficient	• Provides effective and fully developed response • Uses analytical, evaluative, or creative thinking • Is coherent, using techniques such as a consistent theme, sequencing, and a clear introduction and conclusion • Includes details and elaborations that support and develop the main idea • Uses precise language • Uses variety in sentence structure • Contains few errors in grammar, spelling, punctuation, capitalization, and sentence structure; demonstrates a command of these elements and may use them for stylistic effect
Advanced	• Provides a mature and sophisticated response • Uses analytical, evaluative, or creative thinking • Is fully developed, incorporates details and elaboration that support and extend the main idea • Demonstrates use of literary strategies—anecdotes and repetition, for example—to develop ideas • Well crafted, organized, and coherent • Incorporates techniques such as consistency in topic or theme, sequencing, and a clear introduction and conclusion • Uses compelling language, precise word choice • Uses variety in sentence structure • Contains few errors in grammar, spelling, punctuation, capitalization, and sentence structure; demonstrates a sophisticated command of these elements and may use them for stylistic effect in their work

Source: Adapted from *National Assessment of Educational Progress Achievement Levels 1992–1998 for Writing* by S. Loomis & M. Bourque (Eds.), 2001, Washington, DC: U.S. Department of Education.

Because more than half of American students score at or below basic on NAEP writing assessments (National Assessment of Educational Progress, 2003), I recommend using a 6-point scale. Scores of 0, 1, 2, and 3 help delineate exactly how much below basic a student might be. Otherwise, a student scoring at Level 1 who advances to Level 3 over time would still receive the identical ranking of below basic.

The NAEP assesses students at the 4th, 8th, and 12th grade levels in several subject areas—the arts, civics, economics, foreign language, geography, mathematics, reading, science, U.S. history, world history, and writing. As the issue of national examinations heats up, it is inevitable that the NAEP will become a focal point for discussion. Over the years, the NAEP has gained a fine reputation as a reliable and valid indicator of national student achievement (Loomis & Bourque, 2001). The problem with the NAEP has never been the accuracy of its tests, but students' lackluster performance on them.

1

Literacy and
Academic Standards ▪ ▪ ▪

*Only 51 percent of 2005 ACT-tested high school graduates are
ready for college-level reading.*

—ACT, 2006, p. 1

*In 2002, 28 percent of 4th-graders, 31 percent of 8th-graders, and
24 percent of 12th-graders performed at or above the Proficient
level in writing. . . . Only 2 percent of students in each grade
performed at Advanced.*

—National Center for Education Statistics, 2005, p. 50

1996 was a pivotal year. It was the year that Dolly the sheep was cloned
from a cell taken from the udder of an adult sheep, the year of two U.S.
space launches to Mars (Mars Global Surveyor and Mars Pathfinder), and
the year newly reelected President Bill Clinton signed the Telecommu-
nications Act, which helped wire public schools throughout the United
States to the Internet. The year also marked a fundamental change in the
ways that students chose to spend their free time.

In 1996, people in the United States still spent more time reading books
than surfing the Internet. However, since 1996, as use of nonprint media
has surged, reading—especially reading books—has been on the decline.

An overwhelming volume of research (from media research firm Veronis Suhler Stevenson, the U.S. Census Bureau, the Department of Labor, the Kaiser Family Foundation, and the National Institute for the Humanities) indicates that time students spend reading is getting crowded out by time spent with electronic media—particularly, video games and, of course, television.

The Internet

The Internet serves as a vast, immediate source of information. Believe it or not, however, most adolescents do not go online to read Voltaire or Vonnegut, although we might wish they did. Recent studies of teen behavior on the Internet (Gross, 2004; Nielsen, 2005; Rainie & Horrigan, 2005) confirm that adolescents usually surf to find images and music, send e-mail or instant messages, or play online games. Very few students sign onto the Internet looking for reading material. A teen's proclivity for seeking sound and images on the Internet holds true across categories of gender and race.

As indicated in Figure 1.1, the average number of hours per year spent on the Internet increased from around 10 hours in 1996 to 194 hours by 2005. During the same time frame, reading dropped from around 100 hours per year to 84 hours per year (Veronis Suhler Stevenson Communications Group, 2005). Corroborating data from the U.S. Census Bureau (2005) reveal that the smallest segment of book purchasers are age 25 and younger. Although people 35 to 54 years old accounted for about half of all book sales in 2003, people under 25 accounted for less than 4 percent, a percentage that has been dropping since 1996. A study sponsored by the National Endowment for the Arts (2004b) found a precipitous decline in the reading of literature. The steepest declines in reading literature were found among adolescents and young adults.

> Over the past 20 years, young adults (18–34) have declined from being those most likely to read literature to those least likely. . . . The rate of decline for the youngest adults (18–24) is 55 percent greater than that of the total adult population. (p. ix)

Video Games

The Internet is not the only medium to integrate itself into the daily lives of students. The year 1996 also marked the launch of the Nintendo 64

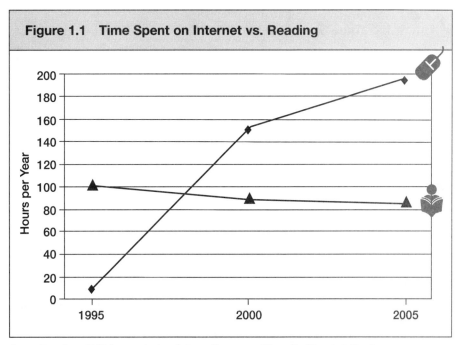

Figure 1.1   Time Spent on Internet vs. Reading

Source: Data from *2004 Communications Industry Forecast and Report* by Veronis Suhler Stevenson Communications Group, 2005, New York: Author. Adapted with permission.

game system in the United States. Soon thereafter, the video game industry began making billions of dollars more than the motion picture industry (Gaudiosi, 2003; Levine, 2006). In terms of hours spent per year (see Figure 1.2), video games have mirrored the rise of the Internet. Half of all people in the United States play video games for an average of 8 hours per week. Of course, video game players are predominantly children ages 5 to 18, who constitute more than half of game players (Entertainment Software Association, 2005).

Last year, I became acquainted with a 17-year-old boy at a local high school who was a video game fanatic. Chris was a good-looking, popular boy who made *A*s and *B*s in his classes, had a girlfriend, and worked part time at a fast food restaurant on the weekends. Although Chris appeared to be a typical high school junior, his schedule was a little unusual. On Sunday through Thursday nights, he ate dinner with his family around 5 p.m. and went to sleep at 6 p.m. Then, he woke up at midnight, logged onto the Internet, and played video games until 7 the next morning when he would get ready for school. According to Chris, his "video game lifestyle" was fully supported by his parents, who seemed thankful that he had few other "bad habits."

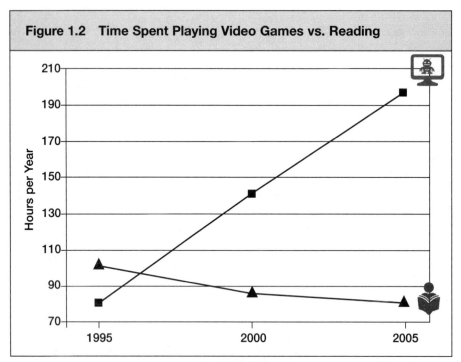

Figure 1.2   Time Spent Playing Video Games vs. Reading

Source: Data from *2004 Communications Industry Forecast and Report* by Veronis Suhler Stevenson Communications Group, 2005, New York: Author. Adapted with permission.

Like most video game players, Chris predicted that the time he spent playing video games would only increase over time (Entertainment Software Association, 2005), although that prospect seems difficult to fathom. When asked how long he planned on keeping up his odd schedule, Chris responded, "For as long as I can."

If you try to start up a conversation with a group of students at school, do not mention books, writers, or the names of historical figures—they will not know them. To see students as young as 5 years old get animated and excited, bring up the titles of the latest video games. In their infancy, video games were developed for a predominantly male audience, but that has changed over the past few years, as females now account for almost half of the video game players (Entertainment Software Association, 2005). More than 228 million video games were sold in 2005, roughly two games for every U.S. household (U.S. Census Bureau, 2005). The largest growth in video games is expected to be in mobile and online gaming (Veronis Suhler Stevenson Communications Group, 2006). About half of American households own a Nintendo game, and the best-selling video game of all time is probably *Super Mario Bros.*, which sold more than 40 million copies (Guinness World Records, 2008). However, when I recently brought up

Mario to a group of middle school children, I was promptly informed that Mario, even in his recently updated form, is "still kind of cool, but way old" these days.

Television

As a medium, television has neared the point of saturation in the United States. On any given day, more than 90 percent of people in the United States tune in to television for at least a few hours. Of U.S. households, 99 percent have at least one television, and more than 70 percent have cable TV. Of those households with incomes over $50,000, cable TV is present in 90 percent of homes (Energy Information Administration, 2006). The average number of TV sets per household is 2.5, and two-thirds of U.S. homes have three or more sets. Over the past few years, the bedrooms of children have turned into media bunkers—68 percent of 8- to 18-year-olds have TVs there, 54 percent have VCRs or DVD players, and 37 percent have cable TV (Kaiser Family Foundation, 2005). The explosion of media available in the bedroom means that "Go to your room" has taken on a whole new meaning. No longer a threat, "Go to your room" has become a treat, equivalent to a trip to the movies or the local arcade in earlier eras.

Since 1996, television has expanded its domain from the privacy of the home into an ever-increasing number of venues. TV screens have become commonplace in classrooms, airports, restaurants, grocery stores, waiting rooms, sports venues, concert halls, and retail stores, and are being built into refrigerators, clock radios, and even wristwatches. Six big-screen TVs greet visitors at the entrance to the beautiful library in my hometown, and they stay on all day. There are four additional big-screen TVs in the hallway leading to the parking garage and a dozen or so other sets scattered throughout the library. In 1996, the average person in the United States watched 15.6 hours of television for every hour of reading; in 1999, television watching crept up to 16.2 hours for every hour of reading. By 2007, the ratio had increased to 21:1. That is, for every hour spent reading, more than 21 hours are spent watching television. The ratio is expected to continue to escalate, although a ceiling seems inevitable (Veronis Suhler Stevenson Communications Group, 2005).

The Move Away from Print

Data on U.S. leisure and sports habits is gathered periodically by the U.S. Bureau of Labor Statistics. Figure 1.3 offers a summary of average hours

Figure 1.3	Average Hours per Day Spent in Leisure and Sports Activities						
Total	Sports	Social	TV	Read	Relax	Video games, Internet	Travel, other leisure
6 hrs., 41 min.	41 min.	1 hr., 19 min.	2 hr., 27 min.	6.6 min.	7.8 min.	1 hr.	1 hr.
100 %	10.3 %	19.76%	36.67%	1.6%	1.95%	14.5%	14.5%

Source: From *Time-use survey, Table 11,* by U.S. Bureau of Labor Statistics, 2008, Washington, DC. Retrieved April 3, 2008 from http://www.bls.gov/news.release/atust11.htm

per day spent in leisure and sports activities for young people ages 15 to 19 in 2006 in the United States.

Perhaps the most startling finding from Figure 1.3 is not the dominance of TV, but the small portion of time given to reading as a leisure time activity during a typical day—6.6 minutes. These 15- to 19-year-olds spent over 900 percent more time (60 minutes) playing on the computer than reading (6.6 minutes), which is consistent with data gathered by Veronis Suhler Stevenson (2005), as shown in Figure 1.1.

Figure 1.4 shows downward trends in hours spent with print materials—books, magazines, and newspapers.

The Quality of Student Writing

The decline of reading is enough to turn some educators into head-shaking curmudgeons. In response to the decline of reading (especially during adolescence), some recent initiatives, such as the federal government's High School Initiative (Chaddock, 2005; McGrath, 2005; Olson, 2005), seek to enhance achievement among high school students through a reemphasis on reading and writing.

The National Assessment of Educational Progress has been testing students on their writing abilities since 1969. Although there have been fluctuations—improvements and declines in the performance of a particular age group or ethnic group from time to time—results in the NAEP have been surprisingly consistent over time. Remember that the NAEP classifies student performance as being advanced, proficient, basic, and below basic. Ever since the administration of the first tests, only a tiny proportion of students—1 or 2 percent—score at the advanced level, a level at which writing should be "detailed and fully developed . . . well crafted and coherent," with "rich and compelling language, precise word choice, and variety in sentence structure" (NAEP, 2003, p. 9).

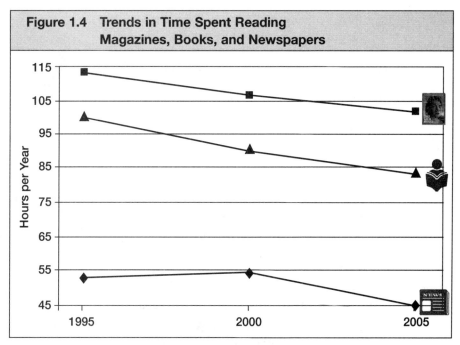

Figure 1.4   Trends in Time Spent Reading Magazines, Books, and Newspapers

Source: Data from *2004 Communications Industry Forecast and Report* by Veronis Suhler Stevenson Communications Group, 2005, New York: Author. Adapted with permission.

In 2002, 20 to 29 percent of students could write at the proficient level, which means that they included "details that support and develop the main idea of the piece" through "precise language and variety in sentence structure to engage the audience they are expected to address" (NAEP, 2003, p. 9). Incredibly, as many as 80 percent of students could only write at the basic or below basic level.

Another alarming statistic surfaced in literacy assessment trends. The National Assessment of Adult Literacy (Kutner et al., 2007) found that the number of 16- to 18-year-olds considered literate actually has decreased since 1992. Figure 1.5 illustrates the average score declines.

Another finding was that the literacy of college graduates nosedived during the same period. "The percentage of college graduates with proficient literacy decreased from 40 percent in 1992 to 31 percent in 2003" (National Assessment of Adult Literacy, 2005, p. 15).

Books Today

In decades past, the unveiling of a new work by a familiar author was a major event. Some select books, particularly those that gained widespread readership, might have been optioned to Hollywood producers

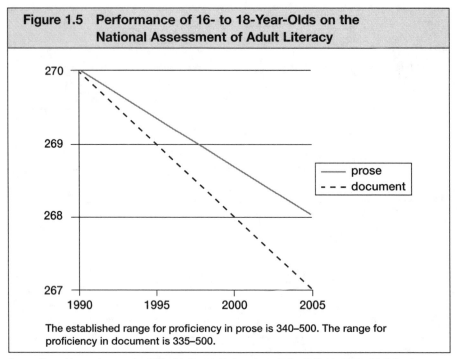

Figure 1.5   Performance of 16- to 18-Year-Olds on the National Assessment of Adult Literacy

The established range for proficiency in prose is 340–500. The range for proficiency in document is 335–500.

Source: From *Literacy in everyday life* by M. Kutner, E. Greenberg, Y. Jin, B. Boyle, Y. Hsu, & E. Dunleavey, 2007, Washington, DC: U.S. Department of Education.

and eventually adapted for film. Over the past few years, however, the relationship between books and films has been transmogrified. Today, rather than provide inspiration for films, books have become subsidiary to the public relations blitz that occurs with the release of a new film. If asked to guess the title of the best-selling children's book of 2004, most of us would be correct in assuming it was *Harry Potter and the Order of the Phoenix* by J. K. Rowling. And so it was—Harry owned the top spot. But in examining the other titles in the top 10 best-selling books of 2004, the number of film tie-ins is astounding (Infoplease, 2008).

10 Best-Selling Children's Books (Paperback), 2004
1. *Harry Potter and the Order of the Phoenix* by J. K. Rowling
2. *Disney/Pixar's The Incredibles* by Irene Trimble
3. *Spider-Man 2: Spider-Man Versus Doc Ock* by Acton Figueroa; illustrated by Jesus Redondo
4. *Shark Tale: The Movie Novel* by Louise Gikow
5. *My Little Pony: Pony Party* by Kate Egan; illustrated by Carlo LoRaso

6. *Spider-Man 2: Everyday Hero* by Acton Figueroa; illustrated by Ivan Vasquez
7. *Spider-Man 2: Doc Around the Clock* by Jacob Ben Gunter
8. *The Sisterhood of the Traveling Pants* (trade paper and mass market) by Ann Brashares
9. *The Polar Express the Movie: The Journey Begins* by Kitty Richards
10. *The Polar Express the Movie: The Magic Journey* by Tracy West

Source: From *Best-selling children's books 2004.* Retrieved April 3, 2008, from http://www.infoplease.com/ipea/A0933506.html.

Nine of the top ten best-selling books were made into films. Eight of the nine that were made into films were never books until the marketing department of the film distribution company decided to hire someone to write a novelization. Lest you think of 2004 as a fluke, please note that the three best-selling children's books of 2003 were *Pirates of the Caribbean*, *Disney/Pixar's Finding Nemo: Junior Novelization*, and *Disney/Pixar's Finding Nemo: Best Dad in the Sea*.

It is difficult to dispute the importance of reading, but the dilemma is that an adolescent must want to read more than he wants to hang out in the media bunker, where the latest, coolest electronic gadget promises vibrant colors, thundering sound effects, and quasi-realistic adventure (Bauerlein, 2005).

Academic Standards

The quiet classroom where students rarely speak or write unless it is expressly pressed on them by fiat is the antithesis of the kind of interactive, multisensory environment that adolescents live and breathe outside of school. The dichotomy is jarring—from arduous drill and chill in school to noisy, fun, exciting games and movies outside of school. Teaching reading and writing through formula, memorization, and workbooks might have been effective once upon a time. However, let us finally admit that these sedentary, abstract, sensory-deprived approaches may be less than optimal today.

Even though traditional methods still have a place in a teacher's tool kit, they do not address the contemporary student's shift away from print and toward film, television, video games, and newer forms of electronic media. The bottom line is that students are reading less and plugging in more. How can a teacher who wants to develop students' literacy teach students who do not read, hate to write, are reluctant to think, and find it difficult to speak intelligibly?

One of the most striking commonalities among the sets of standards developed by professional organizations independently over the past 20 years is the primacy given to literacy. Indeed, it is difficult to be proficient in high school social studies if you cannot comprehend text; it is difficult to be proficient in algebra if you cannot translate symbols into practical operations; it is difficult to be proficient in science if you cannot accurately record the results of experiments; it is difficult to be proficient in English if you cannot write a coherent sentence.

The standards often operate on an implicit assumption that students are able to read and write at grade level. For example, consider two performance expectations relating to a student's knowledge of culture as explicated by the National Council of Social Studies (1994):

> Social studies programs should include experiences that provide for the study of culture and cultural diversity, so that the learner can:
>
> *At the middle school level:* Explain and give examples of how language, literature, the arts, architecture, other artifacts, traditions, beliefs, values, and behaviors contribute to the development and transmission of culture.
>
> *At the high school level:* Apply an understanding of culture as an integrated whole that explains the functions and interactions of language, literature, the arts, traditions, beliefs and values, and behavior patterns.

Many standards from the National Committee on Science Education Standards (1996) are related to literacy. Consider the centrality of oral and written discourse to building scientific knowledge in this standard: "An important stage of inquiry and of student science learning is the oral and written discourse that focuses the attention of students on how they know what they know and how their knowledge connects to larger ideas, other domains, and the world beyond the classroom."

Perhaps surprisingly, seven of ten standards in mathematics (National Council of Teachers of Mathematics, 2000) are related to reading and writing—measurement, data analysis and probability, problem solving, reasoning and proof, communication, connections, and representation.

Of the 12 standards in English and reading (promulgated by the National Council of Teachers of English and the International Reading

Association, cited in this book and provided in Appendix A), all are predicated on a student possessing basic literacy and a desire to learn. For example, Standard 2 requires that "students read a wide range of literature from many periods in many genres to build an understanding of the many dimensions (e.g., philosophical, ethical, aesthetic) of human experience" (National Council of Teachers of English, 1996). Little understanding of human experience is possible for a poor reader who cannot speak clearly or write coherently.

The Partnership for 21st Century Skills (2006) offers an intriguing set of standards that include subject matter and standards for life skills, information technology, thinking, and 21st century content. Sample outcomes for seniors in English are to "identify characteristics of suspect information that may indicate it is an Internet hoax, fraudulent activity, or an unreliable source" and to "construct a virtual museum exhibit depicting the role of the American Dream in classic texts" (Partnership for 21st Century Skills, 2004). Although I learned about the existence of 21st Century Skills only after I finished writing the first draft of *A Teacher's Guide to Multisensory Learning,* the 21st Century outcomes align well with the concepts in this book.

In response to the perceived weakening academic preparation of freshmen entering college, the College Board recently created standards expressly for college-bound students. To date, the College Board has developed standards for English/language arts (2006a) and mathematics/statistics (2006b), and frameworks for science (2006c) and world languages (2006d). When the College Board's standards are examined side by side with other standards, the commonalities become readily apparent. All emphasize the centrality of reading and writing to students' intellectual development.

In a series of reports, the National Commission on Writing (2003, 2004, 2005) has documented the expectation for literacy skills among tomorrow's workers, no matter a student's career aspirations. The commission found that "writing today is not a frill for the few, but an essential skill for the many" (2005, p. 6). The commission highlighted reading and writing as essential skills, absolute necessities for success in the workplace now and in the future.

According to the commission, two-thirds of all salaried employees already have at least some writing responsibility, and 80 percent of companies in the service and financial sectors assess writing before hiring. Work is being transformed from the assembly line, where employees performed repetitive, low-skill tasks, to the think tank, where work has become complex and situational. As a result, the commission advocates putting writing "squarely in the center of the school agenda" (National Commission on Writing, 2003, p. 3) with a doubling of the time spent writing in every class, across all subjects, and at all grade levels.

Unfortunately, the shortcoming of reports and standards is that they explicate what needs to be done, but rarely divulge the protocol to accomplish it. If a student is barely literate and apathetic (or oppositional), meeting standards can quickly seem like an impossible dream. Although it is true that recent sociological and technological trends have militated against engagement and traditional instructional strategies, multisensory techniques can recapture a student's interest and help build literacy—often, believe it or not, to the delight of the student.

2

Multisensory Learning, Engagement, and Achievement ▪ ▪ ▪

From the rich experiences that our senses bring, we construct the ideas, the concepts, the generalizations that give meaning and order to our lives.

—Dale, 1969, p. 187

A few years ago, I asked a group of adolescents to keep a daily journal of their lives in high school—what they learned, how they were taught, what they did before and after school, how they felt about what they did. The overwhelming majority of these students characterized schoolwork as irrelevant, or as one student put it, "boring as crap and worthless." However, outside of the classes—hanging out with friends or participating in team sports or school clubs—students enjoyed school. Some even found *flow*, the term psychology professor Mihaly Csikszentmihalyi (1991) uses to describe optimal experience, a situation where a person meets a challenge equal to the full extent of his or her abilities.

Exhaustive studies of student engagement in high school (Chaddock, 2005; High School Survey of Student Engagement, 2005; McGrath, 2005; National Center for Education Statistics, 2005; Olson, 2005) affirm that most secondary students perceive classrooms as sterile environments where silence, docility, and amiability are valued and assertiveness and imagination are viewed with a certain amount of skepticism. Walking the halls of local schools, it is certainly much easier to find classrooms drowning in ennui than classrooms percolating with joy.

In a study of student attitudes toward high school, Gershman (2004) found that "Miraculous moments of learning and sincere support happen throughout the day, but overall there is a lot of time and money going into an effort that tends to fall flat—unless the intents of public education are to teach punctuality, politeness, orderliness, and respect for extrinsic reward systems—then in that case it is rather successful" (pp. 6–7). Ouch. In a study of adolescent boys, Smith and Wilhelm (2002) found students much preferred playing video games to doing anything at school (not much of a revelation for anyone who has children).

Concerns about student engagement have led to such efforts as the federal government's Preparing America's Future High School Initiative (2003) and the Bill & Melinda Gates Foundation–led National Education Summit on High Schools (Achieve, 2005), all of which seemed to arrive at the same conclusion—schools are failing. "As many as 40 percent of the nation's high school graduates . . . are inadequately prepared to deal with the demands of employment and postsecondary education, putting their own individual success and the nation's economic growth in peril" (Achieve, 2005).

What is wrong with U.S. schools?

A consensus among some researchers (Baines & Stanley, 2003; Bracey, 2000; Civil Society Institute, 2005; Sadowski, 2003) is that an overemphasis on testing is transforming schools—even elementary schools—into factoid factories, where passing the test takes precedence over genuine intellectual and social development.

The charge that schools promote static knowledge under contrived conditions is nothing new. More than 40 years ago, Coleman (1965) criticized schools for their lack of authenticity and vision. For an adolescent, the school's "natural environment is not natural at all, but a sheltered and artificial one which prevents him from having contact with those very problems that can give him maturity. The task then, which I set as an ultimate goal, is to replace these artificial and sheltering environments with ones that reflect the consequences of the future" (p. xi).

Because rewards and punishments are meted out according to the average number of students performing at a basic level on multiple-choice tests, the distance between social, technological, and ethical problems of the real world and the sanctioned school curricula seems greater than ever. Test scores may determine not only a school's level of funding, but also a teacher's salary, the graduation status of students, and the future of the school as an ongoing enterprise. By their nature, end-of-term assessments measure students' ability to recall and manipulate abstract knowledge. Most teachers feel an immense pressure to cover precisely the material that is expected to show up on the exam, no more and no less.

Yet, preparing students for higher test scores by subverting genuine intellectual development is irrational. A student who has fun while he is learning and actually retains the new information is likely to perform better on tests than a student who hates school and remembers nothing two seconds after a lesson. Perhaps it is a vestige of those humorless schoolmasters of the 19th century, epitomized by Mr. Gradgrind in Charles Dickens's *Hard Times*, that many Americans think schooling must involve some amount of drudgery. In the real world, learning can be challenging at times, certainly, but learning can also exhilarate and inspire.

Promoting Engagement Through Direct Experiences

In fact, the relationship between a positive attitude toward a subject and academic achievement in that subject is one of strongest correlations in educational research (Pintrich & Schunk, 2002). An attractive feature of multisensory learning is that the instructional techniques can pique a student's interest so that the desire to get involved can supersede the impulse to sit and do nothing.

Whether influenced by the emphasis on test scores or traditional practices, learning in schools is too often abstract and decontextualized. According to Bruner (1966), experience may be categorized in one of three ways: *enactive* experience, *iconic* experience, or *symbolic* experience. Enactive experience is direct experience. To have an enactive experience, you might walk to a local creek, take a sample of water, and go back to a science lab with an expert environmentalist where you run a series of tests to assess the purity of the water. Iconic experience is a step removed from enactive experience. To have an iconic experience, you might watch a film about an environmentalist who goes to a creek, takes a sample of the water, and runs a series of tests in a lab. A symbolic experience is yet another step removed from actual experience. For a symbolic experience, you would simply read an account of the event, perhaps an article from a naturalists' magazine such as *Orion*.

Because texts are widely available in books and over the Internet, the easiest instructional strategy will always involve the symbolic—in essence, the textbook. Indeed, the textbook is the bastion of symbolic learning—materials are readily accessible, outputs are well defined, and the curriculum (having been sanctioned by the state or school district) is risk free. Nevertheless, because textbooks are dominated by text (verbal symbols), the intended outcomes may be actualized only by a select group of highly accomplished, independent readers. Often, students who have short attention spans or who may be poor readers reap nothing from assigned readings.

If a teacher wanted to teach students about hurricanes, which instructional approach would be best?

1. Require students to read a scientific explanation in a textbook describing how hurricanes form.
2. Combine a brief film clip of a recent hurricane with firsthand narrative accounts and photos.
3. Have students accompany the Hurricane Hunters as they fly jets into hurricanes to gather weather information for the U.S. government.

Undeniably, the third selection offers the most memorable learning experience. Few students are going to snooze or pass notes as their jet cuts through torrents of rain and gale force winds toward the eye of a hurricane. Of course, such an educational field trip would have to be weighed against factors of time, cost, and safety. Selection 2 offers a sensible, safe alternative. However, to execute this instructional approach, a teacher would have to locate an appropriate film, preview it, set it up in class (preferably by showing the film on a screen large enough for students to actually see it), clip newspaper articles, search for images related to hurricanes over the Internet, and figure out how to orchestrate all these individual pieces of information to maximize student learning. Selection 1, reading a purely textual account of a hurricane, is the easiest approach. This is the symbolic experience—the least engaging, least satisfying method of learning about almost anything, hurricanes included.

Now consider most subject matter that is taught in schools. From my experience, the overwhelmingly dominant instructional approach is as follows:

1. Assign a text to be read.
2. Discuss the text in class.
3. Have students respond to questions about the text.
4. Give an exam or a worksheet.

This method assumes that students actually read and understand the text (not a valid assumption in schools where I have worked), and the mode of instruction never ventures beyond the symbolic. Even though a teacher can communicate much information in a relatively brief period of time by delivering the message through the spoken word, such an approach can be meaning free for students, especially those who do not listen well.

According to Moffett and Wagner (1991), classroom activities should move back and forth between personal experience and abstract language. "Sensations are inner coding of outer things. To verbalize them is to transform sensory experience into understandings. By helping learners sense more you may help them to say more" (p. 160).

Dunning (1974) argued that "when kids go out and see real things, the insides of classrooms change. . . . Bringing real world things into class is sometimes hard. But it's the direction to go. Toward the real world." In too many classes, the real world is considered relevant only to the extent that the information might show up on some future test.

In my first year as a teacher, I was given a handout at the school district's teacher orientation. The handout read, "When I read, I remember 10 percent; when I hear, I remember 20 percent; when I see, I remember 30 percent; when I say, I remember 40 percent; when I do, I remember 50 percent. When I see, hear, say, and do, I remember 90 percent." Although the amount learned through a specific sense may not be as precise as those percentages suggest, the idea behind the statement—that students learn more effectively when several senses are engaged—is difficult to dispute. After all, it is through our senses that we come to know the world. Invoking the senses allows our brains to latch on to something concrete, something substantial. By making experience concrete, teachers can provide the necessary scaffolding for students to gain mastery over abstract language.

Dale (1969) characterized the different states of experience in a hierarchy from most abstract (verbal symbols) to least abstract (direct, purposeful experience), as depicted in Figure 2.1.

In Dale's configuration, a word is an example of a verbal symbol. There is nothing about a word itself (other than a word such as *Boom!*) that connotes its meaning. For example, we might know the word *hamburger*, but the word itself does not mimic any feature of something that is edible. If a person were unfamiliar with the English alphabet, she might find it difficult to distinguish between *hamburger* and words that looked vaguely similar—*Hamburg* (a town in Germany) or *humbug!* (something uttered by Scrooge in *A Christmas Carol*). For a writer to communicate to a reader, both parties must agree on what the verbal letters *h-a-m-b-u-r-g-e-r*

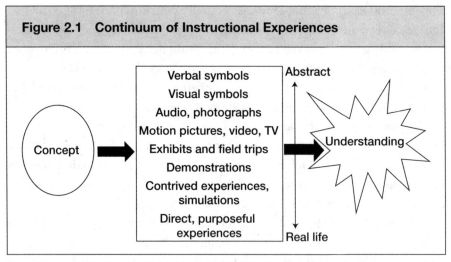

Source: From *Audiovisual methods in teaching* by E. Dale, 1969, New York: The Dryden Press.

symbolize. To make clear the different kinds of experiences represented by each category, I am going to extend the example of the hamburger. How does one come to understand the concept of a hamburger?

Levels of Abstraction

Words are the most abstract representation of a concept. Visual symbols, which might include maps, logos, and graphic designs, are at the next highest level of abstraction. For example, although very young children do not know how to read, they can identify the McDonald's logo and recognize the character of Ronald McDonald. A local vegetarian restaurant I frequent has a sign on its door—an image of a hamburger encircled in red with a large line through the middle of it—meaning no meat is served here.

Recordings, radio, and still pictures are one-way sensory stimulations that communicate through either sound or image. A still photograph of a beef patty being cooked on a grill would be a more recognizable representation for hamburger than the golden arches, especially if a person had no knowledge of fast-food restaurants.

Film and television engage the ear and the eye, and thus are multisensory. More engaging than a photograph would be a film depicting how hamburgers are cooked and consumed at a local McDonald's restaurant.

Going to a culinary institute and witnessing firsthand a variety of ways to cook a hamburger would be superior to watching a film. After watching demonstrations by several cooks, the observer's ideas about hamburgers could be considerably enlarged.

Demonstrating knowledge by modeling appropriate techniques for preparing, cooking, and consuming a hamburger would be better still. This kind of knowledge—learning by teaching—can be quite effective, as the scholarly productivity of teachers and professors around the world attests.

Dramatized and contrived experiences are one step removed from real-life experiences and, accordingly, are very popular with the military. Spending a few days in a simulated battle maneuver in a desert in the southwestern United States would better prepare soldiers for the rigor of war in the Middle East than reading several pages of text or watching a film. Similarly, McDonald's sends most managers to Hamburger University, where they must pass muster in a simulated restaurant replete with cooks, crew, and customers.

Finally, direct and purposeful experiences invoke all the senses— sight, sound, taste and smell, and movement and touch—in real time. Learning about a hamburger using direct experience would involve participating in the work of a cattle ranch, acting as a cook where hamburgers are prepared, and eating hamburgers as a customer in a fast-food restaurant. When feasible, direct experience is the most effective way to learn, whether the subject is making hamburgers, learning how to write a persuasive essay, or solving a problem in physics.

As abstraction increases, sensory reception decreases. Yet most classrooms across the curriculum are dominated by teacher talk and quiet reading (Applebee, Langer, Nystrand, & Gamoran, 2003; Cazden, 1995), neither of which actively engages the senses. Although pure lecturing (meaning talk without accompanying illustrations or other sensory stimuli) can be effective for communicating large amounts of information to bright and willing students, such an instructional approach does not veer beyond the abstract. As Arnheim (1997) noted, "Human thinking cannot go beyond the patterns suppliable by the human senses. . . . language. . . argues loudly in favor of the contention that thinking takes place in the realm of the senses" (p. 233).

Unfortunately, most schools respond to struggling (or remedial) students by forcing them to spend even more time in the realm of the abstract—more work on textual comprehension, more worksheets, more of the back-to-basics approach. Instead of repeated exposure to a narrowed, abstract approach, remedial students might be better served by moving down the continuum of experience shown in Figure 2.1 to activities that are closer to real life. Once students have gathered enough sensory experience in an area, they would be more able to move back to the abstract for analysis and reflection. But many teachers, especially teachers of remedial students, tend to begin their teaching in the abstract and stay there for the duration of the year.

Let me provide an example. Once, I had a student named David who was reading at the 3rd grade level in a 9th grade English class. When I began a unit on *Romeo and Juliet*, I knew from the first day that David would understand little of the plot, vocabulary, or themes. As the unit developed, David failed to turn in most assignments. On the assignments he managed to turn in, he displayed an utter lack of understanding.

Rather than demand that David repeatedly scale the mountain of Shakespearean language, I could have helped him approach Shakespeare from a different perspective. For example, I could have shown a few film clips from the 30 or so filmed versions of the play; shown portraits of the characters of *Romeo and Juliet* rendered by artists such as William Blake, Ford Madox Brown, Frank Dicksee, John Millais, John Stanhope, and John Waterhouse; or played Nino Rota's music based on the play, rock music from Baz Luhrman's 1996 MTV-style film adaptation, Tchaikovsky's *Romeo and Juliet*, Berlioz's *Roméo et Juliette*, or the Prokofiev ballet. I could have also involved David with field trips to see *Romeo and Juliet* being performed on a local stage, or asked that David rehearse the part of Romeo with a classmate in anticipation of a reader's theater presentation. Once David accumulated enough sensory experiences, he might eventually have come to understand the play and been able to comment on its themes. Expecting David to suddenly gain mastery over such sophisticated language and convoluted plot without first giving him some context was ludicrous.

One of the greatest benefits of using multisensory stimuli is that they have the potential to involve students more fully in the learning experience. Imagine that you wanted to learn how to play the piano. If piano were taught as other courses in secondary school are taught, a student would listen to lectures about the history of the piano, read essays about the great composers, analyze famous compositions, and occasionally refer to a diagram of a keyboard. However, a student might not get to touch an actual piano until after the midterm period. By then, the student's interest in the piano likely would have dissipated to nothing.

The Roots of Multisensory Learning

Common sense suggests that students learn in different ways. One of Howard Gardner's (1999) great contributions through the theory of multiple intelligences is the acknowledgment that students are differentially talented. A student can be a brilliant logical thinker but a poor speaker; a superb athlete but an inept architect.

The learning styles movement (Dunn, 1984; Dunn & Dunn, 1989) classifies students according to a preferred way of absorbing and recalling information: auditory, visual, tactile, and kinesthetic. Students who learn best by listening are at an advantage in classrooms dominated by teacher talk. Students who learn best through watching are at an advantage in classrooms where teachers use plenty of visuals. Although some empirical data suggest that a teacher can be more effective if she teaches expressly toward a student's preferred learning style (Dunn, Griggs, Olson, Gorman, & Beasley, 1995), trying to match individual learning styles with instructional strategies would seem logistically impossible in light of a teacher's other responsibilities. Keeping track of the day's lessons; coding individualized education programs (IEPs are required of every student in special education); serving Code 504 students (underperforming students not covered by special education); and assessing the progress of 150 or so other students would be taxing enough for Wonder Woman, let alone most mortals. Under the circumstances, trying to customize instructional strategies to meet individual students' learning preferences or a particular intelligence is not a realistic expectation.

On the other hand, when a teacher uses multisensory techniques, preferred learning styles are invoked as a matter of course—without forcing the teacher into the time-consuming and tedious role of bookkeeper. At its core, multisensory learning is a way of teaching that requires students to activate their full faculties—seeing, hearing, smelling, tasting, moving, touching, thinking, intuiting, enjoying—in a variety of situations.

The Suzuki method, successful with generations of musicians, has long used multisensory techniques. This method requires students to record and listen to their practice sessions, observe other pupils' lessons, watch their teacher demonstrate correct playing techniques, and attend local music events. In fact, all of the strategies of the Suzuki method—field trips, demonstrations, simulations, and real experiences—can be found in the middle to lower part of the continuum of experience, which is closest to real life. Indeed, the Suzuki method encourages students to learn by jumping in. That is, students learn to play by ear first; verbal and visual symbols come only after the student has come to know the joy of playing a song by heart.

Multisensory approaches are also common among teachers of very young children. Fernald (1987), Gillingham and Stillman (1997),

Orton (as cited in Rawson, 1987), and Slingerland (1977) advocate multisensory approaches for teaching phonics and letters to young children. These approaches often involve children seeing a word, tracing its letters with their fingers, and trying to pronounce the word using their knowledge of the sounds of letters. Lacerda (2003) describes this phenomenon in academic terms: "As the number of stored multisensory representations increases, more fine detailed relationships between the acoustic and the other sensory inputs emerge spontaneously from the available correlations between sensory dimensions" (p. 57). By putting together visual cues (the written word), auditory stimuli (pronouncing the word), and kinesthetic activity (tracing the word), children become readers (Henry, 1998; Josh, Dahlgren, & Boulware-Gooden, 2002).

Teachers of students with disabilities have started experimenting with multisensory approaches as well. Originally designed for autistic persons or institutionalized older adults with Alzheimer's disease who did not respond to medication, Snoezelen (pronounced *Sno-zuh-len*) rooms were developed in Holland in the 1970s. The idea was to create an environment where patients could experience stimulation, relaxation, and enjoyment in a completely nondemanding way.

Typical early Snoezelen rooms were equipped with lava lamps, stuffed animals, soothing music, ambient lighting, and a projector displaying images. More recently, Snoezelen rooms have been adapted to meet specific therapeutic and educational goals. For example, some researchers have used Snoezelen rooms to teach life skills to severely disabled school-aged children (Douglas et al., 1998) or to help students with sensory interaction (Pagliano, 1999).

Because Snoezelen became a trademark associated with ROMPA Ltd. of Derbyshire, England, in 1992, most researchers have stopped using the term *Snoezelen* and started using the more generic term multisensory environment (MSE) to refer to any room that has been expressly developed for multisensory interactions. Among severely disturbed patients, Mitchell and Van der Gaag (2002) found that multisensory rooms foster "changes in tolerance levels, group integration, range of vocabulary used, and . . . positive changes in the number and context of interactions" (p. 164). Others (Hope, 1997; Hutchinson & Kewin, 1994; Pagliano, 1999) have documented the positive effects of multisensory rooms on academic and attitudinal benefits for severely disabled and emotionally disturbed students, as well as for students not necessarily classified as needing special services.

Obviously, the ameliorative effects of a welcoming, multisensory environment have implications for the regular classroom. After all, children are "affected by environmental conditions of temperature, light, sound, and the spatial qualities of their classroom settings, as well as by such aesthetic elements as color and texture" (Taylor, Wise, & Wise, 1990, p. 38).

The physical environment of a classroom and the interactions among students, teachers, and materials significantly affect the quality of learning. Neuroscientists have documented "the capacity of brain cells to rewire themselves radically—forming new synaptic connections and dissolving old ones—in response to stimulation" (Horgan, 2004). Because the brain processes information in a compartmentalized manner, different parts of the brain become active when a person reads, speaks, listens, or thinks (Grandin, 1998, 2006a).

Designing relevant and engaging interactions not only enhances student learning, it also affects students' long-term intellectual development. Using multisensory stimuli in instruction increases engagement, promotes deeper participation, and advances the prospect that learning can be fun. According to Paige (2006), "You wouldn't be able to survive without your senses working together." The benefits of multisensory stimuli seem substantial, especially in contrast to the current practice of teaching to the test. Of course, if the score is the goal, multisensory learning can dramatically improve performance on standardized tests, too.

Indeed, a recent, exhaustive report on teaching reading in the United Kingdom found that multisensory appeals were essential tools for maximizing student achievement. "The best teaching . . . was at a brisk pace, fired children's interest, often by engaging them in multisensory activities, drew upon a mix of stimulating resources, and made sure that they received praise for effort and achievement" (Rose, 2006, p. 16).

In a series of experiments over a period of several years, Diamond (Diamond, 1988; Diamond & Hopson, 1998) found that animals (rats, cats, and monkeys) raised in sensory-rich environments developed higher levels of intelligence and lived longer than animals raised in sensory-deprived environments. Furthermore, the physical brains of the animals in sensory-rich environments were larger and healthier than the brains of animals raised in sensory-deprived environments. The link between sensory processing and brain development—in humans and animals—develops in accordance with the quality and nature of the stimuli in the environment (Society for Neuroscience, 2005; Striedter, 2006).

Yet the dominant instructional approach remains the delivery of abstract information in a sensory-deprived environment. A more scientifically valid and infinitely more engaging approach would be to think of the classroom's physical space as a kind of sensory representation of the subject matter and to view the world outside its walls as the laboratory.

Then the curriculum could become not a series of assignments delivered across some dimension of time, but a series of carefully choreographed experiences. The teacher who purposefully crafts multisensory experiences to foster students' social and intellectual development is teaching, whereas the teacher who asks students to read and answer questions is merely assigning.

3

Sight ■ ■ ■

Today we work with the written or spoken word as the primary form of communication. But we also need to understand the importance of graphics, music, and cinema, which are just as powerful and in some ways more deeply intertwined with young people's culture. We live and work in a visually sophisticated world, so we must be sophisticated in using all the forms of communication, not just the written word.

—George Lucas (as cited by J. Daly, 2004)

As the dominant sense, sight serves as the primary tool for orienting the self in the world. Vision is so integral to intellectual development that learning difficulties can sometimes be caused not by brain dysfunction but by problems with the eyes. According to Arnheim (1997), "The visual medium is so enormously superior because it offers structural equivalents to all characteristics of objects, events, relations" (p. 232). If you watch a man trying to lift a box, you can surmise the weight of the box based on your perceptions of the man's stance, the amount of exertion evident in his muscles, the expression on his face, and his relative success.

If the man lifting the box is only a blur in your eyes, then you will not be able to assess the situation with any accuracy. When the sensory building blocks necessary for conceptual development are absent, abstract concepts become difficult, or even impossible. Considering that as many as 75 percent of the activities in a typical classroom rely on interpreting written directions (Richards, 1993), good eyesight is, in many ways, critical to learning.

So, for a student who has problems reading and writing, the first question a teacher should consider is, "How well does this student see?" Dyslexia, once considered a specific kind of cognitive difficulty (seeing letters backward), has come to be viewed as any problem with perceiving and comprehending symbols, particularly letters and words. The emerging definition of dyslexia is that it is a language-based, neurobiological learning disability in which an individual has difficulty with word recognition, spelling, and decoding (Wadlington & Wadlington, 2005). Using this definition, as many as 20 percent of all students can be considered to have some form of dyslexia (National Reading Research Panel, 1999).

A fascinating aspect of the research on dyslexia is the emphasis on using images and other picture-based aids in helping students understand letters and words. One of the most effective techniques for helping dyslexics is the use of strong supplementary visual and multisensory appeals (Abbott & Berninger, 1999; Knight, 1997). Indeed, experts in dyslexia (International Dyslexia Association, 2006) report great success in using picture-based props to aid in the comprehension of text.

Visual props feature just as prominently in the publications of writers who participate in the burgeoning industry devoted to learning styles. Learning styles research finds that most students prefer visual to other stimuli, such as auditory or tactile (Black, 2004; Dunn & Dunn, 1993; Mayer & Massa, 2003; Reiff, 1992). According to learning style advocates, a good rule of thumb for a teacher is "the more visuals . . . the better" (Silverman, 2002, p. 278).

With a power and complexity that would surpass the fastest, most advanced supercomputer system in the world, visual intelligence takes up almost half of the brain's cortex (Bonner & Burton, 2003; Hoffman, 1998). The region of the brain dedicated to vision is intricately connected to the center of emotions, so it is only natural to respond with laughter or tears after witnessing a particularly moving event, such as a wedding or a funeral.

If a student has experienced an injury to the brain, the visual part of the brain can be resuscitated, but the delicate links to emotions cannot. The condition of having a normally functioning visual center but damaged emotional connective tissue is known as Capgras. Students who have Capgras are able to recognize and recall faces and places, but cannot muster the appropriate emotional response to these perceptions. For example, a patient with Capgras would recognize a parent, but the sight of the parent would fail to arouse an affectionate response. In such cases, a student with Capgras would probably suspect that the parent is an imposter—someone who shares the physical attributes of the mother or father but in reality is someone else.

To understand how vision works in healthy individuals, it is useful to remember the discussion in your old educational psychology textbook about the three different kinds of memory—sensory, short-term, and long-term. Sensory memory is instantaneous, but fleeting; short-term lasts a few minutes; and long-term is permanent.

Most of us have experienced the phenomenon of driving a car while trying to find a location, such as a house where a party is going to be held, from a set of written directions. Even though you read the directions before you opened the car door, and then reread them once you started down the road, when you arrive at a stop sign, you cannot recall what the instructions said about which way to turn. Frustrated, you read the directions a third time, but by the time you reach the next stop sign, you discover that you have forgotten them yet again.

Perhaps it will make you feel better to know that when you cannot remember directions, your brain is functioning completely normally. The brain maintains a copy of the text—the sensory input—for only about one second after you stop reading. If the text makes it to short-term memory, then it could be remembered for a longer period of time—perhaps three or four minutes. However, your brain realizes that directions are ephemeral and that you may not need them ever again.

Much more sensory information is received than is transmitted to short-term memory. Relatively little from short-term memory actually makes it into long-term memory, where information is remembered indefinitely. If the directions you are following take you to the location where you will pick up a paycheck every week, then your brain stores such information in long-term memory and will not let you forget it.

Another notable aspect about the visual system is its amazing adaptability. In one study, scientists asked participants to wear goggles that mimicked the view of a wide-angle keyhole. For a few days, goggle-wearing participants stumbled into furniture, walked into walls, and experienced severe disequilibrium to the point of nausea. Because vision is also integrated with all other sensory systems, including the auditory system, participants had grave difficulties locating the sources of sounds while wearing the goggles (Richards, 1993).

However, after two or three days of goggle vision, nausea subsided, participants stopped walking into walls, and they were able to again accurately locate the sources of sounds. In other words, the brain managed to adapt its auditory system to the new sensory data generated by the eyes in only a matter of days (Zwiers, Van Opstal, & Paige, 2003).

Importance of Visualization

Even scholars who specialize in the study of composition have begun acknowledging the ways that visuals and layout can contribute to the effectiveness of a piece of writing. Odell (1981), who once advocated for diversity of audience, purpose, time, and effort with regard to writing instruction, has lately amended his advice to include *visual appeal*. Composition is not just "words, and it's not just words that we use to formulate or convey ideas. Successful communication depends on the look of a piece, the very appearance of the piece on the page. The inclusion of pictures, graphs, charts, or helpful inset boxes highlight key pieces of information that are important for the reader to see in the text" (Odell, 2006).

When given directions to assemble a bookshelf or a bicycle, most of us prefer to work from both words and illustrations rather than from only words. Given the choice between putting together a bicycle through instructions in either text or illustrations, most of us perform better with the illustrations (Prevention, 2006).

Many students, particularly those on the autism or Asperger's spectrum, have difficulty using words to think. Instead of words, many think in pictures or scenarios. For these students, seeing models and getting their hands on the phenomenon itself are essential to understanding. For students who are associative thinkers, the need to visualize is especially acute (Grandin, 2006b). Temple Grandin (2006a), who is an expert in handling livestock and is autistic, emphasizes that visuals help her build connections. "To form concepts, I place pictures of different images into categories and subcategories within categories. The more facts and experiences I can download into my memory, the better I can think; there is more information for my internal search engine to find" (p. 232).

The rule-first approach can decontextualize learning and create feelings of detachment and confusion. Rather than provide the rule and have students apply the rule to a set of exercises, another way to teach is to provide a series of examples, then ask students to figure out the rule from the evidence.

Sometimes, when teaching grammar or parts of speech, a common instructional approach is to emphasize the rule, then assign exercises expressly designed to demonstrate the rule in action. Yet more than 80 years of research (Hillocks, 1999) confirms that participation in such grammar assignments does not improve students' writing. Recently, when I asked a high school student who was completing a grammar worksheet what he was doing, he said, "Working on the assembly line." When I asked him what product he was creating, he said, "I have no idea."

The same kind of logic—applying a rule without sufficient understanding of the concept—is commonly found in the teaching of mathematics. Too often, teachers focus on computation and repetition at the expense of revealing when, where, or why a student might choose to apply such equations in real life. Visual stimuli can help provide a vital connection between computation and conception.

On the other hand, the inability to visualize impedes learning and impairs creative thinking. It is not easy to think accurately about places, people, and cultures that you have never seen. To be effective, visuals should relate to the concept to be learned and help reiterate crucial ideas. Visualization can help a student with spelling, factual recall, mathematics, and spatial relations (Williams, 1983). The work of scientists, engineers, and security analysts increasingly requires sophisticated visualization strategies (Greiper & Sauter, 2005). Many studies over the past few years (Frankel, 2005; McGrath & Brown, 2005; Trindade, Fiolhais, & Almeida, 2002) substantiate the effectiveness of communicating abstract concepts through visual models.

In general, human beings find it difficult to remember information only by hearing it. Brown (1958) found that participants could not remember sounds for more than a few seconds after hearing them. Similarly, Baddeley (2004) found that students had great difficulty learning when they were forced to rely solely on acoustic memory. Lewalter (2003) found that using illustrations significantly enhanced comprehension and problem solving when measured against text-only information on a computer screen. As a rule, the more abstract the concept to be learned, the higher the need for suitable illustrations (Arnheim, 1997).

In numerous experiments with students who had difficulties with reading, visual cues were shown to be quite effective. Typically in those experiments, one group of students read a story and had illustrations to refer to as they read. Another group read without pictorial representations. Not surprisingly, students who were given illustrations scored substantially higher in subsequent tests of recall and comprehension. Even when no pictorial representations were given and students were only prompted to visualize the text, recall and comprehension were significantly enhanced (Hutton & Lescohier, 1983; Leavin, 1973; Pressley, 1979). In a study of the creative processes of Nobel Prize winners, many luminaries credited their ability to visualize as the single most important key to their success (West, 1997).

To aid with visualization strategies, computer simulation technologies have been created in many areas of endeavor, particularly in science and mathematics. After experimenting with virtual examinations of phases of matter (physics and chemistry), a science teacher noted, "A photo or movie may show students the internal geometry of ice, but only virtual reality allows them to enter inside and observe it from any viewpoint" (Trindade, Fiolhais, & Almeida, 2002, p. 486).

Film

A wealth of research has substantiated that students prefer watching film to reading books (Baines, 2008a; Cennamo, 1993; Krendl, 1986; Sherry, 2004), largely because they consider viewing to be a much easier task than reading. Certainly, film does more than text to help students visualize. In fact, sometimes the moving image overwhelms the text. For example, most students who read an excerpt from Ray Bradbury's *Something Wicked This Way Comes* and are later shown clips from the film have all memory of the text obliterated by the pyrotechnics of the film (Baines, 2008a). Similarly a student may read eloquent descriptions of an atomic bomb blast, but until the devastation is seen firsthand (via the images in a film), the power of the bomb is only theoretical.

Film has been shown effective in teaching a spectrum of academic courses, including mathematics, science, foreign language, social studies, and English (Baines, 2008b). Many physical educators use film to demonstrate proper form in athletics—for example, how to properly kick a soccer ball or perform a set shot in volleyball. Film has even been used in public schools to teach social etiquette, address racial tension, warn against sexually transmitted diseases, demonstrate emergency procedures, and inform about an inexhaustible list of other topics (Baines, 2008b).

Although film can be an effective teaching tool, it can be terribly abused as well. For example, a local high school teacher of Spanish in my area decided to show her classes the three-hour-plus U.S. film *El Cid*, about the Spanish hero Rodrigo Diaz who lived in the 11th century. The teacher dedicated five class periods—an entire week—to showing the film, but she did not stop once to ask a question, comment on the authenticity of the production, or ask students to translate the English into Spanish. Obviously, watching an old film, shot in Italy and the United States, starring actor Charlton Heston, has questionable relevance to the language or culture of Spain.

Because students are so inundated with images via the Internet, television, video games, and other contemporary entertainment appliances, films should be used for specific purposes in relatively modest time frames (usually less than 25 minutes). Nevertheless, the proliferation and availability of film provide a rich set of potential resources. Teachers who plan to have their classes study *Romeo and Juliet*, for example, have at their disposal more than 100 film adaptations. After students read the play, the teacher could compile 30-second excerpts from 40 different balcony scenes and show them back to back in only 20 minutes. Through such a tactic, students would gain an unprecedented sense of the characters, dialogue, staging, and possibilities for bringing Shakespeare to life.

Film also provides rich possibilities for poetry and composition. An interesting assignment is to have students adapt a poem or piece of writing into a screenplay, then have them shoot it. Once the students have made a film, they can go back and revise their writing to align with the images and sounds of the film. Inevitably, the exercise of moving from words to image and back to words enhances the quality of student writing by invigorating it with precision and detail (Baines & Kunkel, 2003).

Film can help connect the dots with social studies and science, as well. A comparison of visual accounts of the Iraq War—documentary and Hollywood films; photos from Middle East newspapers and U.S. military sources; television reports from Fox and Al Jazeera—could give students a deep, new understanding of that conflict. Similarly, rather than have students create a poisonous gas in class, a teacher of science might prefer to show a film clip of the chemical cloud that results when bleach and ammonia are mixed together.

Art

A teacher does not need a camera, projector, or even a screen to make learning more effective through visual stimuli. She can use the power of visual media by having students draw in response to reading a text. The quality of a student's drawing does not matter as much as the meaning behind it. The practice of turning abstract text into constructed images helps clarify meaning and aids the teacher in identifying the point at which misunderstanding might occur.

Ekphrasis, writing (usually poetic) in response to visual art, also holds rich possibilities. Mike Angelotti, who contributed Sight Lesson 3 in this chapter, suggests that the best way to begin a writing assignment is to have students make spontaneous works of art through quick drawing. Once the art has been created, words can be used to describe, analyze, and inform. King (1993, 2008) has had great success involving students in finger painting in response to a poem or story. After students read a text, they finger paint for two or three minutes, then explain their impromptu paintings. In explaining their paintings, students reveal the extent to which they comprehended the text.

Using paintings and photographs as accompaniments to texts is an innovative way to offer students multiple perspectives. The Web site Shakespeare Illustrated (http://shakespeare.emory.edu/illustrated_index.cfm), maintained by faculty from the English Department at Emory University, lists a bevy of works of art associated with the plays of Shakespeare. A Google image search on *Ophelia* yielded 53,700 hits. Of course, some hits were photos of pets named Ophelia, but most were photos of actresses playing Ophelia or artists' renderings of the character.

With regard to history, the archive of images on the Internet is boundless. For example, the University of South Florida's *A Teacher's Guide to the Holocaust* (http://fcit.usf.edu/Holocaust/) and the University of Virginia's massive collection of primary source documents from the Civil War called *The Valley of the Shadow* (http://valley.vcdh.virginia.edu/) provide free access to thousands of images and primary artifacts. Visual prompts in math, science, music, and other subject areas can be found by using Internet image search engines, such as Google Image Search or Altavista Image Search. The Internet Archive (http://www.archive.org/index.php) offers free access to items such as images, films, and audio.

If you doubt the power of images to ignite the mental processes, try these scenarios with two of your classes:

1. In one class, ask students to write a narrative of at least a page in length on any topic that they wish.
2. In the second class, lay out copies of paintings (postcard books are a handy resource for this activity). Have each student select a painting that he or she finds interesting or intriguing. Ask students to write a one-page story based on the work they selected.

In the free write class, students will complain that they cannot think of anything to write. Their writing may turn out to be vague, inconsistent, and flaccid. Using the second strategy, students may complain that they cannot limit their stories to a single page. Inevitably, the writing based on the painting will include details from the painting combined with ideas from students' newly fired imaginations.

Implications for Teachers

About learning through sight, it is important to remember two points:

1. Most students prefer visual learning to auditory, abstract, or kinesthetic learning.
2. Student learning is often more accurate and enduring when visual cues are used.

Unquestionably, visual media have become easier to access and create. A teacher who has an Internet connection and a decent color printer should be able to create stunning visuals with little effort and at minimal expense. Adding relevant visual stimuli to a lesson helps students learn more effectively, especially those students who have difficulties comprehending abstract concepts or reading text.

Perhaps the easiest way to enhance the impact of a lesson is to supplement it with multiple visual aids. I remember when I was in 2nd grade and my teacher, Miss Rush, created a wall-size display of the planets. As I recall, the display was on the front wall as we walked into class one Monday morning. During the week, I remember walking up to the display, touching the planets, reading their names, and noticing differences in size and distance from the sun. On Friday, Miss Rush led the class in a brief discussion of the planets and the display. The class spent only a few minutes on discussion because everyone had already learned the names, sequence, and relative size of the planets over the course of the week. I can still visualize Miss Rush's display of the planets in my mind, though I last saw it more than 40 years ago.

Having students create drawings depicting the meaning of unfamiliar words operates using the same principle—the uncanny propensity of visual stimuli to move learning from short-term to long-term memory. Students may forget a definition, but typically will not forget a drawing or an image associated with a definition. The research on the benefits of visual stimuli is persuasive and convincing. A teacher who ignores visual aids does so at the detriment of students' intellectual development.

The following activities use art, film, photographs, and other visual stimuli to hone students' literacy and thinking skills.

Activity	Entry Point	Focus	Preparation Time
Sight Lesson 1 Comic Book Adaptations	Drawing	Reading comprehension	Minimal
Sight Lesson 2 Imagine This!	Poem by Ezra Pound	Style and literature study	Minimal
Sight Lesson 3 Paint-Write	Spontaneous painting	Descriptive writing, poetic writing	Substantial
Sight Lesson 4 Reading Art	Masterworks of art	Reading comprehension, critical analysis, poetic writing	Substantial

Comic Book Adaptations asks students to interpret and reformulate text so that it fits into a storyboard format. Not only do the Comic Book Adaptations activities help students with comprehension, they also help with inference, voice, and tone. Imagine This! has students analyze the techniques of imagist poets, then model aspects of imagist style in their own writing. Paint-Write engages students in spontaneous painting—with fingers, a brush, or even tree branches—in an attempt to graft their thoughts immediately into words. Reading Art uses compelling and controversial art as a springboard for writing. Learning how paintings communicate with nuance and subtlety can help students understand how to inject these traits into their written and oral communication.

Sight Lesson 1
Comic Book Adaptations

Summary: After reading a poem or article, students write a short comic strip detailing the contents of the text.

Senses: Sight and sound

Type of Activity: Individual or pairs

Approximate Time: One day

Objectives: Students translate their knowledge of a poem or story into images to demonstrate and justify their interpretation of a text.

Materials: Pen and paper

Procedures

1. Students read a poem, article, or story (short story or novel). Then students translate the poem, article, or story into a series of at least six storyboards.
2. Students write dialogue and use description from the text or their own words.
3. Students exchange comic book adaptations with at least five other students, comparing their interpretations with those of others (see student sample in Figure 3.1).
4. Points of difference in interpretations are likely and may spark intensive discussion and analysis.
5. The teacher posts the adaptations together on the bulletin board or a wall.

Extension Activities

A teacher might want to assign an essay in which the student compares his comic book adaptation with those of others. The point of the essay would be, "Which adaptation most accurately portrays the story and why?"

Assessment

	1 Unsatisfactory	2 Insufficient	3 Uneven	4 Sufficient	5 Skillful	6 Excellent
Minimum of six story-boards						
Words verbatim from the text or in your own words						
Drawings convey meaning (you do not need to be a gifted artist, but make the meaning clear)						
You read at least five additional storyboards and discussed different interpretations						

NCTE/IRA Standards: 1, 2, 3, 4, 5, 11, 12

Figure 3.1   Sample Student Comic Strip

Sight Lesson 2
Imagine This!

Summary: Students learn about the imagist style of poetry and apply imagist techniques in their own writing.

> *Imagists believed that poetry can be made purer by concentration on the precise, clear, unqualified image. Imagery alone, the imagists believed, could carry a poem's emotion and message. It could do this almost instantly, without all the elaborate metrics and stanza patterns that were part of poetry's traditional mode.*
>
> —John Malcolm Brinnin, "Symbolism, Imagism, and Beyond,"
> in *Elements of Literature: Fifth Course*

Author: David James Poissant, University of Cincinnati

Senses: Sight (visualization), sound

Type of Activity: Begins with a group reading and analysis of poetry and ends with the creation of individual poems.

Approximate Time: Two to three class periods

Objectives: Students will become familiar with the imagist style of poetry. Students will use imagery and free verse to write their own poems modeled after those of the imagists.

Materials: Obtain enough copies of Ezra Pound's essay "A Few Don'ts by an Imagiste" for the entire class and provide several examples of imagist poetry; pen and paper; and photographs, magazine clippings, or works of art that present unique images.

Procedures

Day 1

1. Read a few imagist poems to the class. Suggested authors include Ezra Pound, Hilda Doolittle, Amy Lowell, William Carlos Williams, and Wallace Stevens.
2. Compare and contrast the styles of the authors.
3. Have students brainstorm a list of writing techniques that make imagist poetry different from traditional verse.
4. Read Pound's essay "A Few Don'ts by an Imagiste" and compare the students' assessment of the form with Pound's "rules."

Days 2 to 3

1. Present students with photographs or pictures cut from periodicals, or have students bring images from home.
2. Students must use imagery and simple language to write a paragraph describing their picture.
3. Students search the paragraphs for their best descriptions and phrases and use these to compose their own poems of five to ten lines.
4. Students meet in collaborative pairs and proofread one another's poems, checking to see that each poem meets the characteristics of the prior day's list and avoids breaking any of Pound's cardinal rules.
5. Students may then revise as necessary in class or for homework. Multiple drafts should be encouraged.
6. To complete the lesson, students present their poems, accompanied by the visual aids that inspired the poems, to the class.

The teacher is encouraged to compose a poem of his own to share as a model for the students. Sample poems by student authors are also helpful. The following poems are student examples:

A Sign in Jackson

Driving through Jackson
I saw a sign
glorifying the old,
a testament to time.
The faded letters
spoke of history,
showing the greatness
of a place that most call
nowhere.

The Pink Flower

Among others
this one stood out,
the only pink
against a background of yellow and green.
I wanted it,
but how could I

pick the only one?
It would no longer stand out
but simply be a pink flower.
Better to leave it
the only pink flower.

A Mother's Mother

Eyes sunken, by time,
deep into the surrounding landscape
of her face.

Skin, pale and yellowed
like lace curtains never washed
for fear they will come apart.

Fingers, bony and crooked,
their skin loose and wrinkled.

Hair like a painstakingly curled
helmet of spider's silk,
a mass that seems to float atop her head
rather than rest there.

Assessment Checklist

_____ Identify two stylistic similarities among writers

_____ Identify two stylistic differences among writers (can be different writers than previous two)

_____ List rules for imagistic verse (you make them up based on the readings)

_____ Complete written description of image

Assessment

	1 Unsatisfactory	2 Insufficient	3 Uneven	4 Sufficient	5 Skillful	6 Excellent
Quality of description and relevance to image						
Vivid, precise use of language in poem						
Poem adheres to (or purposefully violates) Pound's rules for imagistic poetry						
Oral performance of poem in class						

Commentary

The Imagine This! activity helps students, through a hands-on approach, understand and appreciate an important movement in early 20th century American literature. It helps dispel students' stereotypes of poetry as confusing, symbolic, or rhyming, and serves as a gateway to preparing students for contemporary American poetry, which is even less rule oriented. Students should also gain an understanding of imagery and free verse as they learn to compose poems in a new way.

NCTE/IRA Standards: 1, 2, 3, 4, 5, 6, 11, 12

Source: From D. J. Poissant, 2007, University of Cincinnati, Cincinnati, OH. Reprinted with permission.

Sight Lesson 3
Paint-Write

Summary: Students spontaneously create paintings, and then they write in response to what they painted.

Author: Mike Angelotti, University of Oklahoma

Senses: Sight, touch, movement, sound

Type of Activity: Individual or group

Approximate Time: Variable, from 10 minutes to several days

Objectives: Get students to write expressively about art. You can adapt the Paint-Write toward a variety of ends—response to literature; descriptive, expressive, or persuasive writing; tapping into creativity.

Materials: Tempera paint (washable kids' paint) with 10 or so colors in separate containers, watercolor brushes, watercolor paper, paper plates to use as palettes, plastic cups or glass jars for water, roll of plastic to cover desktops, masking tape, and scissors. Have students each supply a notebook (individual choice fosters ownership of and commitment to the activity) specifically for sketches and various kinds of compositions—a visual-verbal artist notebook.

Setup: Have all materials easily accessible for students.

Rationale

The first paint-write class is crucial to student acceptance of the process. In general, students need to splash paint on paper and write about it; that is, free paint and free write in an experimental, nonevaluative, nonacademic atmosphere. We have found that most students (and English teachers) have not played with paints since early elementary school and believe that they are without artistic talent, basically because they cannot paint an object to look precisely like that object, and have been told so in no uncertain terms. Consequently, they come to painting with some apprehension.

The focus on process, rather than product, and removal of judgment by peers and teacher, along with demonstration to self through practice, tends to relieve that tension, and replace it with genuine enthusiasm, dedication to personal growth, and productivity. The analogy to personal writing histories is painfully obvious—red ink marginalia and regimented grammar drills, for many, liken the act of writing to placing one's hand on a hot stove. Avoidance results; hence, free painting and free writing are helpful opening activities. Small-group to whole-group show-and-tell sessions tend to help students validate their work and appreciate the work of others. The goal is to connect free painting and free writing, to tap the creative energy common to both, and in the interactions between, develop abilities in both.

Once the flow is established, movement toward more formal writing—often teased out of the free writes, reads, and reflections—typically follows. Students begin to believe that they can become more accomplished writers. With hope and belief come engagement and motivation.

Procedures

1. Students enter the room and immediately begin working and playing, engaging with the paint, which is similar to doodling. They may keep the brush moving during class procedures as long as they are continuously in tune with the class and ready to participate appropriately. Such individually driven multitasking can promote skill development and focus.

2. Using brushes, paint, and water, students intensely fill various sizes of watercolor paper with brightly colored painting. Some students work independently, and others labor collaboratively.

3. Students study some of the completed paintings, free writing reflective pieces or writing poems in response to their own work or that of others, preparing for a paint-write show-and-tell session. Low-key talk relates to ongoing processes, staying on task.

4. The teacher paints, walks among the students, occasionally dipping her paintbrush into student palettes for fresh paint to put on her own paper, stopping to observe from time to time, responding to queries or to what she sees. The teacher casually reminds the visual-verbal artists that process, not product, is uppermost—the goal is to paint nothing, to get out of the way of brush and pen, or to allow creativity to happen. She calls attention to the time remaining until the next event.

5. The next event could be a read, a quick paint, a quick write, a choice piece, a recomposing session—whatever is on the agenda. Student and teacher choices link to student and teacher goals of the moment, and may run from generating word volume through free writes to developing pathways to writing sophisticated, response-to-literature essays and multigenre research papers.

Commentary

In its earliest, most restricted sense, *ekphrasis* referred to the verbal description of a visual representation, often of an imagined object such as the shield of Achilles in the *Iliad*. With its principle of *ut pictura poesis* (poetry as a speaking picture and painting as mute poetry), Horace's *Ars Poetica* expressed the ekphrasitic ideal of giving voice to painting. From Ben Jonson to the Romantics, many poets, most famously John Keats with his urn and Percy Bysshe Shelley with his fallen statue, have allowed art to inspire thought. Rainer Maria Rilke, the Surrealists, and William Carlos Williams continued the tradition in the 20th century (Blackhawk, 2002).

Any student who tries ekphrasis (writing that takes its inspiration from visual art) becomes a participant in the kind of dialogue that has engaged writers and artists for centuries. Listening to works of art and participating in a conversation with them can produce exciting and shifting responses in each of us: poems, stories, self-portraits, essays, and other creative works are generated that "talk back" to the visual stimulus (Foster & Prevallet, 2002, p. xv).

Now when we view Johannes Vermeer's *Girl with a Pearl Earring* as a prompt for Chevalier's novel of the same name and its cinematic adaptation, we know that is ekphrasis. At the least, we have a name and a deeper conceptualization for what English teachers (and others) have been encouraging, in a general sense, for decades—using visual art as a prompt for writing. Having this enhanced perception of what we do at a more conscious level suggests that we can better manipulate the visual-verbal transactions to the mutual advantage of our students as learners and ourselves as teachers.

The difference in the paint-write approach expressed here is that it describes a set of teaching strategies that substantially depend on student development emanating from their individual and collaborative interpretations of and reflections on art of their own making. Students apply paint to paper in a stream of consciousness fashion similar to that employed in free writing, not attempting to paint "something"; hence, the direction, "paint nothing." The resulting paints (see Color Plate 1.1 on p. 183, for example) often resemble abstract art more than anything else, not unlike that of Jackson Pollock.

Judgment is removed from the process, and along with it, anxiety. "Good" and "bad" paintings do not exist. Students then use their own paintings or those of classmates as prompts for free writing, followed by reflective writing on the paint-write just completed. Many combinations of the process are possible: solo, partner, collaborative, small-group, whole-class paints; paint-write, paint-paint, write-paint, write-write; recomposing free writes to more literary writes. Quick paints (1–3 minutes) to fill a page with paint encourage spontaneous painting and discourage judgments and planned painting. Longer duration paints, most effectively introduced later on, encourage reflection and contemplation, more deliberate painting, and contemplative writing. Once students are into it, paint-write innovations emerge from them nonstop. Frequent small- and whole-group show-and-tell sessions allow students to share their own work. Viewing and hearing the work of others can help students validate themselves as writers and painters in this learning community and provide opportunities for meaningful discourse.

The continuing practice of making visual and verbal art addresses meaningful engagement and growth in writing by reluctant and less able learners, as well as those more motivated and advanced. In particular, the process of free painting and then free writing encourages sheer volume of words and a sense of accomplishment by filling a page with self-generated writing. It also features opportunities for student and teacher self-appreciation as visual-verbal artists and learners. It can emphasize collaborative learning, oral language practice, understanding conventions of literary and visual art, portfolio assessment, and other possibilities limited only by the imagination of teacher and student. In brief, paint-write calls on cognitive and emotional play to engage and frame cognitive and emotional growth at the point of individual development. It is at once overtly fun and deeply effective as a set of learning tools.

Color Plate 1.2 on p. 184 is an example of a paint-write combination invented by students—a set of small-group collaborative quick paints and a following quick write collaborative poem. Using a scanner to merge the paints and write, this paint-write was duplicated on a color copy machine for each member of the class and included in the class anthology.

Color Plate 1.3 on p. 185 was one of several student responses to a handout depicting selected Chinese alphabetic characters. The student free painted the image in Color Plate 1.3 from the Chinese character on the chart symbolizing "tranquility," free writing the poem during and in response to the process of free painting.

Color Plate 1.4 on p. 186 is a spontaneous painting I created during a workshop a few years ago. I wrote the poem "And the Teacher Said, 'Paint Nothing'" in response.

Choice in personal writes and paints adds to student ownership and commitment to the whole enterprise, and therefore, to engagement and learning. Expanding the basic paint-write model to include other visual tools, such as cameras and computers, involves extra expense. However, many students already have these tools at their disposal. Beginning with the paint-write seems to work best, likely because of the simplicity and ease of spontaneous, nonjudgmental play associated with the vivid tempera paints—essentially, the familiarity of tools, flexibility and sense of paint-write combinations, and the feeling of accomplishment in painting and writing in just a few class sessions. When the increments of personally meaningful learning are obvious to students, they seem to be more motivated to engage in the activity that gets them there.

At the center is student growth in a democratic classroom that allows students to grow individually in aesthetic forms of choice while also meeting school requirements. In the end, students are more confident as writers, more able, and more willing to write at a moment's notice. They are more in touch with play, free painting, and free writing as learning tools of choice and as effective gateways to more formal written forms. Some students (and teachers) even discover an artistry within that they can grow to a satisfying level of visual and verbal accomplishment.

Assessment

Using a portfolio approach to assessment allows students to choose a minimum number of the various paint-write combinations assigned to represent their efforts over a particular grading period. Students also can be responsible for a daily reflective log and a reflective commentary on the effects of the whole experience. Paints and writes should decorate the room on a regular basis, and students can choose two or three pieces or combinations to include in a class anthology. Outcomes may be designed to engage students in personal writing, create word volume, enhance fluency, and help students move from visual-verbal free play to more formal pieces in realistic stages that advance voice and skill in pressing thought to paper in meaningful ways.

NCTE/IRA Standards: 1, 2, 3, 4, 5, 6, 10, 11, 12

Source: M. Angelotti, 2007, University of Oklahoma, Norman, OK. Reprinted with permission.

Sight Lesson 4
Reading Art (Developing Reading Comprehension Through Art)

Summary: Given the framework of an art critic, students learn to use paintings as springboards for writing and reading.

Author: Debra Winston, Carbondale, Colorado

Senses: Sight, sound, movement

Type of Activity: Individual

Approximate Time: Variable

Objectives: Students learn to appreciate, analyze, and interpret art. Students learn to write expressively about art and to apply fundamentals of art criticism to reading and writing.

Materials: Large art masterworks, tag board, permanent markers, paper and pens, and adhesive that peels off walls.

Procedures

1. Introduce the lesson by telling students they will be learning to study pictures the way some people read books. Then focus on a particular piece of art and model the process for students, asking questions about the images; imagining smells, sounds, and tastes; and interpreting what the author is trying to say. Have the students join in the think-aloud as it progresses and keep a running list of responses on the board. Review the responses, and discuss the synthesis of meaning they represent.

2. Place students in small groups and challenge them to use the same process with a different piece of art. Prepare Figure 3.2 as a handout, with the back side blank, and have students record their thoughts on the form.

3. Ask students to think about what connections they find with the piece, what they think about the artist's decisions and intended meaning, what questions the work brings up for them, what they see as the focal point, which of their senses are activated by the work, and what they interpret overall about the piece.

4. Have some groups "read" their piece of art to the class.

5. Ask students to circle the most powerful words on their own papers. Encourage them to share their choices selectively with their small groups. Circulate and help students find the power words—the words that really connect to the painting.

Figure 3.2   Reading Art Worksheet

Title of Work of Art ⎯⎯⎯⎯⎯⎯⎯⎯⎯⎯⎯⎯⎯⎯⎯⎯⎯⎯⎯⎯⎯⎯⎯⎯⎯

Observers ⎯⎯⎯⎯⎯⎯⎯⎯⎯⎯⎯⎯⎯⎯⎯⎯⎯⎯⎯⎯⎯⎯⎯⎯⎯⎯⎯⎯⎯⎯

What connection can we make to this piece of art? What text, music, plays, dances, or other experiences connect us to this piece of art? (Developing Schema)	When we look at this piece of art, we wonder about . . . ? (Questioning)
What can we assume by looking at this piece of art? (Inferring)	What senses are tapped by this work? What do you experience in terms of smell, taste, hearing, touch, and sight? What do you feel internally? (Creating Sensory Images)
What is the focal point? Where are your eyes drawn and why? (Determining Importance)	What is this piece of art all about? (Synthesizing)

Source: D. P. Winston, 2007, Expeditionary Learning Schools, Outward Bound, Carbondale, CO. Reprinted with permission.

6. In small-group discussions, have students decide which words belong together: Which words should be the first in telling us about the picture? Which words helped them understand the picture? Encourage them to end with a series of words to sum it all up: What is the poem all about? Ask them to use the back of the handout to combine each others' power words to create poetry that reveals what they think about the picture.

7. Walk from group to group, passing out tag board for students to write the powerful words into a poetic form, using a permanent marker. Give each group four dabs of the removable adhesive, so they can post their boards on the walls to create an art gallery. Place the corresponding picture next to each poem. Then have students walk around the room reading and viewing their gallery of ekphrastic poetry and the pictures that inspired them.

8. After they return to their seats, ask them if any group would like to read their poems aloud. If no one wants to read, the teacher can read them. Inevitably, students' reactions are tinged with amazement—"We did that?" They also tend to show perceptiveness when asked what makes a painting good.

Commentary

The following description provides an example of how I carried out this type of lesson as a visitor working with the classroom teacher at one school.

I greet a class of students at Toltecalli High School. Most students who are in this high school have no other options; they have babies or jobs or complications that have kept the local Tucson high schools from being a fit. As I come in with their teacher, the students already look bored, but they also seem a little curious.

When I tell them that today we will be reading art, one young man says, "But Miss, I bleed when I read."

"Wow," I say, "that must make reading very uncomfortable. What bleeds?"

"My head, my nose, blood comes out of my ears. . . ."

Reading is, indeed, a mighty injury to these students. Most of these 16- to 18-year-olds are reading at 3rd- to 5th-grade levels, and they struggle. I believe that the student who spoke up does feel as though he's bleeding when he's reading.

The rest of the students don't interact. They are hardened; their eyes say, "Sure. Show me."

I ask some of the students, in an attempt to make some connection, what they notice when they go to an art museum.

One tells me, "It's all quiet with people just staring like zombies."

"Yeah," I say, "these people are looking at the pictures like some people read books. Today I'm going to show you how to do that."

I quickly move their attention to a large picture by Romaire Bearden titled *Pittsburgh Memories*. I model the use of reading comprehension strategies, partnering with their teacher, taking turns looking at this piece of art by connecting it to our schema, asking questions, imagining smells, sounds, and tastes; we look deeply at the art by asking specific questions and guessing what the author is trying to say. We try to figure out what is most important together. Then we share with the students the synthesis of meaning that emerges after reading all of the recorded responses from this think-aloud.

Quickly, they are placed into small groups and challenged to do the same, this time with other pieces of art. I gave them copies of Figure 3.2 as a handout (with the back side blank) to record their thoughts. In this case, I selected *Miners' Wives* by Ben Shahn for the students to comment on (see Color Plate 1.5 on p. 187).

To get schemas activated, I asked, "What connections can we make to this piece?" then "What music, books, movies, or other experiences connect us to this piece of art?"

Here are some student responses:

"It's like classical music and a violin is being played in a sad tone."

"They are workers, like they are very poor and very dirty, like in a factory."

"Wives are sad or worried for the sake of their husbands."

Then I asked, "I wonder about the artist's choices and meaning. When we look at this piece of art, what do we wonder about?"

And the students said:

"What happened to this woman to make her look so sad?"

"Why are the pants hanging in the corner?"

"Why does she have such big hands?"

"Why are the guys walking away with their heads down?"

Next, I asked students to make an inference. "What can we assume about the lives of these individuals by looking at this piece of art?"

"We might think that these people have a sad life."

"I think she is worried."

"I'm guessing that they are a poor and lonely family."

I wanted students to make multisensory inferences, so I asked what sounds, smells, tastes, and textures the painting implied.

"It smells like smoke and dust from the factory and it looks very cold. I feel like I could hear footsteps in the piece."

Then, I asked, "What is the focal point? Where are your eyes drawn, and why?"

"To the woman because it feels like her eyes are looking into your soul."

"To her face and hands because she is not happy and she is just thinking about something that is bothering her."

Finally, I wanted students to try to pull all the pieces together.

"They work hard and still they are poor."

"I think she is worried because her husband died and that's why the men are walking away."

"The old lady with the baby is upset and maybe the baby will die too."

"And they have a hard life and then if her husband dies she will not have such a good life."

Without any further prompting, students started noticing even more details.

"The woman's eyes are very captivating. I feel that the people in this painting have sad thoughts throughout life."

"You know, I just knew it that somebody died."

I also used *Man with a Hoe* by Jean Francois Millet, which is especially effective in drawing out responses related to the senses.

A student said: "I can smell the smoke, taste thirst, hear the cows, and touch the dirt. I feel that the man is very tired and I see nothing but miles of land." Another said, "I smell slavery," and another commented, "I can smell the dryness of the dirt." One student put himself right into the picture: "My hands are hurting with a splinter."

We went through the rest of the procedures for this lesson, identifying powerful words, sharing choices, combining powerful words to make poems, and holding a gallery walk. We asked students to consider the presentations as works in an art gallery. Instead of just staring "like zombies," students read each others' ideas.

I didn't belabor the debriefing. In the coming days their teacher would use each element of the art comprehension strategies, but in relation to a text. Students would have opportunities to go more deeply into each of the six reading strategies. The power of the moment was that, as a group, they created ekphrastic poetry and proved that they didn't really bleed when they read. They were able to understand and respond to art, and create beautiful poetry.

In response to *Miners' Wives*, one group wrote the following poem.

Hard Violin

Sad worker; so much going on.
Baby filled with sorrow.
Lived, worked; for nothing.
Poor pants in the corner.
Survival's been so much.
Captivating a life-taking news.
Eyes are drawn to a woman that worked hard.
All that's left is nothing
But a sad tone playing.
Now with a new born baby
To nurture all by their lonesome selves

In response to the painting *Man with a Hoe* by Jean-Francois Millet (see an image of the work on display at the Getty Center Los Angeles at http://www.getty.edu/art/gettyguide/artObjectDetails?artobj=879), another group created the following poem.

A Man with a Hoe

Has no place to go
But to work in the heat
In his large warm world
He is hard working but tired
He has a sad life
What is going on in his head
At that very moment?
He is very tired of living that life.

Art that is associated with subject matter also works particularly well, as when the students studied the Japanese internment camps in the United States during World War II. We selected images and photos from the books *Topaz Moon: Chiura Obata's Art of the Internment* by Kimi Kodani Hill (2000) and *Only What We Could Carry: The Japanese American Internment Experience* by the California Historical Society and Lawson Fusao Inada (2000). By using these powerful pieces of art, the students were better able to bring the emotional experience of the internment camps to the surface and into their lives.

Although the initial experience fits nicely into an extended block (75 to 90 minutes) the exercise can easily be spread over two days. And from this base, each reading strategy can be investigated more deeply. This process helps students recognize that discovering meaning in a difficult piece of art is within their reach, as is the meaning in difficult text. They learn by having the tools and taking the time to use them.

Source: D. P. Winston, 2007, Expeditionary Learning Schools, Outward Bound, Carbondale, CO. Reprinted with permission.

4

Sound ■ ■ ■

No legacy and recurrence of inhumanity cancels out the myste-
*rium tremendum, the benediction of music. It is in music and
the indecipherable self-evidence of its effects on our consciousness that reside the lineaments of our possible humaneness. It is
music which carries with it the 'background noise and radiation'
(as cosmology would have it) of creation itself.*

—Steiner (1990, p. 221)

One year, my sixth-period remedial reading class was a complete disas-
ter. I could not seem to garner students' attention long enough to get
them to copy down the assignment for the day, let alone get them interested in actually writing down a few words on paper. I was lost as to what
to do. One day, while scrounging around in the musty book room, I came
upon a long metal structure that had multiple headphones attached to it.
I recognized the object as a multiuser listening station, likely a castaway
from the foreign language department. A second treasure was a massive,
heavy, old, but still intact cassette tape player. Eventually, I took these
devices back to my classroom, cleaned and sanitized them, and tried
them out. Surprisingly, the setup worked perfectly; the quality of the
sound was exceptional.

   As soon as students caught sight of the headphones, they were keen
to discover their use. "We going to listen to Spanish tapes, sir?" a student

asked. I wasn't sure what I was going to do with them, but I knew that whatever I did, it couldn't turn out much worse than what had been transpiring in my class thus far.

In this sixth-period class from the bowels of Hades (actually, this might be somewhat of an understatement), I had 18 boys and 4 girls, and it was the boys who gave me the most trouble. After a few days of stewing over what I might be able to do with the headphone station, I decided that I would use it as a reward. On Monday, I explained the new arrangement. If students participated every day of the week, had no marks for misconduct, and had no zeros on their assignments, then on Friday, after the vocabulary test, they could listen to music on the headphones for the last 20 minutes of class. However, they had to choose from my musical selections.

To my surprise, this simple promise seemed to ignite a few students immediately in terms of both conduct and academics. At the end of the first week, two students qualified to listen to music. That represented two more students than were passing the previous week. These two students gloated over their special status sufficiently to make the other students a little envious. While the two students listened to music, the rest of the class answered questions about a recently read short story.

At the end of the second week, the number of students who qualified for the music station had doubled to four. Although several students had missed the cut-off by only an assignment or two, I was resolute about the requirements—no zeros and no marks for bad behavior.

By the third Friday, eight students qualified for music listening. As there were only eight pairs of headphones, I started to think about adjustments to the qualifications. Instead of good conduct and turning in all assignments, I upped the qualifying criteria to include an average of at least a 75 on their assignments and perfect attendance (including no tardies) Monday through Thursday. This was a significant change, as half of the class typically would be absent on a given day. Initially, the new, more rigorous requirements cut the listening group back to four, but a few Fridays later, the group threatened to exceed eight again.

Finally, I spoke with the chair of the foreign language department and discovered that she had another set of eight headphones that she was perfectly willing to let me borrow (she never used them). I set up a second listening station and added the requirement that students had to read books, write, or draw while they listened to music. Unexpectedly, students did not argue over the new requirement, perhaps because they had heard rumors that I was in trouble with the chair of the English

Department. In fact, the chair was angry at me and probably with some justification. I was using music as a lure—and the music was unrelated to the sanctioned curriculum. Nevertheless, this simple ploy transformed my classroom from a chaotic mess to a somewhat orderly environment. The 20 minutes of music on Fridays seemed like a bargain price to pay for four-and-a-half days of mostly cooperative, interested students.

In retrospect, the scenario seems unbelievable—the behavior of a group of rowdy adolescents improved by the promise of 20 minutes of uninterrupted music one day per week. As a teacher, witnessing the power of a few, well-placed acoustic waves (music) to alter the behavior of adolescents influenced my practice more than any 300 research studies. Perhaps Bunt (1994) had it right when he noted, "As changes occur in our lives, our ideas, and our emotions, these can be articulated symbolically in musical forms. We do not need to know all the details of these ideas and feelings to understand and be moved by the music. Music can act as a transformer of shared meaning" (p. 73).

In many ways, the person who controls the sound in a classroom controls the curriculum. That is why quelling a class before beginning a lesson is essential for the success of most lessons. Indeed, in a class engulfed by noise, learning may be impossible. On the other hand, unremitting silence can lead to boredom and disengagement. A teacher who fails to launch a discussion following an assigned reading knows all too well the terror of silence and diverted eyes. When students have nothing to say, progress can be difficult and cumbersome. A common criticism made by contemporary scholars is that the soundscapes of many classrooms are overpowered by too much teacher talk and too little student comment (Cazden, 1995; Dekker & Elshout-Mohr, 1998; Nussbaum, 1992; Zander, 2003). Whereas too little teacher talk can lead to aimlessness, too much teacher talk can shut down student involvement. Of course, there is a happy medium between the two. Researchers have repeatedly found that well-crafted teacher talk can foster engagement, thinking, and higher achievement (Boyd & Rubin, 2002; Hansen, 2004; Moje, 1995; Prusak, Pangrazi, & Vincent, 2005). Certainly, one aspect of a teacher's job is to instruct, but an equally vital role is to listen.

In listening to a classroom, a teacher must strive to be aware of the sounds that dominate. How often are the voices of students heard? Are deep thinking and participation promoted through questioning? Does talk relate to the topic at hand or is it superfluous?

In the early 20th century, teachers required students to memorize and recite long passages of text while standing by their desks. Now rote memorization is out of vogue, but such a tactic at least guaranteed that students heard masterfully written language in the voices of their fellow students. Today, because some teachers are too busy to make time for reading aloud, some students never learn what eloquence sounds like. They leave school with tin ears, at least with regard to language.

Most teachers are only semiconscious of the ways that sound can influence learning. Yet a student in the back row who fails to hear the soft-spoken teacher at the front of the room is certainly affected by sound. If all teachers had voices like James Earl Jones (the voice of Darth Vader), no doubt student attention would be enhanced. However, even a teacher with a frail, halting voice should strive to accomplish the following:

1. Enunciate clearly in language that can be heard and understood by all students.
2. Modulate the voice for effect.
3. Use silence purposefully (for example, a long pause before offering the resolution to a story).
4. Use props that invoke other senses—sight, touch, movement, taste, or smell.
5. Say something worthwhile.

Usually, teachers fret so much over item 5 that they forget that 1, 2, 3, and 4 have a significant influence on whether a message is received, understood, and retained for longer than a few seconds.

Some innovative programs have attempted to teach children reading and writing through auditory strategies. The most successful of these programs use voice-to-text technologies, meaning that when students speak into a microphone, their utterances are transformed into written text via a computer program (such as Dragon NaturallySpeaking or Philips SpeechMagic). Researchers have found that student performance in reading comprehension, word recognition, and spelling can be enhanced substantially using these sound-based procedures, particularly for students reading below grade level who may also have learning disabilities (Higgins & Rashkind, 2000, 2004; Rashkind & Higgins, 1999).

Also of note is a device called a WhisperPhone, which relies on auditory signals. As students read, they whisper into a phone-like headset, and the voice is carried back to their ears without disturbing other students. Although the device does not translate speech to text, it reportedly increases "accuracy and expression" (Strauss, 2006).

Hearing and Listening

When I was a teenager, I purchased a cheap dog whistle from a reputable firm that did business via full-page ads in comic books. Although the dog whistle did in fact get the desired result from my dog—his ears perked up and he turned his head to the side—I could hear nothing. Strangely enough, my grandmother, who had "selective poor hearing," could also hear the high-pitched sound emitted by the dog whistle. Although she did not hear us when we asked her to take us to the park, she insisted that the high-pitched shriek of the dog whistle gave her a headache.

Relative to other mammals, the human ear is underpowered. It can easily pick up frequencies between 2 and 4 kilohertz, a range that covers the sounds of speech, but it may miss sounds outside of this range (Fountain, 2004). In contrast, the range of hearing for a dog is twice that of a human; a mouse's range is double a dog's range; and a porpoise's range is almost double a mouse's range (Strain, 2006). Thus, when you observe your dog pawing a place against the wall, it might be hearing a mouse noisily scurrying around back there. Whereas a porpoise would be able to discern the sound of an approaching shark from a mile away, the sound of the shark might go unnoticed by a human, even if the shark were swimming alongside.

Until recently, hearing was perceived as a passive process, a simple, biological mechanism that merely received sound waves. However, research has revealed that an optimally functioning auditory system involves active cognitive processing as a matter of course (Bunt, 1994; Gazzaniga, 1995; Plomp, 2002; Wallin, Merker, & Brown, 1999). When cognition kicks in, context becomes crucial. For example, while hiking on a remote mountain trail, the sound of a baby crying may be mistaken for the sound of an animal, whereas the sound of a baby crying would never be mistaken if heard in the maternity wing of a hospital. That is why many scientists prefer to think of hearing "as a holistic rather than an elementalistic process" (Gazzaniga, 1995).

To fully appreciate the complexity of the auditory system, think about the scenario of a lively party. The environment would be filled with music, possibly very loud music. You enter with a friend and chat casually while you check out who else is there. As you listen to your friend make chitchat about buying a new car, your ears pick up the conversation of three women standing nearby. They are saying that an attendee at the party is a talent scout looking for an individual to play the part of a middle school teacher in a movie that has just begun filming. Apparently, the part could be worth hundreds of thousands of dollars for only a few weeks of work over the summer. Although you are enjoying the music and also listening to your friend's humorous monologue about shopping for a new car, you are simultaneously processing the conversation of these three women despite high degrees of interference. Even if bits and pieces of their conversation get drowned out, you are able to fill in the blanks from the context of the conversation.

The same kind of processing occurs when a seasoned teacher is orchestrating a small-group activity. While walking around the room and stopping to help one group, the teacher is also simultaneously scanning the conversations and actions of individuals in the other groups for signs of engagement or off-task behavior. To a neophyte teacher with little experience working in such a context, the task of simultaneous monitoring may seem hopelessly complicated.

In technical terms, a brief summary of what transpires when we hear is as follows: "The peripheral ear, working as a straightforward frequency analyzer, is followed by a second, neural stage in which the spectral components originally belonging to the same sound are reunited in a single percept. Specific processes must be employed resulting in the perception of timbre as the counterpart of the sound's spectrum, pitch as the counterpart of its periodicity, and loudness as the counterpart of its sound level" (Plomp, 2002).

In other words, especially with experience, the ear is able to capture and interpret a variety of sounds almost instantaneously. Surprisingly, the right and left ears appear to process sound differently—the right ear is better at processing speech, and the left ear is better at processing music. This may be why students who are deaf in the right ear have more difficulties at school than students who are deaf in the left ear (O'Connor, 2004).

The Power of Music

Aldous Huxley wrote, "After silence, that which comes nearest to expressing the inexpressible is music" (Huxley, 1931, p.19). Indeed, because music involves several parts of the brain, including areas associated with language ability, emotions, and rhythm, it can have profound effects on our attitudes and learning (Boxhill, 1985; Pinker, 1997). For example, if you went to kindergarten or 1st grade somewhere in the United States, although you have not rehearsed it in years, I bet that you would be able to launch spontaneously into an unabridged version of the alphabet song at this very moment ("A, B, C, D, E, F, G . . ." sung to the tune of *Twinkle, Twinkle, Little Star*). When my son was 10 years old, he learned the names of all the states and capitals by singing a hip-hop tune that he remembers to this day (along with the states and their capitals). Furthermore, if you want to learn the correct pronunciation of a word, the easiest way to remember it is to sing it, preferably using a melody and a beat.

Human response to music, it seems, is built into our genes at birth. Infants as young as 2 months old have been shown to prefer intervals of perfect fifths or fourths over dissonant sounds. According to Trehub (2003), "The rudiments of music listening are gifts of nature rather than products of culture" (p. 673). Commenting on when musical training should begin, Hungarian composer and educator Zoltán Kodály (2008) asserts, "Nine months before the birth of the mother."

In his work with children, Kodály advocated a learning environment full of activity and music—singing, dancing, clapping, and using hand signals. Researchers have found that 1st graders who were taught music through Kodály training showed significantly higher reading scores when compared against comparable groups of 1st graders who had no Kodály training. In one longitudinal study, the reading scores of 1st graders exposed to the Kodály method of learning continued to increase at higher rates for years afterward (Gazzaniga, 1995). The software program "Singing Coach" has shown remarkable success in expanding students' vocabulary. By singing unfamiliar words to musical accompaniment, students learn the pronunciation and meanings of new words. Using a pretest/posttest design, Homan and colleagues (2007) have noted that some students advanced one to three grade levels after participating in only two 45-minute sessions during a 10-week trial.

The power of music is even acknowledged by the U.S. government, as each branch of the armed forces—Air Force, Army, Coast Guard, Marines, and Navy—sponsors several musical groups and provides hundreds of millions of dollars of financial backing (National Endowment of the Arts, 2004). As Langer (1942) has noted, "The real power of music lies in the fact that it can be true to the life of feeling in a way that language cannot" (p. 243).

Music Therapy

In addition to educative and behavioral benefits, music may have therapeutic value as well (Shaller & Smith, 2002). Some hospitals have begun to integrate music into their comprehensive rehabilitation plans. For example, in one study at a hospital, bone marrow patients were randomly assigned to one of two groups—one took part in music and imagery sessions twice per week (in addition to the standard rehabilitative procedures) while the control group received only the standard procedures. Those patients who took part in the music and imagery sessions reported significantly less pain and nausea than those in the control group. In this experiment, the self-reported data were supported by biological evidence—the patients in the music and imagery group actually produced new white blood cells two days faster than those in the comparison group (Daitz, 2003).

For patients recuperating from surgery, music has been shown to have calming effects on nurses and a rejuvenating effect on patients. A harpist placed in a surgical recovery room at a busy hospital in New York yielded faster healing and a more optimistic outlook among patients. In response to the music, one patient said, "I felt if I could just be feeling this calm and relaxed this soon after surgery, things are only going to get better" (Kelley, 2006, p. A14). Apparently, music can influence autonomic and immunologic systems in ways that help the body and mind heal.

One of the advantages of using sound therapy is that music is not logocentric (dependent on words), and thus can work across cultures, age groups, and levels of intelligence. As Spencer (2002) noted, "Music must take rank as the highest of the fine arts—as the one which, more than any other, ministers to human welfare. . . . We cannot too much applaud that musical culture which is becoming one of the characteristics of our age" (p. 48). Because of music's successful track record in terms of rejuvenation and spirit, new uses are being developed in the areas of mental health, medicine, special education, gerontology, autism, and speech. A fascinating use of music has been with children in hospices, places designed for the physical and emotional needs of the terminally ill.

Sweeney-Brown (2005) tells the story of working with a 10-year-old boy named Mark, diagnosed with a brain tumor and given only a matter of days to live. Despite nausea, dizziness, and a rapidly deteriorating condition, Mark came alive when working with a musical therapist, who brought along a set of drums. While playing the drums, Mark became completely engaged. Sweeney-Brown notes, "The sheer aliveness and joy of the music surprises both of us, and Mark seems to gain physical energy as he plays" (p. 57).

Similarly, Eaves (2005) used keyboards and other tech toys to engage teens with muscular dystrophy. Like Mark, the boys with whom Eaves worked became totally captivated by creating and listening to music. The music provided momentary relief and offered a constructive outlet of expression for students who struggled to maintain their dignity amidst faltering physical conditions. Even in the most sophisticated, up-to-date medical setting, "music has an irreplaceable role in comforting children, working with their pain, their suffering, their fears, and their beauty" (Sweeney-Brown, 2005, p. 60).

In another example, to reduce misbehaviors in autistic children, Brownell (2002) used a combination of reading and singing. Several possible outcomes of therapeutic uses of music that Barksdale (2003) notes include to effect personal change, improve social skills, support intellectual development, and contribute to the attainment of self-actualization.

Music and Identity

Perhaps there is no stronger indicator of group identity for adolescents than preferences in music. Indeed, looking back on life in high school, many adults associate particular songs with significant events in their lives (Bunt, 1994). At the last high school I visited, a student informed me that student cliques could be categorized by musical taste: Gangsta rap, hip-hop dance music, top 40, country and western, Spanish, current rock and roll, old rock and roll, punk, Gothic, space music, and classical. Subsets within these musical groups exist. For example, a distinction can be made between students who prefer old-school rap and those who prefer newer rap artists.

Students who like a particular kind of music seem to gravitate toward outward displays of allegiance—dress, language, mannerisms, leisure time pursuits, even attitudes toward learning—that are consistent with the musical genre. About music, Steiner (1971) writes, "Rock and pop breed concentric worlds of fashion, setting, and life-style. Popular music has brought with it sociologies of private and public manner, of group solidarity. The politics of Eden come loud" (p. 116).

Last year, I conversed with a high school student about a string of zeros for work he failed to complete. I was confused because I had witnessed him completing some of the tasks during the class for which he received zeros. After a while, he admitted that he purposefully chose not to turn in several assignments to keep his grade from rising above the *D* level. "Ain't too many rappers school boys," was the rationale he offered. Although I understood his point, I felt obliged to inform him that Kanye West's parents were both professors of English (Tyrangiel, 2005).

Despite its boundary-defining qualities, music can serve as a unifying presence across cultures. For example, a classical music lover might be able to appreciate a hip-hop song, and a rock fan might enjoy a country tune. In a study of social behavior in high school, Milner (2004) found that music often served as the catalyst for fostering communication among groups. Whereas fans of Gangsta rap might not dress or talk like the classical music crowd, both might be able to appreciate a Beethoven symphony. Milner (2004) writes, "The relevant point for understanding contemporary high schools is that where people seek to develop links across social boundaries—as different groups of adolescents frequently do—language and music may be a more available medium than consumer goods" (p. 56).

Implications for Teachers

Whereas learning through music can help something to be remembered for a long time (perhaps indefinitely), an overreliance on purely verbal delivery has been shown to be relatively ineffective. In other words, students remember only a fraction of information from a straight lecture unless the lecturer chooses to also integrate visual, olfactory, or kinesthetic props. A lecturer who uses a variety of relevant, multisensory stimuli can be quite effective.

Perhaps the most striking evidence about sound is its effect on human emotion. There are accounts, for example, of Albert Einstein's love of music (particularly his affection for the music of Mozart) and how music influenced his theories in physics. According to Einstein's son, whenever the scientist "felt that he had come to the end of the road or into a difficult situation in his work, he would take refuge in music. That would usually resolve all his difficulties" (Miller, 2006, p. D3).

Beethoven said that music was the bridge between the senses and the soul (Morris, 2005). Music and sound can be powerful tools, even for teachers like me, who stumble onto them out of sheer luck and desperation. "We do not need to know all the details of . . . ideas and feelings to understand and be moved by music. Music can act as a transformer of shared meaning" (Bunt, 1994, p. 73). The following activities use sound and music in unique ways to foster learning.

Activity	Entry Point	Focus	Preparation Time
Sound Lesson 1 Film Score	Music	Descriptive writing, persuasive writing, vocabulary	Minimal
Sound Lesson 2 Low-Down Character Analysis Blues	Music	Poetry writing	Minimal
Sound Lesson 3 Soundtrack of Your Life	Music	Expressive writing, expository writing	Substantial
Sound Lesson 4 Raider Record	Music	Evaluative writing, criticism, persuasive writing	Substantial
Sound Lesson 5 Adagio Suite	Music and art	Poetry writing	Substantial

In the Film Score activity, students are asked to identify an appropriate soundtrack for a particular passage of text, then justify the music's relevance through a piece of persuasive writing. Low-Down Character Analysis Blues uses meter and a simple poetic pattern to teach students about sentence rhythm, rhyme, and word selection. Soundtrack of Your Life uses students' predilections for contemporary music and their tendencies toward narcissism to encourage self-reflection and to teach narrative and evaluative writing skills. Similarly, Raider Record uses contemporary music as a springboard to teach persuasive and classificatory techniques. Finally, Adagio Suite gives students several quick experiences, including a few interactions with music and images, to which they respond in a series of rapid writing activities. Eventually, students gather together their disparate writings to create a single, longer work. Inevitably, the final product almost creates itself, an aspect of the assignment which most students find fascinating.

Sound Lesson 1
Film Score

Summary: After reading a novel, students listen to five pieces of music. They describe the scene that the music best fits, then select the best overall musical selection for the novel.

Senses: Sound and sight

Type of Activity: Individual

Time: One day

Objectives: Students use their knowledge of a text in writing a response to music. Students write persuasively about music.

Materials: Pen and paper

Commentary: Recently I did Film Score with a class after they had read Meg Rosoff's *How I Live Now* (2004), a story about an adolescent girl who moves from America to live with relatives in England just before the outbreak of a future world war. During the story, the main character, Daisy, falls in love with her older English cousin, Edmund, and becomes a kind of mother figure to her younger female cousin, Piper. Eventually, the war spills over to the farmhouse, and they must flee the area to survive. The group encounters many obstacles, and the family members become separated. Some characters die or disappear. Daisy gets injured and is taken back to America. After a separation of six years, Daisy returns to England and finds Edmund and Piper.

This exercise can be used with any book, although I recommend that you find music that fits the themes.

Procedures
1. Tell students that they are directors of a film. They are adapting *How I Live Now* for film and must select the appropriate music for certain scenes in the book.
2. Write on the blackboard or the overhead projector the list of songs.
3. Students write and draw while the music plays. When the song is over, give students one or two minutes to finish.
4. Once all the songs have been played, have each student select the song that best represents the book's theme. At the end of the paper containing written reactions to the various songs, the

student should explain why the selected song is the most fitting by discussing the book's theme, tone, and plot.

5. The songs I chose for *How I Live Now* were as follows:
   a. Ralph Vaughan Williams, *Fantasia on a Theme of Thomas Tallis*
   b. The Cure, *Friday, I'm in Love*
   c. Hildegard Von Bingen, *Spiritui Sancto*
   d. Frederic Chopin, Etude Op 10. no. 12, *Revolutionary*
   e. Nat King Cole, *Unforgettable*
   f. Brian Jonestown Massacre, *When Jokers Attack*
6. Put students in groups of three or four. Have students share their writing with each other.
7. Lead a discussion of the novel and the music by considering each song and possible scenes associated with it, using contributions from students. See Figure 4.1 as an example.

Extension Activities

A full-blown film director exercise can also be a great deal of fun. Have students choose contemporary actors, actresses, directors, settings, and writers for the filmed adaptation of the novel. Tell students to focus on why these individuals and places would be best for providing a genuine representation of the novel.

Assessment

	1 Unsatisfactory	2 Insufficient	3 Uneven	4 Sufficient	5 Skillful	6 Excellent
Image or written response for each musical selection						
One musical selection selected as most fitting for the book						
Rationale for most fitting musical selection is substantiated through the text						

NCTE/IRA Standards: 1, 2, 3, 4, 5, 6, 7, 10, 11, 12

Figure 4.1   Film Score

A) Williams

The scene where the soldiers come to their house and the girls and boys are seperated. This music would be played when Piper and Daisy are on their way to an Unknown Place (The M'Evoy Rome). It provides a sense of fear and sadness. Daisy is constantly faced with seperation.

B) Cure

The scene when the family goes to the river for the day and has a wonderful afternoon. Edmond and Daisy sit on the Blanket together in love. This song is carefree with an upbeat attitude.

C) Hildecard

This is the scene when Aunt Penn shares the photographs and memories of Daisy's mother with her niece. Daisy is informed of the information about her mother prior to her marriage. This music is somber and is appropriate to set the mood of when Daisy thinks of her mother's death and herself as the cause.

D) Chopin

This is the scenes of piper and daisy traveling on their journey, forced to take of each other, finding their own food and shelter, and hiding from the enemy. They have a feeling of where they are headed, but not certain they are on the right path.

E) Cole

This scene is when Daisy returns to England after six years and is reunited with Edmond, their relationship stands the test of time, and although they were

Figure 4.1 *(continued)*

seperated physically, Edmond often visited her mentally and they stayed connected.

F.) <u>Massacre</u>

This scene is the aftermath of the discovered murders at the farmhouse. Daisy and Piper are confronted with death from a physical aspect to the smell. They end up perserving and finding their home which brought rejoice with the comfort of familiarity.

The best one is "Friday, I'm in Love" by Cure. It is very understandable and relates well to the excitement between the family and Daisy as it's new addition. This song represents love togetherness, and inseperable bonds. Despite all the hardships Daisy has been through, and the war in their country, these kids still find love and happiness. It remindes be of the joy of childhood and living life to the fullest. The song should put any audience member in a good mood and represents the books emotions phenomendly.

Sound Lesson 2
Low-Down Character Analysis Blues

Summary: Writing character analysis blues lyrics provides a refreshing learning experience while examining a work of literature. Specifically, I have used this assignment with *Invisible Man* and *Native Son* because it helps students understand a little about African American culture as well as the protagonists of each work.

Author: Chris Goering, University of Arkansas

Senses: Sound, sight, movement

Type of Activity: Student pairs

Approximate Time: One 50-minute class period

Objective: Students will analyze a character's hardships and problems, will demonstrate an understanding of writing call-and-response lyrics, and will create unity in writing.

Materials: Play samples of songs with call-and-response lyrics. Some excellent choices would be *Texas Flood* by Stevie Ray Vaughan and Double Trouble, *Crossroads* by Robert Johnson, and *Got My Mojo Working* by Muddy Waters.

Procedures

In Advance

Alert students far enough in advance that on Day 1 they will need to come to class having read a novel, story, or poem.

Day 1

1. Place students in pairs.
2. Ask students if they have ever heard blues music. Ask them what they remember about it.
3. Play an example of a blues song with call-and-response lyrics.
4. Read the student example aloud from the bottom of Figure 4.2.
5. Play portions of the prerecorded blues songs.
6. As a class, have students suggest call-and-response lyrics for a minor character in the novel or a famous person in the news. Write the student-generated lyrics on the transparency or blackboard.

Figure 4.2   Blues with Call-and-Response Lyrics

Call-and-response lyrics are structured so that the first line is repeated as the "call" for help and the final line is the "response" or answer to the problem or situation at hand.

The call and response has a distinctive rhythm and rhyming pattern. The consistent rhyming pattern is an end rhyme in which the last word of each line within a stanza rhymes.

a

a

a

b

b

b

c

c

c

Loose rhyming and different rhythms provide individuality and creativity within the call and response. In the following example, a student expresses her feelings about her English class.

Honors English Blues

This is why I sing the blues, the low-down Honors English blues

Yes, this is why I'm singin' the blues, the Honors English blues

Too much homework, no more time, we're all singin' the blues!

Source: C. Goering, 2007, University of Arkansas. Reprinted with permission.

7. Once students have grasped the concept of call and response, brainstorm with students the many different characteristics of a main character. Write out student comments on the blackboard or transparency.

8. Have students write blues lyrics about the character's problems from the character's perspective.

9. After students compose their song lyrics, volunteers share the lyrics they have written with the class by singing them or speaking them.

Extension Activities

Once students learn the call-and-response form, many will begin to use this form of poetry writing as a personal outlet for their own problems. Many students extend this activity on their own time by writing blues lyrics about their struggles: *Homework Blues*, *Driver's License Blues*, *English Class Blues,* and so on. Having students perform these songs in class is highly recommended.

Assessment

	1 Unsatisfactory	2 Insufficient	3 Uneven	4 Sufficient	5 Skillful	6 Excellent
Poem fits blues format						
Poem is written from character's perspective						
Performance—clarity of lyrics and voice						
Performance—creativity and style						

NCTE/IRA Standards: 1, 2, 3, 4, 5, 6, 9, 10, 11, 12

Source: C. Goering, 2007, University of Arkansas. Reprinted with permission.

Sound Lesson 3
Soundtrack of Your Life

Summary: Students select eight major life events and eight songs to go with them. Eventually, each student creates a narrative explaining those choices.

Author: Chris Goering, University of Arkansas

Senses: Sound, sight, movement

Type of Activity: Individual

Approximate Time: Four 50-minute class periods

Objective: Students will write reflectively and personally.

Materials: The Soundtrack of Your Life assignment sheet (see Figure 4.3) contains places for students to write in the names of songs and artists. It may also be necessary for students to consult liner notes in a compact disc (CD) or appropriate Internet sites for lyrics. *The Green Book* by Jeff Green (2002) is a great optional resource which provides a thematic categorization of over 20,000 song titles.

Setup: Play music as the students are entering the classroom.

Procedures

Day 1
1. Play Bon Jovi's *It's My Life*.
2. Discuss the meaning and message of the song and the possible relationships to Jon Bon Jovi's life.
3. Next, have the students discuss this song in relevance to their own lives.
4. After the discussion, have the students choose eight major events in their lives—deaths, first car, entering high school—and then choose a song to go with each event. Some students will need to complete the list as homework.

Day 2
1. Have the students collect the titles of at least eight meaningful songs that correspond to the events they chose on Day 1. The songs should be of a school-appropriate nature.

Sound   73

Figure 4.3   Soundtrack of Your Life: Project Assignment

Music has become an integral part of human existence. It motivates us, calms us, inspires us, at times irritates us, and basically becomes the backdrop against which we live our lives. Songs can bring vivid memories of people, places, and events from our own past and serve to document our thoughts, feelings, and emotions at a given time or place.

Part I Assignment: Imagine you were asked to compile a soundtrack for your life. What songs would you include? Collect the titles of at least eight songs that are meaningful to you and that you feel document something personal in your own life. Just as music producers do, try to create a progression in the sequence of your chosen songs. For example, your songs might be listed in the chronological order of the events they document, or they might be mixed together so that all of the slow songs are not back-to-back. DO NOT just list them randomly. Put some thought into the order of your songs and the complete package you are presenting.

Song Title	Artist or Group
Track 1 _____	_____
Track 2 _____	_____
Track 3 _____	_____
Track 4 _____	_____
Track 5 _____	_____
Track 6 _____	_____
Track 7 _____	_____
Track 8 _____	_____
(extra) _____	_____
(extra) _____	_____

Part II Assignment: Now that you have created the imaginary soundtrack to your life, write a reflective letter (addressed to "Dear Listener") that explains why you chose the particular songs that you did. For each song you will need to reflect on the experiences, people, places, and so on that inspired this selection. Obviously you will also need to explain who you are as a person and then offer some type of reflection on the imaginary album as a whole. Again, for the purposes of this assignment, be sure that this letter is school appropriate. Use the outline below to help you construct this letter. You need to cover each topic listed in the appropriate number of paragraphs; however, the questions listed are there only to help you begin thinking about the topic. You do not need to answer every question or any of the questions as long as you have sufficiently explained the topic of each section. Remember, in reflective writing, longer is usually better!

Figure 4.3   *(continued)*

Topic 1—Explanation of yourself (one paragraph)

This paragraph is basically a brief autobiography:

• Who are you?

• Where are you from?

• Where are you now?

Topic 2—Explanation of this soundtrack (one paragraph)

This paragraph outlines your rationale or purpose in creating this soundtrack:

• What is this album you have created?

• Why are you completing it? ("Because it is an assignment" is NOT an answer!)

• What do you hope to get out of this project?

• What do you see yourself doing with this later in life?

• What goals did you have for creating it?

Figure 4.3 *(continued)*

Topic 3—Explanation of each song on the soundtrack (one paragraph per song)

This section is made up of many smaller paragraphs. Song by song, be sure to explain the following:

• What is the name of the song and the artist?

• Why is this song important to you?

• How does this song connect to your life?

• What does this song reveal about the kind of person you are and what you think is important in your life?

Topic 4—Final remarks and reflection on the soundtrack as a whole (one paragraph)

This paragraph is your conclusion in which you should thank your reader for taking the time to listen to your soundtrack and you can offer any final reflections on this project as a whole.

Part III Assignment: Now that the writing portion of this assignment is complete (deep breath), it is time to present a very small section of your soundtrack to the class. This presentation requires that you read one of your eight events and songs in an author's chair setting (the author stands or sits in front of the class and reads or sings aloud). Also, make and explain a visual aid by creating a CD cover, concert poster, or flyer, or some other idea that somehow represents your soundtrack for your presentation.

Source: C. Goering, 2007, University of Arkansas. Reprinted with permission.

2. By using CD liner notes, the Internet, and *The Green Book*, help students find lyrics that fit their events.
3. It is also helpful to encourage sharing song lyrics or life events in order for students to find songs that fit their musical tastes.

Day 3

1. Now that the students have created imaginary soundtracks for their lives, have each student write a reflective letter that explains why each event and song is included.
2. Create examples or use examples from previous students to help explain the expectations of the assignment.
3. Have students follow the directions in Figure 4.3 for constructing the soundtracks of their lives.

Day 4 (several days after Day 3)

1. This is the day the writing assignment and a visual aid are due for presentation to the class.
2. Students need only share a small portion of their soundtrack; this helps everyone feel more comfortable in front of the class.
3. As the students share their visual aids (usually CD cases of their soundtracks), they begin to understand their peers, which builds a positive classroom climate and mutual respect among students.

Extension Activities

Use this same imaginary soundtrack activity but create the soundtrack to a novel your class is reading instead. This works extremely well because it challenges students to summarize the main ideas of each chapter with an individual song that shares a similar meaning. Other successful and creative ideas include a poster and presentation, an interview with the rock star (student), a CD release party, a mock concert, or a behind-the-music documentary.

Commentary

Soundtrack of Your Life combines students' obsessions with music with personal narrative. The assignment sets a positive tone at the beginning of school by having students share their lives with each other and with the teacher. Through the vehicle of the personal narrative, I learn about my students' backgrounds as I provide them with comfortable ground for their first writing efforts. Of course, the personal narrative—particularly as it connects to music—also engages students in the emotional response that I will expect from them when, later in the school year, they respond to literature.

Assessment

I like to use Soundtrack of Your Life as an activity to get to know students. As such, I do not assess these pieces for a grade. I prefer to comment on the content of what students write and leave evaluations for later in the term.

NCTE/IRA Standards: 1, 3, 4, 5, 6, 7, 8, 9, 11, 12

Source: C. Goering, 2007, University of Arkansas. Reprinted with permission.

Sound Lesson 4
Raider Record

Summary: Students listen to, evaluate, critique, present, and write about music.

Authors: Mark Rabbit and Rob Deckard, Toledo, Ohio

Senses: Sound, sight, movement

Type of Activity: Individual

Objective: Through the use of music, students will learn to write critical, persuasive, informative, and evaluative papers. Students will also learn to think critically, analyze information, and create concrete and supportive arguments.

Materials: CD player, overhead projector, and (if you would like) a VHS or DVD player and video projector

Procedures

Two Days in Advance
1. Inform students that for the next few days they will be doing Raider Record.
2. Students are to bring in a song of their choice. The song's lyrics should not violate school policy with regard to cursing, sex, violence, or drugs (that might eliminate half of the students' first selections).
3. Tell students that each one will make a presentation that includes the following information:
   a. History of the singer or band
   b. Title of the song
   c. Lyrics
   d. Reasons the song was chosen
4. Students should furnish the teacher with a copy of the lyrics the next class period.

One Day in Advance (this activity will likely last 10 minutes or so)
1. Remind students that lyrics cannot violate school policy. Encourage students to be conscious of lyrics that could get them in trouble.
2. The teacher might provide some in-class CDs for students who forget to bring their music with them.

3. Place students in pairs. One student reads the lyrics of the song aloud while the other listens.

4. Students reverse places so that one reads the lyrics and the other listens.

Day 1

1. Set the ground rules. Students should be respectful of each other's music. If they do not like a piece of music, then they should express themselves by citing specific reasons on the assessment sheet. Ask students to use the song rating sheet in Figure 4.4 and remind them that "it sucks" is insufficient.

2. Students will make a presentation that includes the following information:

   a. History of the singer or band

   b. Title of the song

   c. Lyrics

   d. Reasons the song was chosen.

3. A student presents a history of the singer of the band, gives the title of the song, and recites the lyrics.

4. The student plays the song. Because some songs are quite long, you may want to enforce a maximum time limit of 4 minutes.

5. After the song plays, the student explains the reason the song was chosen.

6. After the presentation, students fill out an assessment. The completed sheets are given to the teacher.

7. Proceed in this manner until all students have presented.

8. Before the next meeting of the class, glance over student responses on the assessment rating sheets to ensure that no responses are inappropriate.

Day 2

1. Hand back the song rating sheets to the appropriate student.

2. Using knowledge of the band, song, and the feedback from peers, students write a critique. Students can use the song critique sheet in Figure 4.5 as guidance.

Extension Activities

1. Any teacher who implements Raider Record can choose from among a multitude of assignments. In the past I have had my students write evaluation papers, music critiques, persuasive essays, compare-and-contrast papers, and journal articles. They have

Figure 4.4   Song Rating Sheet

Name:

Title of song:

Song performed by:

Song chosen by:

Overall rating/total points:

Circle the rating in each category, and then add up the total points.

History of the Band

25	20	15	10	5	0
Interesting					Dull
Well done					Poorly done

Lyrics

25	20	15	10	5	0
Powerful					Weak

Why? Give an example.

Song

25	20	15	10	5	0
Loved it					Hated it

Give your comments on the beat, voices, overall sound, and extra considerations.
Beat

Voices

Overall Sound

Extra Considerations

Rationale

25	20	15	10	5	0
Interesting					Dull
Well done					Poorly done

Why?

Figure 4.5   Song Critique Sheet

1. State an overall claim about the music (positive or negative). Your statement can serve as the thesis of the critique.

2. Describe the band (or singer), type of music, sound, lyrics, and feel of the music to give readers basic information needed to understand your argument.

3. Clarify your criteria of evaluation. For example, what makes a great song? (See Figure 4.4 for the criteria.)

4. Once you have established a set of criteria, offer a judgment for each point.

5. Include both negative and positive judgments in your evaluation. Examine your peer feedback. Explain why raters who agreed with you are right and why those who disagreed with you are wrong.

6. Support each judgment with evidence.

7. Write as if you are the expert (you probably are).

---

performed mock interviews with musicians and created their own songs. The opportunities for expansion on this lesson are vast; as long as the music stays fresh, so will the lesson.

2. Inevitably, Raider Record transforms students from timid whiners about writing to cutthroat, hard-nosed, decisive music critics who resist any style that they don't perceive to be sufficiently artistic. I have found that this lesson engages my students to write creatively, precisely, effectively, and purposefully.

Assessment

	1 Unsatisfactory	2 Insufficient	3 Uneven	4 Sufficient	5 Skillful	6 Excellent
The song's lyrics do not violate school policy						
Presentation includes history of the singer or band, title of the song, lyrics, reasons the song was chosen						
Copy of written lyrics given to teacher						
Song is four minutes or less						
Exhibits good listening skills and tolerates different kinds of music						

NCTE/IRA Standards: 1, 2, 3, 4, 5, 6, 7, 8, 9, 10, 11, 12

Source: M. Rabbit and R. Deckard, Toledo, OH. Adapted with permission.

Sound Lesson 5

Adagio Suite

Summary: Students respond to music, art, and poetry in short bursts of writing. Then students put together these short bursts into poems.

Senses: Sound, sight, touch

Type of Activity: Individual

Approximate Time: 2–4 days

Objective: Students learn to use their senses to guide and enhance the quality of writing; students learn to synthesize material from a variety of sources; students work on precision of wording.

Materials: *Adagio for Strings* by Samuel Barber (choose Leonard Bernstein's version), postcards of some of your favorite artwork (available in most bookstores), felt-tip markers, crayons, colored pencils, a copy of Shakespeare's Sonnet 116 (or a favorite poem), paper, pen, blank art paper (larger than 8.5 x 11 inches), and CD player.

Setup: Make sure all materials are readily accessible.

Procedures

1. Tell students to keep all the pieces from this exercise in one place. They should write only on the front of their papers.
2. Ask students to list clichés about love. For example, "love is blind," "all is fair in love and war," "love makes the world go 'round" are clichés. Write them on an overhead or on the board.
3. Ask students to define love for themselves, using a metaphor. For example, "Love is a Rubik's cube. Only four people in the whole world have ever figured it out" or "Love is like a puppy. It will curl up and cuddle with you, and then poop on your floor later." Another student wrote, "Love is like irony, most people who talk about it don't know what it is."
4. Tell students that you want them to select two lines from the poem that is going to be read aloud.
5. Hand out Shakespeare's Sonnet 116. Have a dramatic student with a good voice read it aloud. Tell students to highlight the two most striking lines.

Shakespeare's Sonnet 116

Let me not to the marriage of true minds
Admit impediments. Love is not love
Which alters when it alteration finds,
Or bends with the remover to remove:
Oh no! it is an ever-fixed mark
That looks on tempests and is never shaken;
It is the star to every wandering bark,
Whose worth's unknown, although his height be taken.
Love's not Time's fool, though rosy lips and cheeks
Within his bending sickle's compass come:
Love alters not with his brief hours and weeks,
But bears it out even to the edge of doom.
If this be error and upon me proved,
I never writ, nor no man ever loved.

6. Have students rephrase one line into their own words. For example for "Love's not Time's fool, though rosy lips and cheeks within his bending sickle's compass come," a student might write, "Beauty fades in time, but love endures."

7. Have students rephrase a second line into their own words, but so that the meaning is reversed. For example, for "which alters when it alteration finds," a student might write the opposite meaning—"remains steadfast when circumstances change."

8. Have each student select a postcard work of art. Give students 15 minutes or so to write a story based on the postcard. They should not merely describe the artwork ("there is a woman in a blue dress by an open window"), but should tell a story about it ("Irene had put on the blue dress thinking that it was modest enough for a funeral, but formal enough not to embarrass her family"). See Figure 4.6 for an example of a postcard story.

9. Pair up students. Have one student hand the postcard to his partner and be silent for a minute or two. The partner should try to think of a story that might also work with the postcard.

10. Have the student who wrote the story explain it without reading from his paper.

11. Have each pair discuss the postcard, the writer's story, and the reader's story.

12. Switch places and repeat the process so that the partner gets to explain and discuss her story.

Figure 4.6   Postcard Story

Delerious and hop-headed, that thrings can banjo-sitter seeps out onto the boulivard, like reefer smoke, underneath the tawdry moan of a licorce stick while the jug-band on the corner bangs a washboard a timpani and blows a kamolike a trumpet. The street cars horn chimes in.

Ignacious Codwallup swaggers like he's got a strait-razor in his boot-sock because he probably does. He's a real cool jive, slinging cat from the bowery, and he swings the piano likes he's mad at it.

The whole town is hot with bath-tub hooch or windsor whiskey still tasting of the acrid rust of ship's haul or the earthy sweat of the boot it was kept in.

Across the street a couple of swells eye a dark bird in a red dress.

"Hey there pork-pie"

She bowls to Ignacious.

"This here club is the jumpingest joint in town. It's the cat's pajamamas"

The guy in the bottom left boks like the the joker.

13. Have each student write down a favorite phrase, plot twist, or sentence from the partner's story.
14. Hand out large paper, crayons, colored pencils, and felt-tip markers.
15. Tell the students that the musical piece they are about to hear is about love. Have them draw or write what they think the composer is trying to say about love and life. Have students identify the dominant colors and tastes of the piece. They can add words, thoughts, or memories if they wish, though images, colors, and tastes (or scents) are preferable.
16. Give students a few minutes after the music has stopped playing to finish their drawings and think about what they have drawn.
17. Tell students that they are going to explain their drawings to their partners, who are going to write down exactly what they say. Give students one minute to think about what they are going to say. Color Plate 1.6 (see p. 188) is an example of one student's drawing.
18. Have the partner write down verbatim what the student says about the drawing. About the drawing in Color Plate 1.6, the artist wrote, "It tasted like grape juice. I drew a brown vine because that's what the cello sounded like—purples and blues and reds. Then when it got all dramatic and bloated and swollen, I drew the paisley."
19. Students should take all these different pieces, spread them in front of them, and then write a poem.
20. You may provide formats for poems (e.g., sonnet, limerick, villanelle, or pantoum) or have students write in free verse.
21. Students write their poems, basing them on the short bursts of writing they have collected.
22. Peer edit if you wish.
23. Have students read their poems aloud.

Here is an example of a student-written poem:

Love Is Like the Gossamer Tatters of Grocery Bags

Tangled and torn together
On a barb wire fence

Gossamer tatters of grocery bags
Like ghostly tendrils
On a barb wire fence

Undulating in an ugly place of rust and carburetors
the ghostly tendrils
Rippling magic mystery and whimsical hope

Undulating in an ugly place of rust and carburetors
Clap together
like hands.

Extension Activity

Students might be encouraged to put their poetry to film or in a PowerPoint presentation with music and sound.

Assessment

	1 Unsatisfactory	2 Insufficient	3 Uneven	4 Sufficient	5 Skillful	6 Excellent
Student participated in previous activities (please attach all writing)						
Language is original and vivid						
No clichés						
Poem is written in appropriate form (pantoum, villanelle, sonnet, other)						
Exhibits good listening skills and is a good editor for peers						

NCTE/IRA Standards: 1, 2, 3, 4, 5, 6, 7, 8, 9, 11, 12

5

Smell and Taste ■ ■ ■

Taste and smell are the senses least used for learning in the classroom. Nevertheless, much about the olfactory system is relevant to teaching. Humans are highly responsive to smells and tastes, although responses may be unconscious. Smells and tastes linger in the brain far longer than other kinds of memory and have been shown to influence health, belief, behavior, attitude, and productivity.

Smell

Smell is the sense of memory and desire.

—Rousseau

Rousseau was astute in asserting that smell ignites memory. The sense of smell can endure long after facts, conversations, and the memory of people and places have faded. A 5-year-old boy who gets a whiff of a cake being baked in an oven can remember and identify the precise smell decades later, even if he smelled the aroma only once and has not experienced it since (Vroon, 1994). It is not uncommon for some elderly Alzheimer's patients to forget their spouses and children, yet they can recognize the aroma of a freshly baked apple pie and the fragrance of a rose.

Compared with visual and auditory memory, smell is more enduring. Furthermore, little to nothing can interfere with a smell except other smells. For example, most of us find it difficult to remember a telephone number if there are other stimuli happening at the same time—people shouting epithets nearby, a large man in a bright red beard singing an aria, two women on the other side of the room hurling wine glasses against the wall. Because olfactory processing can operate without engaging the brain, chaos would have no influence on the identification of aromas in such a room. Sometimes the sense of smell stimulates bodily functions even when the brain is unconscious. For example, if the scent of peppermint is used in a room where a woman is sleeping, her heartbeat will quicken and electrical impulses in the brain will increase (Badia, Wesensten, Lammers, Culpepper, & Harsh, 1990).

The sense of smell is largely overlooked in education, although smell can influence attitude, the brain, and behavior. For example, say you are considering the purchase of a new car. You happen onto a car lot and look at a car which happens to be your favorite color and has all the options and features you desire. Suddenly, the dealer offers to sell you the vehicle at $10,000 below the invoice price. When you test-drive the car, you are overpowered by the scent of burning oil. The smell likely would not only dissuade you from purchasing the car, it might also affect your attitude toward the manufacturer of the car and the salesperson. For the remainder of your life, whenever you happen by the car dealer's place of business, it is likely that your brain will ignite with the acrid scent of burning oil.

If linked to particular events or tasks, smell can evoke emotions and memories. Teacher Amie Gabriel (1999) tested the effects of four different scents—cedarwood, lavender, rosemary, and wintergreen—on student behavior. She found that fewer students misbehaved in scented conditions, particularly with lavender or rosemary. Some students complained that cedarwood, a tree that has an odor similar to pine, made the classroom "smell like a bathroom," exemplifying how a particular scent can become associated with a place, as pine-scented cleaners have come to be associated with cleaning the bathroom.

Smells do not have an influence on performance per se; however, smells can initiate a conditioned response, such as associating burning oil with inferior quality automobiles and pine with bathroom cleanup. While particularly revolting scents can negatively affect an individual's mood (Ehrlichman, 1995), pleasant scents can lead to optimism (Baron & Thomley, 1994; Knasko, 1992, 1995). In Japan, where much attention is paid to the sense of smell, many corporations routinely infuse the work environment with particular scents in the belief that such a strategy leads to higher productivity and lower stress (Hashimoto, Yamaguchi, & Kawasaki, 1988; Shimuzu Ltd., 1990).

Because olfactory processing occurs in a distinctive location with few direct connections to the newest part of the brain, the neocortex (where language processing occurs), neuroscientists suspect that the sense of smell is the oldest of the senses. Unlike the eyes and ears, which are densely networked with several regions of the brain, the olfactory sense is connected almost exclusively to the limbic system, the center of emotions. That is why a fragrance usually elicits a reflex action rather than a thought. For example, when most humans suddenly find themselves in the vicinity of a pig farm, the response is not intellectual, but instinctive—"Yuck! What is that odor? Let's get out of here!"

Recent research confirms the mystical properties of the nose. Scientists have found that an intact olfactory organ is a necessary precondition for the displaying of sexual behavior in most animals. For example, the queen bee is recognized by other bees through her distinctive scent. In animals, scents can bring with them pheromones, chemicals that can attract members of the opposite sex. All the more reason for boys and girls to shower after physical education class!

Smell researchers (Cutler et al., 1986; Roach, 1999) have found that pheromones in males' perspiration have psychological and physiological effects on women. The scent of men's sweat decreases tension, increases relaxation, and affects the timing and length of women's menstrual cycles. The hug that a wife gives her husband at the end of a long day may be motivated by affection, but it holds some biological benefit for the wife as well.

In another study of the effects of the odor of sweat, it was found that gay men preferred the sweat of other gay men and heterosexual women while heterosexual men and women liked the scent of gay men the least. Apparently, gender preference has a component that is reflected in body odors, and in the biological response to body odors (Martins et al., 2005).

In an experiment to ascertain the extent to which individuals could recognize their own scents, one hundred people wore shirts for 24 hours (using no soap or deodorant, etc.), then put their soiled shirts into bags. A few days later, when the hundred individuals were instructed to find their smelly shirts from the collection of bags, 75 were able to sniff them out. Of the 25 who did not identify their shirts, most were smokers or menstruating women (Lord & Kasprzak, 1989).

Another study required mothers to identify the swaddling clothes that had been wrapped around their babies immediately after birth only through scent. Although the swaddling clothes were identical and mothers were asked to examine the clothes weeks after the birth, 80 percent of women correctly identified their child's swaddling clothes using only the scent as a guide (Porter, Cernoch, & McLaughlin, 1983).

As recently as the 19th century, doctors relied on the sense of smell as a primary tool in diagnosis. They sampled the aromas of sweat, urine, breath, and blood in ascertaining a patient's health. Some historians conjecture that the development of the stethoscope (invented in 1816) was hurried along by doctors' aversions to handling potentially vile substances. At different points in history, smell has been assumed to possess mythic powers: Homer advocated burning sulfur to rid buildings of airborne bacteria; Hippocrates proposed combating the plague by burning wood; and in the Bible, the breath of beautiful, young virgins was assumed to have restorative powers for King David (Vroon, 1994).

Unlike sight and touch, the brain takes some time to assess olfactory stimuli. When you are walking on a mountain trail and spot a boulder coming down the mountainside directly toward you, the brain immediately alerts you to the danger and you jump out of the way. When you place your fingers into a pan of boiling water, the message of pain sent to your brain is instantaneous—Ouch! However, the brain usually takes 12 seconds or so to determine the features of a smell. In most cases, the brain's first response to a new smell is one of apprehension.

Although some smells have cultural overtones, most smells are greeted with praise or condemnation uniformly across cultures. In general, people prefer the aromas of fresh food, drink, and flowers, and dislike the smell of decomposing animals, rancid food, and body waste (Schleidt, Neumann, & Morishita, 1988; Turin, 2006). Nevertheless, even pleasant smells can become disgusting at a certain level of concentration. You may be surprised to learn that the perfume industry uses indole, a compound found in skatole, the substance that puts the stink in excrement. Although indole smells of flowers in low concentrations, in high concentrations it smells like . . . well, you know.

With over 400,000 distinct odors in the world today, most dictionaries offer precious few words to characterize them. Yet, words can have a profound effect on how an aroma is perceived.

A study by psychologists at Brown University (Herz, Beland, & Hellerstein, 2004; Herz, Schankler, & Beland, 2004) found that a "borderline smell" (the researchers mixed dirt, rain, and hot buttered popcorn) may be classified as good or bad, depending on the mood of the individual at the time the scent is encountered. When individuals were feeling frustrated, they found the borderline scent annoying, but when they were feeling happy, they found it pleasant.

Lindstrom (2005) claims that when a Hershey's chocolate shop in Times Square began using a heavily scented chocolate aroma in the environs of the store, its revenues increased 81 percent. Similarly, when a branch of Barclay's Bank started brewing fresh coffee in the mornings, patronage increased by 12 percent, according to Lindstrom. Certainly, the sense of smell is gaining some interest in business—Singapore Airlines has patented the aroma of the hot towels its flight personnel distribute before meals, and the Westin Hotel chain is trying to assert ownership over the scent White Tea, a fragrance in use in all of its hotels. A study in casinos found that scented slot machines received 45 to 53 percent more traffic than unscented machines (Hirsch, 1995).

Some studies (Lehrner, Eckersberger, Walla, Potsch, & Deecke, 2000) have even shown that a slight fragrance of oranges can help reduce anxiety, promote serenity, and foster positive moods among patients in a waiting room at a dentist's office. Surely, if altering scents can calm the nerves of patients waiting for a root canal, it can also work for students preparing to take an exam.

Despite years of attempting to classify smells (Cox, 1975), researchers have been unable to break smells down into convenient building blocks the way words can be broken into morphemes and sound into waves. A Dutch physiologist with the formidable name Zwaardemaker (Pace, 1898) created a classification system of nine classes of smells, described as follows (with two examples for each class):

- Ethereal—chloroform, ether
- Aromatic—lavender, lemon
- Balsamic—vanilla, jasmine
- Amber—musk, urine of the civet (a cat)
- Alliaceous—rotten eggs, potassium bromide
- Empyreumatic—coffee, tobacco
- Hircine—cheese, sweat
- Repulsive—potato, bugs
- Disgusting—dead animals, Venus flytrap

Obviously, the sense of smell is ripe for teaching a wide assortment of vocabulary and for translating aromas into words. Recently, some

American businesses have started exploring the potential of olfactory stimuli. For example, in 2004, Procter & Gamble launched an air freshener called Scentstories, which diffuses a series of different aromas over the course of two and a half hours. Current stories include Wandering Barefoot on the Shore and Relaxing in the Hammock. According to researchers in consumer behavior, fragrance has become an essential consideration for home and workplace, on a par with furnishings and interior design (Green, 2006; Spangenberg, Crowley, & Henderson, 1996). Rooms in some expensive, new homes are even being planned to include both air monitoring and scent programming technologies.

Although such considerations may seem extravagant, the quality of air in a classroom is vital to good health and proper functioning of the brain. A recent study of children with asthma traced their condition to poor air quality in and around the public schools the students attended (Fernandez, 2006). In a room without windows and proper ventilation, the carbon dioxide that students exhale has no place to go. As a result, the amount of oxygen in a room gets displaced by carbon dioxide, which in turn can cause drowsiness and promote increased levels of allergens. The Environmental Protection Agency estimates that students miss more than 10 million days annually as a result of the contaminated air in school buildings (Smith, 2006).

Taste

Korsmeyer (1999) noted, "Tastes convey meaning and hence have a cognitive dimension that is often overlooked. Foods are employed in symbolic systems that extend from the ritual ceremonies of religion to the everyday choice of breakfast. Perhaps most obviously, eating is an activity with intense social meaning for communities large and small" (p. 4).

If you doubt the link between food and socialization, try serving frog legs to your family on Thanksgiving or escargots in garlic sauce to the boisterous crowd gathered in your backyard on July 4th. Of course, sometimes food represents nothing more than sustenance to get through the day (Telfer, 1996). But at other times food is rife with meaning.

In the Christian ceremony of communion, for example, bread is equated to the body of Christ, and wine or grape juice is symbolic of the blood of Christ. In the Jewish and Muslim faiths, pork is considered inedible. Yet in certain restaurants in rural Kentucky, there is nothing on the menu except pork, corn cakes, and potato salad. According to the Bible, it is not a book, song, or a jewel that lures Adam and Eve from Paradise, but the bite of an apple.

Many foods have an interesting etymological history. Pretzel means "folded arms" in Italian. Developed in 610 CE in northern Italy, the pretzel was designed to represent folded arms in prayer. The Latin word *prestiole* means "little gift," and the Italian word *bracciatelli* means "small arms" (Panati, 1987). Monks baked pretzels and gave them as rewards to students who properly recited their prayers.

Croissants were first baked in 1683 to represent the shape of the flag of the Turkish army (the crescent), which was attacking the city of Vienna. Bakers created croissants both as a celebration of the successful defense of the city and as an act of disdain for the Turkish army. Armed with croissants, Viennese citizens were given the opportunity to "chew up" the vanquished enemy (Elkort, 1991). In an alternative version of the story (Ayto, 1990), the history of croissants is traced to the vanquishing of Muslims from Buda and Pest in 1686. In either case, the croissant was representative of more than just a piece of bread.

In most classrooms, food is rarely consumed unless a teacher is offering candy as a reward. Obviously, most students have ready access to sweets at home, but when candy becomes a reward that can be eaten during class time at school, it is transformed into the realm of the symbolic.

Taste invokes the other senses too—smell, obviously, but also touch (the texture of food), sight (how the food looks), and even sound. Incredibly, cereal makers spend a great deal of time and money trying to find an appropriate sound to accompany the consumption of their products. A rather plain rice cereal became one of the bestselling cereals in America because its advertiser marketed the sounds of "snap, crackle, and pop" as if these auditory signals had some culinary significance.

As early as 365 BCE, Plato identified the four basic tastes—sweet, sour, bitter, and salty—that are still recognized by dieticians today. Across cultures, sweet and salty are considered desirable; the allure of sour varies; and bitter flavors are deemed undesirable. Plato considered taste and touch "lower" than the other senses, such as sound and sight. Sound and sight were thought to be "distant senses," meaning that a person could use them without coming into contact directly with the thing being experienced. However, with taste, one must hold the food, then consume it. In a way, food merges into the body and becomes a part of it.

Although the sense of taste naturally serves helpful purposes, it also can lure a human toward excessive eating, which can lead to obesity, problems with health, and early death. Aristotle believed that the natural human tendency was to overindulge in pleasures of the body, so he postulated that eating a minimal amount of food and abstaining from alcoholic beverages were more virtuous than eating too much and getting drunk. As with self-indulgence, Aristotle considered gluttony to be unsuitable for the disciplined mind. "Of vices of the body, then, those in our own power are blamed, those not in our power are not. And if this be so, in the other cases also the vices that are blamed must be in our own power" (Aristotle, 1976, p. 126).

As artists, musicians, and literary critics can be trained, so food critics can learn to make eating an aesthetic experience (Petrini & Watson, 2001). Shows on radio and television that depict gourmands demonstrating their taste buds in action seem to be proliferating. There is even the Food Network, a cable channel that boasts 60 television series and hundreds of videos.

In *Phaedo* (Plato, 1977), Socrates characterizes delicious food as a hindrance to the intellectual development of a philosopher. Most teachers have similar qualms about the effects of food on the academic achievement of their students. Undoubtedly, eating can distract students from the lesson at hand in several ways, especially if their stomachs are growling from hunger. Because most students have intense (sometimes emotional) reactions to food, any academic work involving food must be purposeful and planned well in advance.

Implications for Teachers

The immediacy and intensity of the olfactory system make it a powerful instructional tool, but integrating smell and taste into a coherent instructional plan is no easy task. If nothing else, a cognizance of the potency of the olfactory senses would be useful for teachers. This might be manifested by an awareness of the quality of air in a classroom; a knowledge about how odors can attract and distract; a consciousness of the powerful, symbolic properties of food; and a predilection for using these dynamic senses in creative, constructive ways that enhance student learning.

Some suggestions for how a teacher might integrate the olfactory senses in a real classroom to enhance achievement follow.

Activity	Entry Point	Focus	Preparation Time
Smell and Taste Lesson 1 Aroma from Another Room	School building	Science, descriptive and expressive writing	Minimal
Smell and Taste Lesson 2 Readers' Café	Snacks, beverages, art, and books	Reading, speaking, informational writing	Substantial
Smell and Taste Lesson 3 Candy Freak	Playing around with candy	Vocabulary, science, mathematics, descriptive and persuasive writing	Substantial
Smell and Taste Lesson 4 Scent of My Soul	Scented candles or other examples of distinctive scents, guided writing	Quality of expression, symbolic language, poetic writing	Substantial

Aroma from Another Room forces students to think out of the usual box of visual description by having them offer details about a site on school property using only words that characterize smell, taste, and sound. Readers' Café turns reading into a social event as students read books, create posters, then wander around the room and talk about literature with their peers. Candy Freak allows students to momentarily take on the mantle of candy connoisseur as they get to measure, weigh, smell, and taste a variety of chocolates. Little do they know that as they search for the right word to represent the glorious sensations experienced by their taste buds that they are expanding their vocabularies, picking up concepts from physical science, and learning to write persuasively at the same time. Finally, with Scent of My Soul, students learn about autobiography, biography, literary devices, and informational writing by investigating a subject of infinite interest—themselves.

Smell and Taste Lesson 1
Aroma from Another Room

Summary: The student writes a short descriptive essay using a minimum of visual description and a maximum amount of words describing smells, sounds, and emotions.

Senses: Smell, sight (visualization), sound

Type of Activity: Individual or pairs

Approximate Time: One day

Objectives: Students write using only words that describe smell, sound, and emotion. Students use their deductive powers to figure out the room being described.

Materials: Pen and paper

Rationale

Students often neglect to address sound, smell, and emotional states of mind when they write. Aroma from Another Room forces students to think about experiences and words that describe those experiences in a new way.

Procedures

1. Have students think about any area on school property that has a distinctive smell. Some possibilities include the following:
   a. Current classroom
   b. Other classrooms (science lab, mathematics, social studies, foreign language, choir, band, English, shop, auto mechanics, etc.)
   c. Gymnasium
   d. Cafeteria
   e. Parking lot
   f. Principal's office
   g. Assistant principal's office
   h. Counselor's office
   i. Locker rooms
   j. Bathrooms
   k. Storage closets
   l. Area near a dumpster
   m. Soccer field
   n. Library

      o. Locker

      p. Custodial office

      q. Hallway

2. The student writes a description of the area, paying special attention to sounds, smells, and emotions (see the sample description in Figure 5.1). Emphasize to students that the purpose of the exercise is to make plain through the description which room is

---

Figure 5.1 Aroma from Another Room: Student Sample

Darkness fills the room like a musty old blanket because my teacher isn't here yet and the lights haven't been turned on. There are no windows to let in the outside light. Mr. Nisley, the custodian, has unlocked the doors to let in the droopy shufflers waiting at the door. I feel tired and wish I wasn't here. Remote, quiet conversation and the tread of footfalls echoes in from the hall. As we enter, yesterday's smells rush past us, desperate to escape their overnight prison. Someone had a banana in the room and the peel sits moldering blackly on top of a heap of wadded paper in the trash can near the door. Paper smells of all kinds—big, cheap tan paper that rips when you try to use your eraser; nappy textured watercolor paper that the teacher hoards until you beg, glossy, thick, special-purpose paper waft their flat-chemical and earthy scents into the room. Water plink-plinks from the leaky faucet in one of the deep sinks somewhere in the darkness at the side of the room. With the room lit only from the hall, I can see the counters lining the long back wall, littered with cans, boxes, jars holding an assortment of wasted brushes, bottles of glue, and buckets filled with sponges. A half-used roll of scratchy brown paper towels dips its crumpled leading edge over the counter almost to the floor. Slick black-topped tables hover over stools crammed beneath, and easels hunker low, hunched old men clustered together in the corner.

    Mrs. Yonky, my teacher, her voice more nasal and strident than usual, blusters in briskly calling out, "Bus duty, bus duty . . . ," far too loudly for so early in the morning. She flicks on the fluorescent lights and abruptly, the paint-dappled floors, like some quirky abstract work, dance into prominence. Crusted glue splotches on the tables become visible in the glaring light. I aim for a seat as far away from the buzzing, flickering light fixture hanging just out of parallel with the ceiling near the back wall. Angst-riddled art plasters the walls, black, purple, and red predominant. The stiff old wheels whine out a protest as I pull my work-in-progress from the rolling rack shelves. I collect a cracked, red plastic cup half-filled with shards of oil pastels from the supply counter. Acrid, powdered tempera dust shrouds large areas of the counter with a blue sheen and whips into the air as people brush past. Wiping the top of the stool with the inside bottom of my t-shirt, just to be sure, I sit down and try to get lost in my work.

being described (not to disguise it). Each student should have a minimum of 10 olfactory words and 2 metaphors or similes.

3. After students have finished writing the descriptions, have students count off from one to however many students there are in class. Students write the number they say in the top right-hand corner of the paper.

4. On a new sheet of paper, students draw a line down the middle of the paper. Then, they number their papers along the left margin according to the number of students in class (Each number represents a student's paper).

5. Students read 10 papers (alter this number as you wish). If a student is reading a description with #3 in the top right corner, then he writes on line #3 on his paper.

6. On the left side of the paper, the student writes his best guess at the room being described. On the right side of the paper, he writes the phrase or sentence that tipped him off.

7. If the papers are read aloud, the teacher should highlight particularly effective wording.

8. Students turn in their description papers and their papers reviewing their peers' descriptions.

Extension Activities

1. A teacher may want to offer rewards for the best aromatic description or the description that was most often correctly identified.

2. A teacher may want every student to read her description out loud and have students guess as a group.

3. This exercise could be used between classes as well. That is, students in fifth period class could try to guess the locations that students in second period described.

Assessment

	1 Unsatisfactory	2 Insufficient	3 Uneven	4 Sufficient	5 Skillful	6 Excellent
Minimum of 10 olfactory words						
Two good metaphors						
Variety of sentence structure						
Cohesive organization						

NCTE/IRA Standards: 4, 5, 6, 11, 12

Smell and Taste Lesson 2
Readers' Café

Summary: Students create a poster and an information sheet about a book they recently read. Then, for half of the time, they sit in an area designated as a "booth" and discuss it with other students. For the other half of the time, students walk around, munch on snacks, sip tea (or water), and talk about books.

Senses: Taste, sight, sound, movement

Type of Activity: Individual and group

Approximate Time: Designed to be completed in two days

Objectives: Students represent themes pictorially, write a précis, and get to talk about their books with other students. The hope is that momentum will build for reading and discussing books.

Materials: Large, poster-size paper, colored pens and pencils, tea, snacks

Rationale

I worry that adolescents often choose to do anything with their leisure time except read books. Although Readers' Café may seem a little fluffy, students seem to enjoy the time to relax and talk about books. The idea of talking about books (without being forced to participate) may be a first-time phenomenon for many students.

Procedures

In Advance

Each student selects a book from the library (or better yet, the teacher suggests a book for each student). The student comes to class on Day 1 having read the book, with the book in hand.

Day 1
1. Distribute one poster-size paper and one 8.5 × 11 inch paper to each student. Show students a sample of what their work might look like (excerpts from a student's poster are shown in Figure 5.2).
2. On the poster, the student writes out and draws the following:
    a. Title of the book and author
    b. Three images representative of theme
    c. Genre
    d. Very brief summary of the plot
    e. One significant event in the book

Figure 5.2   Readers' Café

The Elements

Sometimes the weather is our greatest enemy - other times it's our best friend.
• The snow helped to hide Siv's feathers, but the wind hindered flight.

The History of our Land

History

Historical knowledge breeds apprecation and dainty of arment circumstances.
• King Coryn Knows that he's part evil since study his history.
• Power struggles present throughout.

Firesight

Discerning hope and light in the face of destruction.

• Grank's quest to save his friend's brings peril but his magic capabilities along with his positive attitude soften the blows.

A. Grank

B. Grank is a middle-aged owl. He's male and spotted.

C. He's gifted in the way of foresight, but sometimes acts nastily and emotionally

D. "Yes, I had begun to think of this egg and myself as "us". Destiny had bound us together as strongly as if I were this chick's father."

E. Grank and I are both nocturnal.

3. On the 8.5 × 11 inch paper, the student writes out the following for the character profile:
   a. Name of protagonist
   b. Age, gender, physical appearance
   c. Intelligence, including common sense
   d. Representative phrase (something he or she says in the book)
   e. Extent to which character is like me

Day 2

1. Divide the students into two groups.
2. Students in the first group move their desks to the outside walls of the room, creating an open space in the center. Students attach the posters to the wall behind their desks. (It would be nice to allow posters to remain for a week or two after this activity.) Students in this group place their character profile sheets on top of their desks and sit or stand at their booths.
3. Distribute five copies of the Reader's Café Evaluation (Figure 5.3) to each student in the second group. Students can review any five of the books represented in the booths. If space is available, consider creating a quiet work area where students can sit and fill out the evaluation sheets after visiting the booths.
4. Tell students in the second group that they have 25 minutes (alter the time as you see fit) to walk around, discuss books, fill in five evaluation sheets, munch on snacks, and drink whatever beverage you have provided.
5. Students turn in their five evaluation sheets.
6. Switch positions. Students who were walking around (the second group) attach their posters on the wall and sit or stand near their posters. Students previously in the booths (the first group) receive five Reader's Café evaluation sheets.
7. Members of the first group walk around, discuss books, fill in the five evaluation sheets, and munch on snacks.
8. Members of the first group turn in their five evaluation sheets.

Extension Activities

1. A teacher may want to offer rewards for the best poster or best character profile.
2. A teacher may want to allow students to choose from among the books presented the day after Readers' Café. As several students may desire to read the same book, the teacher should create a process for ensuring a fair distribution of hot books.

Figure 5.3   Readers' Café Evaluation

Person you are evaluating_____

Title of the book_____

Author of the book_____Genre_____

Evaluation (1–10)_____

A few words about the plot

_____

_____

_____

_____

_____

_____

_____

_____

_____

_____

Does their presentation make you want to read this book?

1	2	3	4	5
absolutely not	probably not	maybe	probably	definitely

How well prepared was this person?

1	2	3	4	5
not prepared	little effort	all right	well prepared	impressive

Comments

_____

_____

_____

3. Readers' Café can be repeated as a "best books of the year" event.
4. A teacher may assign a student to dress up as the author or a character in the book.

Assessment for the Poster

	1 Unsatisfactory	2 Insufficient	3 Uneven	4 Sufficient	5 Skillful	6 Excellent
Title, author, genre						
Three images representative of theme						
Brief plot summary						
One significant event						

Assessment for the Character Sketch

	1 Unsatisfactory	2 Insufficient	3 Uneven	4 Sufficient	5 Skillful	6 Excellent
Name, age, and physical appearance of main character						
Intelligence and common sense						
Representative phrase						
Extent he/she/it is like me						

NCTE/IRA Standards: 1, 2, 3, 4, 5, 6, 7, 8, 9, 10, 11, 12

Smell and Taste Lesson 3

Candy Freak

Summary: Students read an excerpt about candy. Then they rate a series of candy bars on a variety of criteria. Eventually, students create a persuasive paper based on the results of their critique of the candy.

Senses: Taste, smell, touch, sight, sound

Type of Activity: Pairs

Approximate Time: Up to three days (more with the extension activities)

Objectives: Students learn to attach words to sensory stimulation in real time. Students learn how to write persuasively.

Materials: At least five different kinds of candy, a transparency, and multiple copies of the Candy Assessment (Figure 5.4) for each student. Each pair of students needs one assessment for each candy bar to be evaluated. Also, each student will need a copy of the Candy Freak Sensory Words list in Appendix B.

Procedures

In Advance

Send a note home to parents advising them that your class will be using candy as props for a writing assignment. You need to know if your students have any dietary restrictions, such as allergies to peanuts or chocolate. If you have students in your classes that cannot have candy, find out from their parents which foods are safe.

Days 1 to 3

1. Distribute copies of the Candy Freak Sensory Words list (see Appendix B) to the students.
2. Tell students that they will be writing a sensory essay similar to the one you're reading aloud to them. The word list is not exclusive but is designed to help them find precise words to describe and evaluate a series of candy bars.
3. Read aloud the sample student essay in Figure 5.5.
4. Have students peruse the sensory word list for 5 or 10 minutes and ask questions about unfamiliar words.
5. Distribute the Candy Assessment (Figure 5.4). Place students in groups of two.

Figure 5.4   Candy Assessment

Name of Candy:

Characteristic	Data/Comments/Description	Value (1–10)	Score	Value × Score
Appearance				
Size				
Quality of Ingredients (list and comment)				
Aroma				
Texture				
Taste				
Aftertaste				
Total				

Figure 5.5   Model Persuasive Essay

Oh, the songs of the angels pale in comparison to even the aroma of the ineffable glory that is a Pearson's Mint Patty. What can even be said, truly, when the words of this too pallor language of ours cannot even express fully such trivial items as infinity, eternity, and the sweet hereafter? How then can one even begin to grasp the individualized packets of eternity and pleasure that are Pearson's Patties? How can these dollops of quintessence be put into words? Verily, I submit that they cannot, but even so I will try.

To begin—the aforementioned aroma. Even before the shimmering silver shell of packaging is removed, one cannot help but be struck deaf and dumb (at least momentarily) by the towering magnificence of the staggeringly delightful, sweet odor of mint. The wonder that is real peppermint oil colors the mind's eye instantly with a vision of a field rolling in mint leaves. Truly, a vision of the fields of heaven themselves, perhaps even completed by visions of a cherub of dark chocolate with wings of silver, depending on how, shall we say, lucid one is at the time, dear reader.

Despite the titanic might of the mint aroma, do not think for a second that it is "too much" or that it is alone. Truly, the mint is a revelation that there cannot be too much mint, and the scent of each patty makes one apt to grab at least one more. An epic test in self control, eating each one is. However, as I said, the mint is not alone. No, if it was, it might be, perhaps, too much for the mortal coil to withstand, akin to what would have happened to Moses had he looked on the full glory of God (which, for the record, is something that tends to burn mortals to a cinder). Delectably dark—as dark as the mortal sins, midnight under a starless sky, or simply all the way to #000000 on the HTML color chart—it balances the heaven of the mint with a hint of hellfire—the brimstone sparkle of delight in indulgence. Yin to mint's yang, one could say.

Oh, the sparkle of metallic, regal joy that is the packaging. Honestly, all I have ever caught is the silver. My fervor to partake of the patties has always eclipsed my desire to slowly inspect the packaging, though I do suppose that someday I could take a longer look at any which now make up the three or four inch cushioning which envelopes my floor.

The dark, circular shards of rapture themselves are roughly the size of an overgrown quarter (though only slightly so), in other words, perfect for one zealous bite or two more restrained ones. (What good is restraint in the world of candy?) The palate is utterly overwhelmed by this legendary mint endeavor—all senses at the mercy of the one. So powerful, so enthralling, so mind blowingly mesmerizing is the mint that one initially forgets that ah, there is chocolate dark and shadowy here too.

(Figure continues on next page)

Figure 5.5 *(continued)*

The outside is smooth, with ripples as a crystalline pond just barely blemished by the throw of a stone. Only this pond's surface is dark chocolate. Beneath its surface lies a prize far greater than any fish or Moby Dick. The creamy, silky mint dances as a mouthful of palatable pleasure. Once one swallows, and the initial dance is done, the afterglow of the candy is delightful in its own right: the aftertaste is crisp and clean. Each breath, both in and out, propagates the remnants of the mint-a-li-cious exaltation, and it is then that the wisps of dark chocolate make themselves known to the taste buds.

So is the majesty that is the mint patty, and may it never be diminished. Yea, unto the ends of the universe may it be so. Lesser candies may continue to resort to the flaccid appeal to hunger cures, but the mint patty shall eternally be about flavor, and none shall be beyond the exultation of Pearson's.

6. Students are to write the name of the candy bar being assessed on the Candy Assessment form. In the Data/Comments/Description column, they write out descriptions of each characteristic of the candy, using words from the sensory word list when needed.

7. Place the transparency of Figure 5.4 on the overhead projector.

8. Simulate eating a piece of candy and responding to each characteristic carefully. Encourage students to help you fill out the transparency by suggesting words from the sensory word list.

9. Once the Data/Comments/Description column has been completed, move to the Value column. In this column, students decide on a value score for each characteristic. For example, most students will care primarily about taste. So, taste may receive a value of 10. If students decide that appearance is not important, then they may give a value of 1 for appearance.

10. Using the transparency of Figure 5.4 on the overhead, solicit responses from students regarding the values you should attach to each characteristic.

11. When you are finished, students discuss and fill in the value column on their own sheets.

12. Simulate an evaluation of a piece of candy. You may want to exaggerate your movements and expressions to give students the flavor of the assignment. First, comment on the candy's appearance both in its wrapper and out of the wrapper. Attach a value to Appearance in the Score column. Next, carefully measure

the candy, record the measurements and comments about the appropriateness of the size, and attach a value to Size in the Score column. Proceed in this manner until you have given a score to every characteristic, including aftertaste.

13. Emphasize to students that you are especially interested in their written comments. Remind students about the vividness of the language from the brief student essay from the read-aloud.

14. Multiply the Value column by the Score column for each characteristic. Put the product in the Value × Score column. Add all entries and fill out the Total box.

15. Students should fill out one Candy Assessment form for each piece of candy they sample.

16. Tell students that everyone gets a piece of candy. Both students in the group should evaluate the same candy at the same time, discuss the taste, and record data and comments in the appropriate boxes on the assessment form.

17. Students should share writing tasks. One student records responses for one candy, another student writes for a second candy, then back to the original student for the third candy, and so on.

18. Hand out the candies.

19. Most of the time, students will become intensely engrossed in tasting, smelling, measuring, recording, and most importantly— finding the right words to represent their sensations, thoughts, and feelings.

20. Once students complete an assessment sheet for all candies, then they create a persuasive essay on which candy is the best of the bunch. If your students need help structuring their persuasive essays, you can use the guidelines from Figure 5.5 as a handout for students.

21. Students read their persuasive essays aloud to the class.

22. Students vote individually for the most persuasive essay by jotting their name and the names of the authors of the best essay on a piece of paper. Students cannot vote for themselves.

23. Count up the votes and declare a winner. (I usually declare a winner the next day.)

24. Purchase a modest bag of candy for the winners. (I try to give a bag of the candy they wrote about as their reward.)

Extension Activities

You may choose any kind of food that you want, though candy seems to have widespread appeal. Several different kinds of writing (not just persuasive) are possible with this activity, including descriptive, informative, and narrative.

Assessment for the Essay

	1 Unsatisfactory	2 Insufficient	3 Uneven	4 Sufficient	5 Skillful	6 Excellent
Clear position						
Joke, story, or quotation at opening						
Descriptions, facts, statistics, examples, expert testimonials						
Anticipate opposing argument						
Respond to anticipated criticism						

NCTE/IRA Standards: 1, 3, 4, 5, 6, 7, 11, 12

Smell and Taste Lesson 4
Scent of My Soul

Summary: Students respond to a variety of prompts and pen several pieces of writing on the road to creating an autobiographical, highly metaphorical poem. Students transpose the poem to film.

Senses: Smell, virtual taste (that is, students imagine tastes, though they do not actually eat anything in class—although this dimension could easily be added), sight, sound, movement

Type of Activity: Individual and group

Approximate Time: Designed to be completed in small exercises over several days. Eventually, students create a poem from the compiled pieces.

Objectives: Students learn techniques for writing descriptively, create a character sketch, and pen an original, autobiographical poem displaying lively use of language.

Materials: At least a dozen scented candles (different scents), colored pencils or crayons, paper, and the list of sensory words from the Candy Freak activity (see Appendix B). Alternatively, consider cloves, vanilla flavoring, maple syrup, garlic, bleach, pine cleaner, men's or women's perfume, vinegar, cut-up onion, bacon, ammonia, popcorn, roses, oranges, lemons, cantaloupe, dill pickle, pineapple, celery, cranberries, coffee, tea, bacon bits, and carbonated beverages. You will need a camcorder if the goal is creating a film, or a computer with Microsoft PowerPoint if the goal is creating a slideshow.

Rationale

Often, poetry gets a short shrift. Some teachers are frightened of trying to teach poetry for fear that students will resist or revolt. Others claim that any words strung together, however clumsily, constitute a poem. (Remember "found poetry"?) With Scent of My Soul, students dive into poetry, wrestle with words that adequately express their thoughts and feelings, and show that they care about the aesthetic effects of the words they write.

Procedures

Day 1

1. Ask students about their favorite color. Next, ask, "Does this color represent you?" A student may love the color blue, but think that yellow better represents her personality, for example. Although there are numerous books available on color theory (e.g., red is associated with passion, energy, and courage), I usually do not bring in any of those resources. Rather, I prefer that students select a favorite color based on their instincts—what they like. Students write out "My soul is _____" and fill in the blank with a color.

2. Distribute a copy of the sensory words (see Appendix B) from the Candy Freak activity.

3. Students list foods and tastes, and smells that are of the color they chose (5–10 minutes). Encourage students to use descriptive language. For example, rather than write "apple" for the color red, a student might say, "a red apple, so big it looks like a red pumpkin" or "a cinnamon red-hot candy that tastes sweet but burns your lips."

4. Pass around scented candles (or other materials). Ask students which scented candle they like best.

5. After students have decided on their favorite scent, have them describe it as best they can. Students should use not only descriptive words from the sensory words list but also phrases of their own choosing. Encourage students to describe associations with the scent. For example, the aroma of apple may make a student think about "Aunt Emma's home-cooked apple pie that she would always bake for us when we came over to her house on Sunday afternoon. Dad would turn on the television and look for a football game while Mom and Aunt Emma would talk in the kitchen."

6. Students make a list of objects associated with the color, taste, and scent (5–10 minutes).

7. Place students in groups of two or three. The focus will be on one student's color at a time. The first student reveals the color she chose. The other group members think for a minute, then do a free association aloud (meaning they say anything that comes into their minds in relation to the color, keeping in mind taste, smell, touch, sound, and sight). The student writes out everything her partners say, even if some of it seems to be off topic.

8. Repeat the process until all students have revealed their colors and everyone in the group has been the focus for the free association.

9. Ask students to read their entire lists aloud to other members of the group.

Days 2 to 3

1. Ask students to share any lists that have particularly vivid language. Draw attention to unique, interesting descriptions.

2. Tell students they are going to write a description of themselves and their peers. Encourage students to use precise language. They should be cognizant of the feelings of others. No insults will be tolerated.

3. Read aloud a favorite character description from a book or article. Ask students to note any parts that seem particularly effective.

4. Put students in different groups of three.

5. Pick one member of the group on which to focus.

6. Give two copies of the peer description handout (Figure 5.6) to every student. Students should keep all their writing until instructed to do otherwise. For 10 minutes, the other members of the group write about the physical characteristics of the person in focus by filling out the Peer Description sheet. Students may write complete sentences, jot down phrases, or simply list words.

7. While his peers are writing about him, the person in focus responds to the prompts in the Description of Me guidance sheet (Figure 5.7).

8. After time is up, peers read aloud their notes to the person in focus. The person in focus does not read the piece about himself.

9. Switch until every student has been the person in focus.

10. This time, the other members of the group write a series of metaphors or similes about the person in focus for 10 minutes (Item 2 in Figure 5.6). The metaphors are likely to be based on the words they have already used. For example, if a student noted that another student had a great sense of style, she might write, "She looks like the girl on the cover of *Vogue*" or "She could be Halle Berry's younger sister."

11. Again, on completion, students read their metaphors to the person in focus.

12. Students switch until everyone has had the opportunity to be the student in focus. As before, when others are writing about

Figure 5.6   Scent of My Soul: Peer Description

1. Physical appearance

   Typical clothes

   Clothes when he/she dresses up

   Face, complexion

   Hair

   Body

   Way that he/she walks

   What does he/she do when he/she walks into a crowded room?

   Most distinctive characteristics

2. Metaphors

   Animal

   Plant

   Object

   Landscape

   Music, sound

   Taste

   Touch

   Famous person

   Someone else you know

him, the student in focus writes metaphors about himself on the back of the Description of Me sheet (Figure 5.7).

13. Finally, students give each completed Figure 5.6 to the student they wrote about.

14. Ask students to compare their own observations and metaphors with those of their peers in a quick piece of writing (perhaps take 10 or 15 minutes).

Day 4 (half day)

1. Students spread out Figure 5.6, Figure 5.7, and the comparison paper in front of them so they can see them all at the same time.

2. Students use these materials to write a character sketch about themselves.

Day 5 (half day)

1. Place students into groups.

2. Give each student a yellow and a pink highlighter.

3. Students exchange papers with each other.

4. Students highlight effective phrasing in yellow.

5. Students highlight mundane words, clichés, and well-worn phrases in pink.

6. Students return papers and writers make any corrections they deem fit.

Day 6

1. Distribute Form of the Loose Villanelle (Figure 5.8) and read aloud or distribute Model Pantoum (Figure 5.9).

2. Students write a pantoum, using excerpts from their previously penned papers or new inspiration.

3. Students transpose their poems into films.

4. A student can either superimpose the lines of his poem on the film or read his poem aloud during the film.

Figure 5.7   Description of Me

Physical appearance
    Typical clothes

    Clothes when you dress up

    Face, complexion

    Hair

    Body

    Way that you walk

    What you do when you walk into a crowded room

    What you will look like in 10 years

Favorite foods
    Describe them

Favorite possessions
    Describe them

    Explain why they are important

Psychological profile—what motivates you?
    Money

    Love

    Power

    Attention

    Charity

    Friendship

    What else?

A big fear

A dream

Important relationships

If you inherited 10 million dollars, what would you do with the money?

On the back, write at least seven metaphors that would help describe you.

Figure 5.8   Form of the Loose Villanelle

The villanelle has 19 lines and six stanzas. Each stanza has three lines, except the last stanza, which has four lines. The first and the third lines of the poem repeat as refrains, so make sure those lines are particularly good. The most important rhyme is between the first and third lines. Because there are so many possibly rhyming lines, do not end line 1 or 2 in a word like *orange*. Instead, use an easy-rhyming word such as *red, blue*, or *sun*. When you cannot think of a rhyming word, try one that sounds somewhat close. The structure is:

> *line 1–a–1st refrain*
> *line 2–b*
> *line 3–a–2nd refrain*
>
> *line 4–a*
> *line 5–b*
> *line 6–a–1st refrain (same as line 1)*
>
> *line 7–a*
> *line 8–b*
> *line 9–a–2nd refrain (same as line 3)*
>
> *line 10–a*
> *line 11–b*
> *line 12–a–1st refrain (same as line 1)*
>
> *line 13–a*
> *line 14–b*
> *line 15–a–2nd refrain (same as line 3)*
>
> *line 16–a*
> *line 17–b*
> *line 18–a–1st refrain (same as line 1)*
> *line 19–a–2nd refrain (same as line 3)*

Note: For a sample of a great villanelle, see Sylvia Plath's "Mad Girl's Love Song."

Figure 5.9   Model Pantoum

The pantoum is a verse form that uses four lines in a stanza. The second and fourth lines are repeated in the first and third lines of the next stanza.

The Cycle
The soul is a model prisoner
Content in captivity
Consistency of cell walls
Free us

Content in captivity
We dance we
Free us
Circumstance of gravity

We dance we
Twist and twirl and cradle sky
Circumstance of gravity
Plummeting ever earthward

The soul is an infant
A budding being
Waking in life yet dreaming
Still of ancient times

A budding being
The soul is old indeed
Still of ancient times
Wandering souls remember

The soul is old indeed
Reflecting being
Wandering souls remember
The cyclical nature of all things natural

The line was created by
Man and man alone
This room, page, street
Just imagine the world before

Figure 5.9   *(continued)*

Man and man alone

Laid claim, plans, brick
Just imagine the world before
Linear injustice crept in

Laid claim, plans, brick
Laid it all on the line
Linear injustice crept in
And usurped the cycle

The soul accepts this wreath of oxygen
Animated by breath
Rise and collapse with it
Tether so subtly and bind with it

Animated by breath
I picture my soul as a balloon
Tether so subtly and bind with it
Confide in it

I picture my soul as a balloon
A tree trunk, a raindrop, an atom
Confide in it
As mother
As soul
As other

Extension Activities

1. The teacher may want to assign a storyboarding activity prior to the making of the film.
2. Students could also transpose their poems into PowerPoint presentations.
3. Always have the student read her poem aloud in a presentation. As the words occur in the film or PowerPoint presentation, the student speaks the words, too.

NCTE/IRA Standards: 1, 2, 3, 4, 5, 6, 7, 8, 10, 11, 12

6

Movement and Touch ■ ■ ■

Proficiency and learning come not from reading and listening but from action, from doing, and from experience.

—C. Cook, *The Play Way* (1917)

In a typical classroom, students take their seats before the bell rings and remain there for the duration of the period. In general, students are expected to remain quiet, obedient, still, and docile.

For a moment, imagine you are an adolescent again. Your body is in hormone overload, your mind is racing with vague desires, and your emotions soar and fall encounter by encounter, moment by moment. The prospect of sitting in a plastic and metal chair and listening to an older person talk about a subject in which you have minimal interest for an extended period of time does not thrill you. You would rather be doing almost anything besides sitting and listening, except for maybe sitting and filling in the blank spaces of a seemingly senseless worksheet. You feel like screaming, running, talking, listening to music, or playing video games, but instead you are required to sit motionless for most of 420 minutes (seven hours), Monday through Friday. What do you do to release the tension and pent-up energy?

To cope with such a sedentary existence, students may develop unusual, at times ungainly, coping mechanisms. In high school, I used to bounce my legs up and down under the desk constantly, scribble little drawings in the margins of my papers, and write poetry. But I was a compliant nerd. Other students channel their energy by using pencils as drumsticks and books as drums, endlessly brushing and combing their hair, picking at parts of their faces (sometimes the nose, mouth, ear, or blemishes), applying makeup, shuffling through backpacks or purses, writing notes, squirming and stretching, talking, and, of course, raising hell (also known as misbehaving) in the classroom. Gensemer (1979) notes that when the mind "cannot handle . . . nervous energy, the excess spills over into the rest of the body" (p. 37).

After teaching English, reading, and social studies for a period of years, I returned to the university to obtain certification in physical education, just so I could get outdoors and move around for part of the day. Eventually, the principal assigned me a split schedule. In the morning, I would teach in a shirt and tie in the classroom; by afternoon, dressed in shorts with a whistle around my neck, I would be on the playing fields.

As a teacher, I know that it is sometimes difficult to conjure ways to get students out of their seats for academically sound reasons. Sometimes, the problem is simply a matter of space. I once taught in a tiny portable building in which 35 student desks were jammed side by side. The student desks in the front row were less than three feet away from the whiteboard, so anytime I wrote on the board, my butt was practically in the faces of the students in the front row—an unpleasant situation for all of us.

Teaching with Movement

Even under such conditions, or perhaps especially under such conditions, movement can be an effective way to teach. After all, it is almost impossible to fall asleep while the body is in motion.

Using movement as a learning tool does not have to involve fancy, elaborate techniques. One fun exercise is to pose a series of true-false questions to students. Students stand to signify that they believe a statement to be true or false, the teacher keeps track of votes, and, after everyone has stood, the correct response is revealed. This technique is useful for teaching simple grammatical concepts, too—helping students to distinguish between lie/lay, it's/its, and who/whom, for example. In lieu of standing, a teacher might suggest that students flap their arms or jog in place near their desks.

Science teachers have long illustrated the molecular structures of solids, liquids, and gases through movement. They bunch all the students together and tell individual students to move around very little to demonstrate solids; for liquids, students are more dispersed and encouraged to become somewhat more active; to represent gasses, students are spread out and told to run and jump around.

Sometimes just bringing a class outside and asking them to describe the phenomena they encounter—the grass, a tree, the football stadium, the sound of cars passing by, the school building—is a way to use movement to initiate thought. Ludwig van Beethoven took a stroll in the woods to sort out and hone his musical ideas, humming and singing melodies with great exuberance, oblivious to onlookers. Immanuel Kant walked the same path in his German village at the same time every day as he considered problems of logic, theology, and philosophy. Ralph Waldo Emerson liked to invite a friend along for a long walk when he had important matters to discuss. Similarly, when Emerson's children became depressed or angry, he would ask them to venture outside in the belief that nature would help restore their equilibrium. Emerson (1994) wrote, "If a man would be alone, let him look at the stars. The rays that come from those heavenly worlds will separate between him and what he touches. One might think the atmosphere was made transparent with this design, to give man, in the heavenly bodies, the perpetual presence of the sublime" (p. 3). Throughout time, writers and thinkers have used movement to get their intellectual processes into gear.

Unfortunately, the "sit down and shut up" methodology predominates in too many classrooms. This technique may seem necessary when 35 students are crowded into a tiny room and scores on spring's standardized exam serve as the sole criteria of success. However, "sit down and shut up" can sterilize learning and promote negative attitudes toward academics.

A conventional response to poor results on standardized tests is elimination of all curricular areas that involve any kind of movement— art, music, shop, and physical education. This is more bad news for students who are already bored, sluggish, and out of shape. For the record, the prevalence of obese adolescents ages 12 to 18 has tripled (to 15 percent) since 1980 (Ogden, Flegal, Carroll, & Johnson, 2002). Three of four adolescents in high school do not attend a daily physical education class (Burgeson, Wechsler, Brener, Young, & Spain, 2001); one in three engage in no vigorous physical activity (U.S. Department of Health and Human Services, 2004).

Retreating from physical movement is shortsighted and potentially harmful to academic achievement. Gibson (1988) has documented that movement and touch are essential for the proper maturation of the mind, especially in the early years. Researcher Jean Piaget (1953) termed the first stage of development the "sensorimotor stage" to emphasize the importance of movement to cognitive functioning. Like Piaget, Kephart (Godfrey, Newell, & Kephart, 1969) hypothesized that the earliest demonstration of intelligence in children is expressed through movement. Young children who have limited interactions with the environment are likely to experience serious learning difficulties in school. Without adequately developed motor skills, a child is unable to discern and interpret much about the world around him. "Intellectual deficiency is tantamount to a disrupted and undeveloped motor system" (Bell, 1971, p. 111).

Adolescents, particularly slower-than-average learners, may learn more effectively when motor skills are invoked in teaching academic subject matter (Kephart, 1971). That is, linking movement and touch to intellectual development is an astute strategy for adolescents, as many "concepts are ultimately anchored in motor experience" (Bell, 1971, p. 125).

One way to integrate movement and action into instruction is to consider transforming typically passive activities into active ones. For instance, rather than have students read a story aloud in round-robin fashion, a teacher could consider turning the story into a reader's theater, where students role-play, add dramatic interpretation, and spontaneously perform as they read. So much of school focuses on a student "taking in"—for example, information, study skills, models, and suggestions. But time also should be devoted to expression—to perceptions, thoughts, feelings, and meaning. As H'Doubler (2002) has noted, "To know is the essential first step, but it is the expression of what we know that develops character and a sense of values" (p. 11).

Drama can engage students in real-world applications of thinking and literacy. It is a way of allowing students to play with language and to explore new ideas without having to face the consequences usually associated with making a mistake (Apter, 2003). Drama and performance are often "where the life change experiences happen for students" (Ririe, 2002, p. 63).

Getting students to participate in drama may seem difficult initially, but students warm to it quickly. An entire K–12 language curriculum could be predicated on making drama and movement the focal points of instruction—in fact, it already has been (Hoetker, 1975; Moffett & Wagner,

1991). According to Heathcote (as cited in Johnson & O'Neill, 1984), "Drama is such a normal thing. It has been made into an abnormal thing by all the fussy leotards, hairdos, and stagecraft that [are] associated with it. All it demands is that children shall think from within a dilemma instead of talking about the dilemma. That's all it is; you bring them to a point where they think from within the framework of choices instead of talking coolly about the framework of choices" (p. 119).

Through drama, students can experiment with expression in a safe and stimulating environment. Engaging in drama can help students learn about their talents and limitations in ways that would be impossible in a classroom dedicated to quiet seatwork.

Importance of Touch

Over the past few decades, the touch of a human being has come to elicit suspicion and alarm, especially in public schools. Sadly, incidents of sexual misconduct by adults in authority—clergy and teachers—have made even the most innocuous gesture rife with sinister potential. Because of Americans' creeping concerns over sexual abuse, many schools advocate that teachers make no physical contact whatsoever with students. If teachers strictly abide by such directives, they may communicate to students a sense of uncaring and arrogance. In his prognostications about the future, Naisbitt (1982) warned against allowing anomalous events to shutter basic human needs.

There is nothing inappropriate about a pat on the back for a job well done or a nudge on the arm as an indication that "I want you to succeed." A simple touch can convey a great deal. The oldest record of a handshake was to symbolize a transfer of power from a god to a human in Egypt, circa 2800 BCE (Panati, 1987). In the Bible, the touch of Jesus revives a leper and gives him hope for a new life (Mark 1:40–45). Touch therapy is the foundation of medicine as developed by Hippocrates in 400 BCE. Human touch constitutes a baby's first sensations of the world; the hands of a mother connote security and provide a sense of belonging.

A few minutes after my son was born, he was whisked away to the neonatal intensive care unit because he had a potentially dangerous fever. The neonatal nurses prodded and examined him, then placed a breathing apparatus over his mouth and nose and moved him to a clear plastic box. My wife and I were both extremely worried about his health, so I spent much time gazing through the large hospital window at him, staring as he slept. Unfortunately, the birth had turned into a daylong ordeal for my wife, who was near total exhaustion. A few minutes after the birth, when we were moved to a different room, my wife had to make the journey in a gurney.

After a few more hours of waiting, my wife finally demanded that she be allowed to see her newborn boy. A new nurse on duty, distressed that a mother had not seen her baby since a brief glimpse just after the birth, wheeled my wife down to the neonatal intensive care unit.

There, in the clear, glass box was our son, screaming and fidgeting.

"He's been like that for quite a while," said the neonatal nurse.

As soon as my wife picked up our son, his crying ceased.

The physical need for touch does not end in infancy. "The need for touch . . . increases with age and wisdom. Physical, psychological, and emotional touches are all essential for the proper establishment of internal sources of security, self-image, trust, and interdependence. They are needed for normal growth and development and are essential for a healthy aging process" (Fanslow, 1990, p. 543).

The boom in high-touch health care—chiropractics and massage have become multibillion-dollar industries—may be a response to the increasing sense of detachment engendered by the no-touch movement (Barnes, Powell-Griner, McFann, & Nahin, 2004).

Indeed, researchers are discovering that touch can be more effective for the slings and arrows of aging—arthritis, aches, and depression—than prescription drugs. But touch therapy has proven effective with women and men of all ages and especially with children who have autism, attention deficit hyperactivity disorder (ADHD), depression, bulimia, anorexia, chronic fatigue, and even drug addiction (Field, 2001). In general, patients who are given a personalized approach, replete with appropriate touching (or massage, in the case of physical ailments), have demonstrated faster healing and lower anxiety levels (Fraser & Kerr, 1993). In an examination of healing processes across cultures, Bloom (2005) found touch and a caring disposition to be essential for recuperation. He writes, "Perhaps some of the popularity of massage therapy and chiropractic treatment comes from the experience of feeling healed after the laying on of hands" (p. 256).

Certainly, one of the most alluring aspects of new science museums, such as the Center of Science and Industry in Columbus, Ohio, for children is that exhibits are designed with touch in mind. Similarly, when park rangers design exhibits, they include areas where children can feel the fur of mammals, the skin of reptiles, and the scales of fish.

Clearly, the human touch can be nurturing. In contrast, withholding touch can have adverse emotional consequences. For example, when medical personnel avoid physical contact with patients, patients often become withdrawn and less responsive. They may begin to view their ailment as making them unattractive, or even repulsive (Fraser & Kerr, 1993).

For people with problems with low vision or near blindness, touch can be used as a sensory substitute to aid with daily life. According to researchers (Lenay, Canu, & Villon, 1997), *haptic* (meaning touch) appeals provide the best sensory substitute for blindness or low vision. A Tactile Vision Substitution System, or TVSS, converts images captured by a video camera into tactile signals, which stimulate the skin on the back, chest, or eyebrow. Similarly, researchers (Bach-Y-Rita, Kaczmarek, Tyler, & Garcia-Lara, 1998) have described an undetectable system of vision through touch in which a tiny camera is attached to a pair of glasses. The camera wirelessly transmits signals to a dime-sized electrotactile receptor on a dental retainer. This technology has enabled even blind patients to exercise some degree of ambulatory freedom.

Using haptic appeals can also be a way of teaching students who have difficulties with reading or spelling. Even older adolescents can learn proper spelling by tracing words with their fingers or feeling letters cut out from sandpaper. Researchers have found that although low-vision students may be slower readers (especially if they trace several words as they read), they "can read as accurately as can sighted children" (Gompel, Van Bon, & Schreuder, 2004, p. 771).

As with most multisensory appeals, movement and touch maximize their effectiveness when reiterating lessons taught through the visual, auditory, or olfactory senses. For example, a teacher who wants students to learn about the contribution of a certain author might introduce the writer by

- Reading excerpts aloud in class.
- Playing parts of the work from a book on tape.
- Assigning students to perform a reader's theater.
- Bringing in a large, poster-size picture of the author.
- Having students dress up and act as if they were the author.

If education is an attempt to "awaken in the young a capacity to recognize the good and the worthwhile" (Arnold, 1988, p. 103), then movement must be integral to instruction. Nothing awakens students more than getting them off of their butts and moving around, speaking, and performing.

Implications for Teachers

Of all the senses, touch is the most valuable, at least according to Helen Keller. Keller (1980) writes, "I have met people so empty of joy, that when I clasped their frosty finger tips, it seemed as if I were shaking hands with a northeast storm. Others there are whose hands have sunbeams in them, so that their grasp warms my heart" (p. 144).

Despite all we know about the biological benefits of a hug or pat on the back, many teachers shy away from such common, friendly gestures. Despite all we know about the need for children to move around and interact with the world, most classroom instruction is still reliant on the delivery of seatwork to silent students. The expectation for dormancy is all the more striking considering the natural hyperactivity, curiosity, and joie de vivre of children. In light of such developmental realities, integrating more hands-on activities into instruction seems like an idea whose time has come. Any excuse to get students out of their seats, moving, and thinking would be a welcome relief from the staidness of the typical classroom. Drama, role-play, tactile manipulation, acting in real time, and hands-on learning are proven ways to increase student engagement and intensify learning.

The following lessons incorporate movement and touch into learning activities.

Activity	Entry Point	Focus	Preparation Time
Movement and Touch Lesson 1 Red Carpet Conversations	Imagined conversations between unusual interlocutors	Grammar, quality of writing	Minimal
Movement and Touch Lesson 2 Quadrama	Different kind of book report	Literary interpretation, literary terms, quality of writing	Minimal
Movement and Touch Lesson 3 Truth Commercials	Video	Research, persuasive writing, presentation and speaking	Substantial
Movement and Touch Lesson 4 Indiana Jones and the Participial Phrase	Film clips	Sentence combining	Substantial

Although speaking is an activity in which students engage daily, few teachers remember to include speaking as part of the curriculum. In Red Carpet Conversations, students actually engage in simulated conversations with celebrities and friends, then operationalize their dialogues into longer pieces of writing. Rather than use the same-old, same-old book report, Quadrama reveals a new, hands-on, artistic way for students to communicate about books. The Truth Commercials lesson uses simulation, advertising, and the lure of film to teach research skills and rhetorical devices. In Indiana Jones and the Participial Phrase, the teacher dresses up as an adventurer and gets to crack a whip to teach sentence combining, bringing new meaning to the phrase *hands-on learning.*

Movement and Touch Lesson 1

Red Carpet Conversations

Summary: Creating a conversation between two famous people is a fun, creative, and humorous lesson that teaches students how to apply writing rules that include punctuation, quotation marks, and indentation. Although the two famous people that the students choose may have nothing in common, it is hysterical to see how students have them meet and fill in the content of their conversation.

Author: Lesley Kahle, 7th Grade English teacher, Orange Grove Magnet School, Tampa, Florida

Senses: Movement, sound, sight

Type of Activity: Individual

Approximate Time: Three 45-minute class periods. I give students a class period to write their rough drafts and a class period to edit and start their final drafts. I allow students to take home their conversations for further revisions before turning in the final paper.

Objectives: Students will use dialogue writing rules to create a conversation between two famous people that they randomly choose from a basket, brainstorm the conversation, write a rough draft, use peer or adult editors, and write a final draft.

Materials: A basket, small slips of paper, an overhead or chalkboard, and pen and paper or computer.

Setup: Write or type up a list of famous people. The following are some of the categories of famous individuals or celebrities I have pulled from: talk show hosts, musicians, professional athletes, actors/actresses, presidents, authors, cartoon characters, and cultural icons. On individual small slips of paper, write 60 or more names—one on each sheet—and place them in a basket.

Procedures
1. Distribute Red Carpet Conversations: Guide for Writing Dialogue (Figure 6.1) and go over the basic rules.
2. Clarify what magic words are and how they improve dialogue.
3. Choose two names from the basket and brainstorm as a class a conversation between the two people.

Figure 6.1   Red Carpet Conversations: Guide for Writing Dialogue

1. Quotation marks (" ") always go around the exact words that were spoken or what the person thought.

2. Commas (,) question marks (?), exclamation points (!) and periods (.) always go inside the quotation marks. Commas separate dialogue from the speaker.

3. Each time, be sure to include who is speaking or thinking. Example: "Good morning class. Now it's time to write dialogue," said the cheerful teacher.

4. You can improve your dialogue by using stronger verbs instead of the tired word *said*. Example: "Oh, good!" responded the eager students.

5. The very best dialogue writing also includes some "-ing" or magic words to show what the speaker is doing while talking. Example: "Now what shall we write about?" asked the cheerful teacher, turning off the overhead projector.

   Magic Words: after, when, because, as, that, while, who, although, almost, with, since, before, by, in, on, even though.

6. Always begin a new paragraph and indent every time the speaker changes.

Example:

   "We could also write up a conversation between kids who are planning to build a fort," added another student because that was exactly what he was doing at home.
   "There are so many wonderful conversations we could write about, but we'll have to choose just one to write together," instructed the teacher, passing out writing paper to everyone.

Source: L. Kahle, 2007, Orange Grove Magnet School, Tampa, FL. Reprinted with permission.

4. With student input, model and write the beginning of the conversation on an overhead, following the dialogue writing rules and using magic words.

5. Allow students to choose two names randomly from the basket.

6. Distribute Red Carpet Conversations: Writing Rubric (Figure 6.2) and go over the criteria for how the students will be assessed.

7. Students brainstorm the conversation between the two individuals, including the setting and an event or conflict that happens between the two people. The teacher reads aloud the student sample dialogue in Figure 6.3 to help the students get an idea of how others have tackled the project.

8. Students construct a minimum of a two-page rough draft of their Red Carpet Conversation.

9. Students peer edit by having two peers act out the conversation while the writer makes notes. The writer revises.

Figure 6.2   Red Carpet Conversations: Writing Rubric

Name:

Names drawn:

Task	Author	Points	Teacher
1. Created a conversation between the two names chosen with a minimum of two pages in length, including a brainstorm, rough draft, and final draft.		20	
2. Quotation marks exist around the exact words spoken.		10	
3. Punctuation for dialogue is inside the quotation marks and punctuation is at the end of each sentence.		10	
4. Included who is speaking after the dialogue.		10	
5. Included at least eight instances of magic or -ing words that show what the speaker is doing while talking.		10	
6. Indented to show change in speaker.		10	
7. Good revision has taken place by two other writers. (Proof is shown below for each.)		10	
8. Show, not tell technique used, and did not use the word *said*.		10	
9. Author has scored himself or herself in each category.		10	
Total:		**100**	

Teacher comments:

Editors (Minimum of two)

Name: Signature

1.

2.

Name	What did you find to help the author?

Source: L. Kahle, 2007, Orange Grove Magnet School, Tampa, FL. Reprinted with permission.

Figure 6.3   Red Carpet Conversations: Student Sample

That's Hott

"So, Snoop, we should make another movie together," stated Paris Hilton as she and Snoop Dogg sat in a New York café.

"Fo rizzel!" agreed Snoop as he was taking a bite out of his scone.

"That would be so cool! We should ask Clint if he will direct, call him up." suggested Paris.

"Aight," affirmed Snoop while dialing Clint Eastwood's cell phone number.

"Hello," answered Mr. Eastwood on the set of his new movie *Million Dollar Baby*.

"Yo, dis is Snoop. Paris and me dun both agreed that we should make another movie together and dat you should direct. You down wit dat, homie?" Snoop asked Clint.

"Sure, I already have some ideas. Let's start filming immediately. I can hold off on *Million Dollar Baby* for awhile. Meet me at the New York airport tomorrow at 3:00 p.m. That should give Paris some time to wake up. My people will call to give you more information. Pack for warm weather. We're going to Fiji. Gotta go, bye," Clint replied, hanging up right away.

"Man, that boy can talk a lot, but at least we got our movie," Snoop told Paris as he put away his phone.

"That's hott, I need to go pack!!!" yelled Paris as she bolted out the door.

"Wowwww . . . this place is pretty!" oohed Paris as she strutted off the private plane with her dog Tinkerbell in her arm.

"Dis is da bomb dizzel, fo rizzle my nizzle," complimented Snoop in his own language.

"My driver will take you to the hotel so you can unpack. We will start filming tomorrow. I will meet you there around 1:00 p.m. Be ready to start by 3:00 p.m. Don't party too late; we need you fresh for tomorrow. Bye," explained Clint.

"Well, we are here," Snoop stated as he stretched his legs after just getting out of his limo.

"Why did he have to make it so early?" whined Paris as she moped out of her very own stretch limo.

"Ummm, guys." Clint piped in as he shuffled over to the two actors, "there is a problem."

"Don't play wit' me foo', the 'Dogg' don't deal wit disasters now," commented Snoop anxiously.

"Well, we need to leave the island immediately. The Fiji government has put out a warning that the volcano located in the center of the island is scheduled to erupt at 7:00 p.m. tonight," explained Clint with an embarrassed tone.

"That's hott," whispered Paris.

"Literally," added Snoop.

---

10. Students choose a peer. Together they read the two parts of the conversation.

11. Students turn in their final drafts.

Extension Activities

An idea that works well in conjunction with this lesson is script writing. It is a relatively simple step to bring their conversations to life through the stage or a screenplay. Students can act out the conversation live or videotape scenes and play them for the class.

NCTE/IRA Standards: 1, 2, 3, 4, 5, 6, 7, 8, 9, 10, 11, 12

Source: L. Kahle, 2007, Orange Grove Magnet School, Tampa, FL. Reprinted with permission.

Movement and Touch Lesson 2

Quadrama

Summary: Students create an artistic representation of a recently read novel, merging drawing and writing with knowledge of literary terms.

Author: Robert Masters, Temperance, Michigan

Senses: Touch and sight

Type of Activity: Individual

Approximate Time: It will take 30–40 minutes to explain the directions and rubric, show the class how to make a side of the quadrama, display examples, and field any of their questions. After the overview of the project is complete, it is up to the teacher to establish the amount of class time, if any, to be devoted to working on the project. The project itself can take 4–5 hours or longer to complete (not counting reading the novel).

Objectives: Quadrama is designed to make the students not only read a novel for understanding but also to give their visual interpretation of events and literary devices. It is not enough to read a book and be able to explain the plot with writing. The expectation is that a student can show the scenes that represent the major elements of the story's plot (introduction, conflict, climax, resolution). A quadrama can be done with a class novel or individual reading.

Materials: Students will need but are not limited to the following materials: construction paper or poster board, glue, markers or colored pencils, and any other craft-type materials.

Procedures

In Advance

Before doing a quadrama, all students should have read a novel.

Day 1

1. Distribute How to Make a Quadrama (Figure 6.4) as a handout for students and explain the six components that are necessary to complete the project, as outlined in Requirements for the Quadrama (Figure 6.5).

Figure 6.4   How to Make a Quadrama

1. Fold a standard piece of paper from the top right corner to the opposite side.

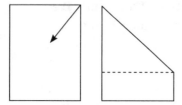

2. Cut off the bottom strip of paper not included in the fold.

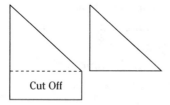

Cut Off

3. Unfold the paper to reveal a square with a diagonal fold line. Fold the opposite corners together to form an X. Unfold the paper for a square.

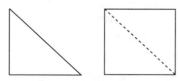

Unfold to form square   Fold opposing corners to form X

4. With scissors, cut one of the folds to the middle of the X.

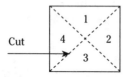

Cut

5. Overlap parts 3 and 4 and fold together to form the bottom. This will give you one side. Then repeat the process three more times for a total of four sections. Finally, attach the four sections by gluing sides 1 and 2 to sides 1 and 2 of the other section.

3 and 4 Glued Together

Source: B. Masters, 2007, Sylvania, OH. Reprinted with permission.

Figure 6.5   Requirements for the Quadrama

DUE DATE: _____

This is a project that accompanies the novel you are reading. In class I will show you how to set up the quadrama, but the project itself will be done on your own. The following requirements must be included in order to receive full credit on the quadrama.

1. Introduction: A scene depicting the main characters and setting of the story.

2. Conflict: A scene depicting the main problem of the story.

3. Climax: A scene depicting the most exciting part of the novel, when the conflict is about to be resolved.

4. Resolution: A scene depicting what happened after the conflict was resolved.

5. Each of the four parts (intro, conflict, climax, resolution) must be explained in writing on the bottom of the corresponding scene or section. A minimum of 50 words per section is required.

6. The four scenes must be in 3D picture format.

Besides grading you on the requirements above, I will also be looking at the effort, creativity, and neatness of the quadrama.

Source: B. Masters, 2007, Sylvania, OH. Reprinted with permission.

2. Once the requirements are explained and student questions are answered, demonstrate how to make one side of the quadrama.

3. Repeat the process, but this time have students follow along and model what you do. Help students who have difficulties.

4. After all students have completed the side, show a finished quadrama (see Figure 6.4).

5. Once everyone has seen the finished product, pass it around and allow students to ask questions.

6. Explain the grading process of the quadrama by handing out the rubric in Figure 6.6.

7. After the initial day of explanation, the students may work independently on the project at home or during class. The time and place where the project is to be completed are at the teacher's discretion.

NCTE/IRA Standards: 1, 2, 3, 4, 5, 6, 7, 8, 9, 10, 11, 12

Source: R. Masters, 2007, Temperance, MI. Reprinted with permission.

Figure 6.6   Rubric for the Quadrama

Name: _____

Artistry	Writing	Technical
___ **Color:** Use of varying colors	___ **Word Requirement:** 50 words minimum per scene	___ **Appearance:** Proper size and shape
___ **Background:** Full and complete background	___ **Coherency:** Writing is understandable and legible	___ **Directions:** Followed requirements
___ **Detail:** How much detail is in the four scenes	___ **Knowledge:** Four parts are correctly explained	___ **Effort:** Project neatness and presentation
___ **Creativity:** Use of different materials to make Quadrama		
Comments:	Comments:	Comments:

Each section is worth 10 points

_____Total points out of 100

Source: B. Masters, 2007, Sylvania, OH. Reprinted with permission.

Movement and Touch Lesson 3
Truth Commercials

Summary: The Truth Commercials lesson is an eye-opening experience that gets students involved in research, writing, media literacy, and original thinking. Students actually create a 30-second public service announcement (PSA). Of course, if a camcorder or cassette recorder is not available, students can always perform the commercials live using props.

Author: Lesley Kahle, Orange Grove Magnet School, Tampa, Florida

Senses: Movement and touch, sight, sound

Type of Activity: Individual, then later with a partner

Approximate Time: Six 45-minute class periods

Objectives: Students will use research skills to discover facts of a topic (in my example, the hazards of tobacco use), become acquainted with the format for a script, and bring to life an original idea for a 30-second audio or video Truth Commercial.

Materials: Media center access, cassette recorder, video camcorder, tripod, TV with VCR, access to MTV to tape a few commercial examples, an example of a script, pen and paper or access to a computer.

Procedures

In Advance

Videotape two to three Truth Commercials from MTV and reserve the media center for two days of research. Select and find an example of script writing so you can go over the format of that genre. Make a content frame on which students will record their research.

Days 1 to 6

1. On Day 1, have students view the examples of Truth Commercials and explain to them that they will be creating original, 30-second audio or video commercials of their own that will first require them to complete some research. Discuss with students the four major hazardous areas of tobacco use: cigarettes, secondhand smoke, spit tobacco (also known as dip), and chewing tobacco.

2. Go over the Truth Commercials Assessment Sheet (Figure 6.7) with students so they understand all parts of the assignment and how it will be evaluated.

Figure 6.7   Truth Commercials: Assessment Sheet

Objective: To promote youth and adult awareness of the hazards of tobacco use.

Rubric Checklist: Place the score that you think you deserve on the line.
There will be two tape recorders and VHS camcorders for student use in class.

Requirements

Topics for commercials and public service announcements:
____ One of the following cancer prevention areas is your topic for the contest:
"Smoking—It's a Killer"
"The Smoke Around You . . . Secondhand Smoke"
"Quit Spitting"
"Don't Bite Off More Than You Can Chew"

Research: (50 Points)
____ Use the Research Fact Sheet to document 20 facts on the hazards of tobacco (see Figure 6.8). (Five on each type: cigarettes and cigars, secondhand smoke, spit tobacco, and chew tobacco).
____ Underneath each fact on the sheet, write down the name of the book, Web site, or other resource where you found the information.

Script (the written version of your commercial): (50 Points)
____ Script written by you (but anyone can star in your commercial).
____ Script is original (created by you, not copied) and uses a narrator as the only speaking voice.
____ Everything to be acted out is written out, along with the set directions.
____ Script length is at least a half page typed and double spaced, or one page handwritten in blue or black ink (skipping lines as in double-spaced type).
____ Targeted audience for the commercial is young adults, ages 11 to 16.
____ Script follows typical script-writing format.
____ Brand names or any trademarked items *cannot* be used, and no one can be seen smoking *real or fake* tobacco products.
____ Brainstorm/open mind (10 Points)
____ Rough draft (20 Points)
____ Final draft (20 Points)

Commercial: (100 points)
You can work with a partner and choose which of your screenplays to develop into a commercial.
____ Your commercial is between 25 and 30 seconds long for a video. Cassette tapes must be 15 to 20 seconds long. Any additional time will disqualify the entire commercial.
____ Your radio public service announcement (cassette tape) or video public service announcement (VHS tape or DVD) has been submitted. Adapter tapes or VHS camcorders cannot be submitted. You must transfer the video to a regular tape or DVD for submission.
____ Your full name and project title are labeled on the cassette tape, VHS, or DVD.

Source: L. Kahle, 2007, Orange Grove Magnet School, Tampa, FL. Reprinted with permission.

3. Spend Day 2 and Day 3 in the library allowing students to become familiar with the various resources in the media center while they research 20 facts on the hazards of tobacco use or on their own topics. Make a generic chart similar to the research fact sheet example in Figure 6.8 and distribute to students. The form will guide them to collect five different facts about four different elements of their topic.

4. On Day 4, show students some examples of script writing. Next, students begin brainstorming their ideas for commercials and begin writing their scripts in class. Ask students to finish their scripts as homework, allowing them extra time to develop their ideas.

5. On Day 5, allow students to partner up and select one of their scripts to be filmed or recorded. Students then can film or record their commercials, which will be played on Day 6. See Figure 6.9 for an example of a PSA script written by a student.

Extension Activities

1. As a springboard for teaching the elements of a narrative, ask students to pick the most powerful fact from their research. This fact becomes the problem or conflict in a narrative.

2. After doing an assigned PSA, have students choose a topic of personal concern on their own and create another script and PSA.

NCTE/IRA Standards: 1, 2, 3, 4, 5, 6, 7, 8, 9, 10, 11, 12

Source: L. Kahle, 2007, Orange Grove Magnet School, Tampa, FL. Reprinted with permission.

Figure 6.8   Truth Commercials: Research Fact Sheet Example

Directions: Research and fill in the chart with five hazardous facts about each type of tobacco. Under each fact, write down the source and page number where you found your information.

	Cigarettes and Cigars	Secondhand Smoke	Spit Tobacco	Chew Tobacco
Fact #1				
Sources				
Fact #2				
Sources				
Fact #3				
Sources				
Fact #4				
Sources				
Fact #5				
Sources				

Source: L. Kahle, 2007, Orange Grove Magnet School, Tampa, FL. Reprinted with permission.

Figure 6.9   Student Sample of Public Service Announcement

20-Second Lesson

(Open on homemade graveyard with gravestones, flowers on the ground near gravestones)

(Female student stands in front of the graveyard. She is wearing a black skirt with lace on the edge over black panty hose. Also a black dress shirt with a black hat.)

STUDENT:

Here is all you need to know about smoking in twenty seconds.

(takes a deep inhale to prepare herself to say the facts and quickly says the facts)

Cigarette smoke contains 69 chemical compounds that can cause cancer. Cigarette smoke contains the radioactive isotope polonium-210. Two thousand teens start smoking every day. Some tobacco companies add urea to cigarettes and cigars. Cigarettes and cigars will eventually kill one-third of the people who use them.

(Again takes a breath to refresh herself)

There you have it. Smoking—it's a killer.

(Points to the graves behind her.)

Movement and Touch Lesson 4

Indiana Jones and the Participial Phrase

Summary: Students learn to avoid choppy sentences by using participial phrases.

Author: Matt Copeland, Washburn Rural High School, Topeka, Kansas

Senses: Movement, sight, sound

Type of Activity: Individual

Approximate Time: 50 minutes

Objectives: The student will define and identify a participial phrase, construct sentences using participial phrases, and practice sentence-combining skill.

Materials: Copy of *Raiders of the Lost Ark,* TV and VCR, adventurer hat, leather jacket, and bullwhip.

Procedures

In Advance

As ridiculous as it may sound, dressing the part of Indiana Jones makes a tremendous difference in student reception to this lesson. Students will forever associate participial phrases with "that Indiana Jones thing."

Day 1

1. Activate prior knowledge of participles and participial phrases by brainstorming definitions of each of these terms and reviewing present and past participial forms.
2. Act out two nearly simultaneous actions (for example, picking up a piece of paper and pointing at the chalkboard).
3. On a piece of paper, have students identify each of these actions in a complete sentence. (The teacher picked up the piece of paper. The teacher pointed at the chalkboard.)
4. Discuss with students how rough and choppy these two sentences would sound in a piece of writing. Then explain that using a participial phrase can help to correct this problem.
5. On the chalkboard, model for students how to combine these two sentences using a participial phrase. (Picking up the piece of paper, the teacher pointed at the chalkboard.)

6. Distribute the chart for recording actions (Figure 6.10).

7. Model how to complete the chart using the example sentence in Step 5.

8. Show the first 10 minutes of *Raiders of the Lost Ark*. When students observe two simultaneous actions, they are to stand up for a second or two, then sit back down and write the actions on the chart. The actor for each pair of actions must remain the same.

9. Students proceed in this manner until they have documented 10 simultaneous actions from the movie.

10. For each pair of actions on a student's completed chart, have him construct a sentence using a participial phrase.

11. Have students pair off to check their partners' sentences for proper use of participial phrases.

12. Have students return to a prior piece of their own writing and combine at least two sentences using participial phrases.

Assessment

	1 Unsatisfactory	2 Insufficient	3 Uneven	4 Sufficient	5 Skillful	6 Excellent
Standing up for simultaneous activities						
Simultaneous worksheet on recording actions completed						
Ten original sentences created from worksheet on recording actions						

NCTE/IRA Standards: 1, 2, 3, 4, 5, 6, 7, 8, 9, 10, 11, 12

Source: M. Copeland, 2007, Washburn Rural High School, Topeka, KS. Reprinted with permission.

Figure 6.10   Indiana Jones and the Participial Phrase

When you notice two nearly simultaneous actions, stand up. Then, sit down and record the actions below.

Action A	Actor	Action B
Example: picked up the paper	the teacher	pointed at the chalkboard
1.		
2.		
3.		
4.		
5.		
6.		
7.		
8.		
9.		
10.		

Source: M. Copeland, 2007, Washburn Rural High School, Topeka, KS. Reprinted with permission.

7

Sense of Play ■ ■ ■

Play is by its very nature educational. And it should be pleasurable.
When the fun goes out of play, most often so does the learning.

—Oppenheim, 1984

The goal for most teachers today should not be aligning curriculum or preparing students for standardized examinations, but engaging the hearts and minds of their students. In the days of yore, knowing how to plan for lectures, textbook quizzes, quiet seatwork, and homework was considered a sufficient repertoire for teachers. The only problem with these strategies is that most students today consider them the equivalent of watching cabbages grow. Passive techniques lose their effectiveness when learners are not born gifted or blessed with innate enthusiasm for learning.

To force students into a humorless straitjacket of drill, silent reading, and worksheets is to invite oppositional behavior and apathy. After all, at least according to Plato, man's essential nature is to play.

For schools who fail to maintain adequate academic achievement, the typical administrative response has been to banish play so that students can focus more intensely on academics. In an exhaustive study of achievement in the K–12 schools of 30 Organization of Economic Cooperation and Development countries, it was found that no correlation existed between the amount of homework and students' levels of achievement. In fact, in countries where more homework is given, national achievement is actually *lower* than in countries where almost no homework is assigned (Baker & LeTendre, 2005). Similarly, researchers have not found a correlation between achievement and high-stakes testing, as measured by international tests of achievement (the Program of International Student Assessment, or PISA, and the Trends in International Math and Science Study, or TIMSS) or state exams (Baker & LeTendre, 2005). Thus, the contention that higher academic achievement can be attained through more testing, longer school days, and additional homework has zero empirical support.

Nevertheless, play has been abolished for many children ages 3 to 6 in Head Start programs in an effort to cultivate alphabet awareness and early reading (Zigler, Singer, & Bishop-Josef, 2004). Where underachieving students are concerned, the opposite response would seem more beneficial—more real-life experiences, not fewer; more sensory stimulation, not a harder return to text; more play, not less. Whereas increasing testing and homework may actually denigrate student achievement, play fosters creativity, cooperation, openness, and intelligence (Hair & Graziano, 2003; Russ, 2004; Shiner, Masten, & Roberts, 2003). Play occurs naturally, without coercion. A teacher who can turn learning into play makes life richer and students happier.

What difference does happiness make? According to Klein (2006), a researcher who has studied the effects of happiness on attitude, success, and quality of life:

> Happy people are more creative, and, as many studies show, they solve problems better and more quickly. Happiness makes people smart, and not just momentarily, but permanently. Positive feelings stimulate growth in the nerve connections in the brain—happiness and new mental associations go together. Finally, happy people are also nicer people. They are more aware and more likely to see the good in others. They are more likely to act altruistically and they are more successful mediators in resolving conflict. (p. xviii)

It should be no revelation that to learn the rudiments of any subject area, a student must first decide to become willingly involved. Toward this end, the entry point for lessons, especially at the beginning of the term, should be accessible, low-stress, and fun. The teacher's job, as a guardian of students' intellectual capital, is to gradually demonstrate to students how to play appropriately. High standards and academic rigor are admirable goals, but cannot be achieved without the willing participation of those involved—the students.

Implications for Teachers

When a teacher in Florida was struggling to get his students to learn vocabulary, he thought up a game he eventually decided to call Vocabulary War (Baines & Kunkel, 2003). In this activity, teams of students compete in a timed, simulated game show based on their knowledge of meanings and spellings of words. Before Vocabulary War, the teacher struggled to get his students to complete a worksheet on vocabulary, let alone attain a passing score on a state exam. After Vocabulary War, students began begging him for vocabulary words, and the grades for the class zoomed into the A and B range and stayed there for the remainder of the year.

One day, the assistant principal caught students trying to enter the teacher's classroom in the early morning hours before school. When asked what they were doing, the principal was startled to learn that the students were trying to get the day's vocabulary words so they could get an early start preparing for a session of Vocabulary War that afternoon. Imagine. One day, you think students couldn't care less about vocabulary and that they will never learn any new words. The next day, students are trying to break into your classroom so that they can get the newest set of vocabulary words. In this case, the difference in student attitudes and performance was attributable to a single strategy—turning vocabulary study into an enjoyable activity.

The following lessons incorporate a sense of play into learning activities.

Activity	Entry Point	Focus	Preparation Time
Play Lesson 1 Triple Loops	Collaborative writing	Response to literature, literary analysis, expository writing	Minimal
Play Lesson 2 Cut-Up Poems	Scrambled words	Poetic writing, sequencing	Minimal
Play Lesson 3 Between the Ears	Drawing	Main idea, inference, comprehension	Minimal
Play Lesson 4 CSI: Contextual Semantic Investigation	Investigation	Vocabulary development, reading comprehension	Substantial

The final activities in this book use what I call the sixth sense—the sense of play—to engage students in academically challenging activities. The Triple Loops activity uses collaboration and conversation to get students to revise. How many times have you handed back a composition for revision only to have the student cross out a *the* and substitute an *a*? Triple Loops circumvents such trivialization and forces students to look more deeply at their writing. Cut-Up Poems force students to think sequentially and poetically, even if they typically resist such an approach. Between the Ears uses spontaneous student drawings to assess reading comprehension and to spark discussions of a text, character, or theme. CSI: Contextual Semantic Investigation transforms a research-based approach to learning vocabulary in context into an exciting detective game.

The secrets to these final activities, like the secrets to all the activities in *A Teacher's Guide to Multisensory Learning*, are predicated on student engagement and intensified learning experiences. If the senses are stimulated, the mind is focused, lessons relate to real life, and school assignments become play, then students' immense intellectual and social potential begins to blossom. The assign-and-assess approach, dominant in K–12 schools for more than 100 years, has had its day. It is time to wake up to the power of experience, the richness of participation, the wonder of the day at hand. It is time to engage the minds of our students with lessons worth learning.

Play Lesson 1
Triple Loops

Summary: Students learn to revise using subtle, highly interactive, collaborative strategies.

Author: Pamela Sissi Carroll, Florida State University, Tallahassee, Florida

Senses: Sight, sound

Type of Activity: Starts as individual (Phase 1: Loop), moves to pairs (Phase 2: Loop de Loop), becomes collaborative (Phase 3: Group Loop)

Approximate Time: In a normal five-day school week, the teacher could schedule the Loop phase on the first day, the Loop de Loop phase on the second and third days, and the Group Loop phase on the fourth and fifth days. Final results would be shared with the class on the following school day.

Objectives: Students will develop confidence and expertise in assessing their own writing and in assessing the work of classmates.

Materials for Phase 1 and Phase 2: Plenty of paper for experimenting with phrases, sentences, paragraphs, or other language maneuvers.

Materials for Phase 3: Sheets of large paper—butcher paper or poster-size paper and markers, or two overhead transparencies and markers, per student group, unless whiteboard space is plentiful.

Procedures

Phase 1—Loop (Individual Activity)
1. All students respond to a common journal writing prompt by writing for the specified period (about 10 minutes).
2. After they have written their entries, have them reread their words carefully and circle the one sentence or phrase that is the most powerful, meaningful, or well-written.
3. Instruct the students to start a new journal entry with the words within that loop (about 10 minutes).

Commentary About Phase 1: Students are often surprised to see how their own words have the power to generate more words. Phase 1 is particularly enlightening for students who are frequently certain that they have nothing to say when asked to write. They can be encouraged to return to earlier journal entries or other pieces of writing to loop on their own in order to discover topics.

*Note that looping is an idea that has been used by many fine teachers; I do not mean to suggest that it is my idea. Its origin has simply long ago escaped me. I do believe that its place in this kind of sequence, and its use as a vehicle that leads toward teaching collaborative coauthoring skills, however, is unique to this Triple Loop activity sequence.

Phase 2—Loop de Loop (Pair Activity)

1. All students form into pairs and face each other (any left without a partner will be included in a triad).
2. Students read aloud their looped pieces to their partners, then exchange papers and read the other's paper quietly.
3. After hearing the piece and reading it start to finish, each partner circles what he or she believes to be the most powerful, meaningful, or well-written phrase or sentence in the partner's piece.
4. He or she then uses that phrase or sentence as a starting point for a third piece of writing, again composing for approximately 10 minutes.
5. After time is called, the partners again face each other, and again read aloud their own compositions to their partners. This time, however, the starting line will be familiar to the partner because the writer's piece begins with words from the partner's original looped writing.
6. After the writing is shared orally, the partners should discuss their choices with each other, and then write down the reasons for their choice for the Loop de Loop.

Commentary About Phase 2: This phase is a point in which the writer learns not only to determine what works in his or her own writing, but to notice and articulate what works in a classmate's writing as well. In addition, Phase 2 requires that the student adapt to the partner's way with words in order to begin a paragraph or other piece of writing with some of those words. This kind of flexibility will be important in the Group Loop phase, when the final goal of collaborative coauthorship is addressed.

Phase 3—Group Loop (Collaborative Coauthoring Activity)

1. Two pairs combine to form groups of four.

2. Each group selects a scribe (one who has legible handwriting and who can write fairly quickly), a revision leader, a lead writer, and a speaker/timekeeper. If you need to form larger groups, double up the jobs as appropriate, so that everyone in the group has a specific task.

3. Students repeat the procedure for reading their own writing aloud to the members of the group, but this time, they read the products of their Loop de Loop session, in which each student started a piece of writing with the partner's words.

4. After each person in the group has read aloud, the group members begin to circulate the papers around the circle. Each member reads each paper, and loops the most powerful, meaningful, or well-written phrase or sentence that he finds in each paper. Each student uses a different color pen or pencil (or initials his or her loop so that the writer will be able to match the loop with its designator).

5. After all of the strongest phrases and sentences are identified, the scribe merely transcribes all of the looped items onto the board or paper or overhead film so that all group members can view them easily.

6. The revision leader leads the group in determining which of the items listed are redundant, which are really not as strong they looked originally, which are more eloquent than others that make similar statements, and so on. The group determines, based on its conversation, which phrases and sentences should remain, which should be deleted, and which should be revised. The revision leader continues to lead the group until the revisions are completed, while the scribe records the revisions for the group.

7. The writer leader takes over as the group's leader and, with the group's input, determines which of the phrases or sentences offers the strongest possibility for a new opening point.

8. The groups begin with that opening and move through the next portions of the text together, drawing when they can from the other strong phrases and sentences, but not restricting themselves to those, since the direction of the piece that they compose together may move far from the original pieces.

9. The groups should be given ample time to compose their coauthored pieces.

10. The speaker/timekeeper reads the coauthored version aloud to the class and turns in the paper.

Commentary About Phase 3: In this phase, students are not merely dividing up a page and suggesting that one write the first few lines, another the next few lines, and so on, as has often been the practice in traditional group work. Instead, they are using their combined skills and talents to generate and compose ideas, to edit and revise, to read critically, to seek the value in others' writing as well as their own, and eventually to publish.

Triple Loop Lesson Plan with Student Samples

Following is an example of incorporating the Triple Loop activity sequence into literature instruction. I have chosen, for this example, a prompt that a teacher of 11th grade students has used to spark their initial prediscussion responses to Naomi Shihab Nye's poem "The Lost Parrot." In this poignant poem, two voices join the narrator's. A teacher encourages a reluctant student to write and to put his ideas on paper; she uses the kinds of questions that the best teachers among us use—gentle, quiet, yet direct. The child, Carlos, stalls and refuses to write; while the class moves past him, he cannot take his mind off the one subject he cares about: his parrot—the one that left.

Phase 1—Looping

1. The teacher reads the poem aloud, dramatically distinguishing between the boy's voice and his teacher's.
2. After listening to the poem, each student writes a journal entry for 10 minutes in response to this prompt:

> Nye spaces out the words in the line that Carlos says in this way:
> "I don't know where it went"
> What kind of effect does that spacing have when you hear that line, and when you see it?

In response, one of my students, Zachary, writes:

When I first heard the poem, I thought that it sounded like Carlos was confused, like he didn't know what he wanted to say right then. But then when I read it again, I thought it might sound like Carlos is about to cry about the fact that he can't find his parrot and he is frustrated because everyone else keeps saying he ought to forget about it and do other things and move on. It made me think that we jump to conclusions all the time about why people are acting like they do. None of Carlos's school friends probably knew anything about Carlos except that he missed his parrot. Maybe it was one that his granddad had given him and then his granddad had died. Maybe he had found it when it was a tiny baby bird and he had raised it even when everyone else said it was sure to die. It could have been the only thing that Carlos had that he could call his own, and that was why he couldn't think of anything else. When the teacher says, "Write more," and he tells her he can't because "I don't know where it went," his words sound almost like he is stumbling down a street or through a field, looking and looking without any real hope that he will ever find the bird that means everything to him. It is a sad line and a sad poem.

3. Zachary rereads his paragraph and circles the phrase, "his words sound almost like he is stumbling down a street or through a field." He then starts a new piece of writing from there. Instead of writing a paragraph, he decides to try to write a poem in response to "The Lost Parrot":

His Words
Stumbling
Down the street
Through the field
Don't know
No parrot
No hope

Commentary on Phase 1: Although Zachary deleted some of the words of his original Loop, he clearly uses them to generate his second piece of writing in response to Nye's poem.

Phase 2—Loop de Loop
1. Zachary and Lisa share their Loop products. They read each other's work aloud.
2. After Zachary reads his poem and Lisa reads her paragraph, Lisa marks these words in Zachary's poem:

His Words
Stumbling

3. She then responds to his poem with the beginning of a story:

> His words stumbling, the man came into the vet clinic with a dog in his arms. The dog, he explained to the woman behind the counter, wasn't his, but he was sure it was somebody's, and either way, he couldn't just keep driving past it and let it get hit by a car out there on West Tennessee Street. He told the woman that he had been a client there on Northwood for almost 15 years, until his old dog had to be put to sleep, and that had been almost six years ago. He said he knew that whoever was looking for this dog must be frantic, that he knew he would be—that he had lost his dog once, for five days, and thought he'd go crazy with grief until some near-neighbor found it and brought it home. "Just look, it has such a good clean collar and trimmed nails on its paws. It is a pet person's dog, for sure. Probably used to sitting inside eating bologna off a plate. Might have gotten out of an RV during the football game last week. I spotted it near the stadium first, then off the side of Tennessee for three days in a row, sitting in the same place. Thought it must be hurt, but it don't seem like it now. Just seems like it wants to rest a little and get on home."

Note: For the sake of space, I will limit the example to one person's work in each phase. Please note, though, that each partner in Phase 2 and each group member in Phase 3 is responsible for responding to a classmate's writing and for producing his or her own writing, too.

Phase 3—Group Loop

1. During the Group Loop, Zachary and Lisa joined a group with two other students. Together, they decided to place the best excerpts into one of three categories:
   a. Keepers
   b. Don't know
   c. Don't seem to like it as much now. Just seems like it wants to rest a little and get on home.
2. At first, Zachary pushed for the group to try to write a poem together, but decided, with the group, that the poem he had written was actually a bit too depressing. The group decided to use Lisa's story about the old man and the dog as the focal point for its coauthored text.
3. They worked to finish and polish it, focusing primarily on dialogue.

Assessment

A benefit of the Triple Loop activity sequence is that the assessment of writing is an organic part of the process. Students assess their own and their classmates' work, focusing on the best parts, and moving on from those parts to develop them. Of course, a letter grade could be attached to the process and product at any point.

Final Commentary

My experience as a teacher of writing has been that writing prompts are most meaningful and have the greatest potential for generating substantive class discussion and further writing when they are related to literature that the students are or have been engaged in studying. When I taught middle school, I spent three or four years assigning journals in which I asked students merely to write entries on "any topic that they chose." I believed, then, that my generosity in giving them the full universe of topics would allow them to break all the barriers that school's restrictions placed around their creativity and would free them to write artistic pieces with clarity, fluency, and style. What I read, page after page, was more akin to the notes that I intercepted as I walked between rows of students when they were supposed to be reading silently but were writing to each other instead—messages about what was going on during the weekend, about who liked whom, about who had gotten in trouble and why, and what they hated about the stories they were being told to read.

Despite the disappointing results, I continued to ask the middle school students to keep journals. I encouraged them to turn down any pages that they did not want me to read, in naïve and selfish hopes that they would protect me from learning too much about their personal lives, because I was unsure that I would know how to intervene when I learned too much about the problems that many of the young adolescents were living through. Yes, I knew the potential benefits of journaling: writing journal entries has the potential to help the middle school students articulate ideas in writing, to write for a specific audience (even when that was just me), and to write on demand and for a specified time (the first 10 minutes of each class session). What I learned from my middle school students was that they actually preferred a sense of starting place and of direction; they preferred to be shown the neighborhood in which they could roam instead of being offered the entire universe of possibilities as relatively inexperienced writers. With a bit of structure and direction—a writing prompt that invites them to explore the neighborhood in which they will wander—their creativity is released into action.

For the Triple Loop activity sequence, and for the journal to be a useful writing tool in other ways, students need to see it as a place in which they can write drafts that they will feel comfortable manipulating in various ways—reducing or discarding parts, adding and intensifying others. But providing a prompt, instead of asking for a diary entry, provides them with a solid starting point for their growth as writers, too.

NCTE/IRA Standards: 1, 2, 3, 4, 5, 6, 9, 10, 11, 12

Source: P. S. Carroll, 2007, Florida State University, Tallahassee, FL. Reprinted with permission.

Play Lesson 2

Cut-Up Poems

Summary: Students create original poems from the words of another poem.

Senses: Sight, sound

Type of Activity: Individual

Approximate Time: 30 minutes. You can either have one student construct a poem each day (selecting a different student to write the poem for the day until every student has done it) or you can provide every student or pair of students with a cut-up poem.

Objectives: Get students to play around with language, learn a few new words, figure out an appropriate sequence, and write an expressive poem.

Materials: Cut up one of your favorite poems or purchase instant poetry kits (such as the *Magnetic Poems* or *William's Wit Kit*, a collection of magnetic words taken from Shakespearean sonnets). For this lesson, I will use Emily Dickinson's poem "It's All I Have to Bring Today."

Setup: Cut up each word of the poem and put them in an envelope. Prepare an envelope for each student or a pair of students. Distribute the complete poem at the very end of the lesson only after students have created their own poems from the words.

Procedures

1. Hand out the scrambled words (or a sheet with all the words on it). Emphasize to students that the purpose is to create a great poem, not to guess the meaning or style of the original. See Figure 7.1 for an example.
2. Tell students to create a poem from the words provided in the envelope. They should try to use all the words, but if they have a few left over, that's acceptable. Some students will want to sneak in words of their own. Let them.
3. Once students have finished, have them read their poems aloud. The variety and quality of poems is often striking.

Figure 7.1   Cut-Up Poem

Directions: The words below are from "It's All I Have to Bring Today" by Emily Dickinson. Rearrange the words to create your own poem. If you wish, you may leave out some words and add a few if necessary.

Words cut up from "It's All I Have to Bring Today" by Emily Dickinson

all, all, all, all, and, and, and, and, and, be, bees, beside, bring, clover, could, count, dwell, fields, forget, have, heart, heart, heart, I, I, in, it's, meadows, my, my, my, one, should, some, sum, sure, tell, the, the, the, the, the, this, this, this, to, today, which, wide, you

Student sample:

My heart dwells

In wide clover fields

Counting bees to the meadows

Sure today forgets the sum

Of all my fears

This heart, it's all I have

Besides this moment

Which I bring you

Original poem:

"It's All I Have to Bring Today" by Emily Dickinson

It's all I have to bring today—

This, and my heart beside—

This, and my heart, and all the fields—

And all the meadows wide—

Be sure you count—should I forget

Some one the sum could tell—

This, and my heart, and all the Bees

Which in the Clover dwell.

Enrichment

After every student has written a poem from the cut-up words in the envelope, I recommend assigning a student the task of combining one line from each poem into a class poem.

Commentary

The Cut-Up Poems activity offers easy entry points for writing and is especially suited for students who have difficulty coming up with the first few words in a writing assignment.

Assessment

I usually use Cut-Up Poems as a warm-up activity, to get students to think in novel ways about words and poetry. I write comments on their creations but do not give them grades. Of course, if a student pens a particularly compelling poem, I will feature it on the bulletin board.

NCTE/IRA Standards: 1, 2, 3, 4, 5, 6, 9, 10, 11, 12

Play Lesson 3

Between the Ears

Summary: Students draw the outline of the head of a character (for those who are artistically challenged, a circle will do). Then they draw five representative images that depict the values of the character, along with a brief explanation.

Senses: Sight, sound

Type of Activity: Individual

Approximate Time: One day

Objectives: Students analyze a character in a story to infer motivations, values, and thoughts.

Materials: Large, poster-size paper and colors

Procedures

1. On the blackboard or overhead transparency, list the names of as many characters as you and the class can remember from a recently read book. Recently, I used this activity with Sherri Smith's novel *Lucy the Giant* (2002), about a 15-year-old girl who leaves her alcoholic father in Sitka, Alaska, for an adventure on a crabbing boat near Kodiak, Alaska.
2. Assign students to examine the motivations, values, and thoughts of one of the characters listed. I recommend assigning as many as possible, including minor characters. When two or more students do the same character, the results can be very interesting.
3. Students draw five images inside the outline of a head that represent the thoughts of the character. Students must be able to provide evidence from the text to substantiate the images.
4. Refer to the list of characters again. Ask students to show their drawings to the class and explain each image. Check for comprehension or misunderstanding as students make their presentations. Compare multiple drawings of the same character. Highlight particularly astute analyses. Figure 7.2 is a student sample of Between the Ears.

Extension Activities

After doing Between the Ears and pondering the motivations and values of a character, it is a simple step for students to use their drawings as the basis for a character sketch or a literary analysis.

Figure 7.2   Between the Ears: Student Sample

Assessment

	1 Unsatisfactory	2 Insufficient	3 Uneven	4 Sufficient	5 Skillful	6 Excellent
Minimum of five images representative of character						
Reason for choosing the five images clearly explained with references to the text						
Presentation of findings was clear and con-vincing						

NCTE/IRA Standards: 1, 2, 3, 4, 5, 6, 7, 8, 9, 10, 11, 12

Note: A few years ago, a student informed me that James Percoco (1998) in his book *A Passion for the Past* advocates a similar activity, which he calls "historical heads." Indeed, the activity could work especially well with historical figures, writers, and politicians.

Play Lesson 4
CSI: Contextual Semantic Investigation

Summary: Students use graphic organizers, group work, and think-aloud protocols to "investigate" the meanings of unfamiliar words.

Authors: Michael W. Kibby, William J. Rapaport, Karen M. Wieland, and Debra A. Dechert, University of Buffalo, Buffalo, New York

Senses: Sight, sound

Type of Activity: Individual or group

Approximate Time: CSI is designed to be completed across several instructional days. Although it is broken up into three segments of approximately 45 minutes each, teachers should feel free to modify the plan to suit their schedules and resources.

Objectives: Students learn vocabulary in context.

Materials: Make one copy per student of the Instructions for CSI hand-out (Figure 7.3), five copies per student and three transparencies of the CSI Case File handout (Figure 7.4), and a transparency of the Activating Background Knowledge handout (Figure 7.5).

Rationale

What does a reader do when he comes across a word with an unfamiliar meaning? If the reader decides that the word is needed to understand the text, he has three choices:

1. Look up the unfamiliar word in a dictionary.
2. Ask someone else what the word means.
3. Try to figure out the sense of the word.

The first solution is not always viable, for a number of reasons. The reader might not have a dictionary at hand. Even if a dictionary is accessible, the word might not be listed, the dictionary entry might offer multiple meanings, or the meaning might be too obscure. Alternatively, the definition of the target word might be so complex that it creates another context, which requires looking up or figuring out the meanings of still more unknown words. For example, a student recently used the *Merriam-Webster Online Dictionary* to find the meaning of *infract*. The meaning she found was "to infringe." Not sure about the meaning of *infringe*, she looked it up, finding the definition "to encroach." Again, not knowing

Figure 7.3   Instructions for CSI

1. Focus on Hard Word: Have you seen/heard the word before? Does the word have any identifiable structural cues (e.g., prefix, affix, root)?

2. Reread: Reread the sentence with the hard word (maybe the preceding sentence) to gain full meaning.

3. Part of Speech: What part of speech is this word?

4. Summarize Meaning: In your mind, summarize the meaning you gained from everything in the text you have read so far.

5. Activate Prior Knowledge: Think about what you already know about the topic and how your prior knowledge might be linked to the hard word.

6. Connect: Connect meaning gained from reading with prior knowledge so that all you know about this topic is at the forefront of your thinking.

7. Reword: Reconstruct the target sentence so that the target word is in the subject position.

8. Thinking or Reasoning: Use the following suggestions to guide your reasoning about what you have learned from the text about the hard word.

a. For nouns— these processes are not linear, and are listed in no particular order	General meaning: How does this word relate to the meaning of the passage or the meaning of the immediately surrounding text?
	Class membership: What category of person or thing is this?
	Properties: What properties does this person or thing have?
	Structural information: What is the size, shape, parts, and so on, of this person or thing?
	Visualize: Can you build a picture in your mind of what this person or thing might look like?
	Acts or functions: What kinds of actions does this person or thing carry out? To whom or what are these actions done?
	Agents: Who does something to or with this person or thing? What do they do to or with the person or thing?
	Ownership: Can this thing be owned? If so, by whom?
	Comparison-contrast: Is the person or thing compared or contrasted to some other person or thing?
	Synonyms: Can you think of another word or phrase that would easily replace this word and make sense within the text?
b. For verbs— these processes are not linear, and are listed in no particular order	Transitivity (knowing if the unknown verb is solely an action, an action done to another person or thing, or an action done to another person or thing to or with something may provide much information about the unknown verb): • Is this word the actual action (intransitive—action only; e.g., John sang). • Is the action done to another thing (transitive—verb and direct object; e.g., John sang "Happy Birthday"). • Is the action done to another thing to/with something (ditransitive—has direct and indirect object; e.g., John sang "Happy Birthday" to his sister).
	Synonyms: Can you think of another word or phrase that would easily replace this word and make sense within the text?
	Class membership: What category of action is this?
	Properties: What properties does this action have?
	Visualize: Can you build a picture in your mind of what this action might look like?
c. For modifiers	Contrasts: Does this hard word appear to contrast the subject or action it modifies to another subject or action with which you are familiar?
	Parallelism: If the grammar of the hard word's sentence/clause (modifier-subject/action) is parallel to another, what clue does that offer?

9. Hypothesis: State your hypothesized or predicted meaning of the hard person, thing, or action.

10. Confirm: How sure are you that the meaning you hypothesized is correct?

Source: M. Kibby, W. Rapaport, K. Wieland, and D. Dechert, 2007, University of Buffalo, Buffalo, NY. Reprinted with permission.

Figure 7.4   CSI Case File

Before reading: What do I know about this topic?

_____
_____
_____
_____
_____

Copy the target sentence:

_____
_____
_____
_____
_____

Target word and part of speech:

_____

Check one:
- ☐ Noun
- ☐ Verb
- ☐ Modifier (Adjective or Adverb)

Reword the context to make the target word the subject of the sentence:

_____
_____
_____
_____
_____
_____
_____

My Hunches and Evidence

Source: M. Kibby, W. Rapaport, K. Wieland, and D. Dechert, 2007, University of Buffalo, Buffalo, NY. Reprinted with permission.

Figure 7.5   Activating Background Knowledge

The title of the story we are going to read this week is "The Lottery Ticket." This story was written by Russian author Anton Chekhov. What does the phrase "The Lottery Ticket" bring to mind?

Read the first paragraph of the story. Can you make predictions about this story based on the title and this first paragraph? Brainstorm in your researcher notebook.

Please share some of your predictions with the class.

Complete the following focused free write in your researcher notebooks.

"In what ways, if any, would winning the lottery change your life?"

Source: M. Kibby, W. Rapaport, K. Wieland, and D. Dechert, 2007, University of Buffalo, Buffalo, NY. Reprinted with permission.

encroach, she looked this word up, finding its definition to be "to enter by stealth." Finally, she asked her teacher, who told her "*infract* is the verb form of *infraction,* which means breaking the law."

The second solution, asking someone who knows the word's meaning, is easier—provided there is someone nearby to ask, which is not always the case. The knowledgeable person would most likely require contextual information and would probably say, "Read me the whole sentence."

The third solution is to hypothesize possible meanings from textual constraints. *Textual constraints* means that information across the text is used to figure out the meaning—not just the sentences located near the unknown word.

One of the characteristics that distinguish highly successful readers from less adept readers is an interest in learning new words. Rather than consulting a dictionary or asking another person to learn about a new word, successful readers make guesses at word meanings based on textual constraints, prior knowledge, and their powers of reasoning. Inferring the meaning of an unfamiliar word takes skill, strategy, and practice. The more practice with unfamiliar words, the better a reader becomes at decoding them.

Helpful Hints for Teachers

- Students will have varying degrees of word consciousness, or awareness of unknown words (Kibby, 1995). CSI requires students to select unknown words from their texts while reading, but this does not mean that students should identify all unknown words. By discussing the text in a global way, the teacher can gain awareness of which important words students are ignoring or misinterpreting.

- Not every hard word needs to be known. If lack of knowledge of a specific word does not interfere with comprehension, the student probably should ignore the word and keep reading.

- Some students may require guidance in the construction of meaning of new words. Word maps can be used to teach students about the types of information—category, properties, and illustrations—that contribute to word meanings (Schwartz, 1988; Schwartz & Raphael, 1985) or concept development (Peters, 1974–75). The software package Inspiration is an excellent tool for graphically representing a word's meaning.

- If too many words in a text are unfamiliar, attempts to infer word meanings from context will not be very productive. A teacher should limit the number of target words for CSI. Tell students the meanings of the other unfamiliar words in the text in order for them to infer successfully the meaning of the target word. The best texts for CSI are those that contain only a handful of unfamiliar words.

- Teachers must model the thinking process using words unfamiliar to them and most of their students. Because teachers usually know many more words than their students, finding unfamiliar words in your teaching materials may happen only rarely. Good sources for strange and unusual words includes www.thefreedictionary.com and www.phrontistery.info.

- The student does not have to figure out the correct meaning of the target word but should generate a reasonable hypothesis that can be defended with textual cues and prior knowledge. The reader's goal should be to derive a sense of the word given the context.

- The senses of new nouns are generally much easier to figure out than the senses of new verbs or new modifiers.

- Seeing a new word in just one context provides some useful information, but experts agree that multiple contextual exposures are required to develop a thorough and in-depth understanding. So the teacher should consider finding supplemental texts with which to confirm or revise initial hypotheses about word sense.

Procedures

In Advance

For homework, students find a difficult word in context, print out the passage, and bring it in to stump the teacher.

Day 1 (first day of CSI unit)

1. Distribute a copy of Figures 7.3 and 7.4 to every student.
2. Students present their challenging words and their contexts to the teacher. For an example of how a teacher might respond, see Figure 7.6.
3. Display the transparency of Figure 7.4 (or draw it on the board) and model strategies as students provide the challenging words ("I do, you watch").
   a. Begin by rearranging the target sentence to put the unknown word in the subject position.
   b. Discuss background knowledge about the topic.
   c. Search for clues within the text that give a sense of the target word's meaning.
   d. Consult Figure 7.3, Instructions for CSI, for ideas of clues to look for, depending on the part of speech of the target word.
4. Students listen and watch.
5. Students reconstruct the steps the teachers took by filling in Figure 7.4, using Figure 7.3 when needed.
6. For the purposes of demonstration, I use Anton Chekhov's "The Lottery Ticket," available at http://fiction.eserver.org/short/the_lottery_ticket.html
7. Display the transparency of Activating Background Knowledge (Figure 7.5). Ask students what they know about lottery tickets. Stimulate discussion, asking students to make predictions as to what the story might be about.
8. For homework, ask students to read a story in the literature book or read "The Lottery Ticket" independently and to underline or highlight the hard words.

Figure 7.6   CSI Teacher Response

> **Reclining on a sea of pillows in her suburban San Antonio bedroom and picking leisurely at a snack, Pamela Hoy contemplates her good fortune. How wonderful to be able to work in the bedroom of her own home!**
>
> Hoy is not just another stock-optioned **sybarite** achy with ennui; she's pregnant. After a trip to the emergency room two months ago, Hoy was told she'd gone into labor and was given medication and ordered to spend the rest of her gestation lying on her left side.
>
> Spencer, T. (2000). Take two naps and fax us in the morning. http://money.cnn.com/magazines/fortune/fortune_archive/2000/05/15/279755/index.htm

Student: [Reads the target text from the magazine article.] OK, I am looking at the sentence and the words around it. The "sybarite" part, it's obvious that. . . . [She reads target sentence aloud.] "Hoy is not just another stock-optioned sybarite achy with en . . ." How do you pronounce it? [Teacher assists, and student repeats.] "Ennui. She's pregnant."

Teacher: What is the word that stumps you?
Student: Sybarite is definitely it.
Teacher: [Probing to make sure.] So you know what ennui is?
Student: I have a sense of ennui. If you have ennui, it's a sort of "it's about me" kind of a thing. [Pauses.] Well, no, I guess that wouldn't be it.

Teacher: My understanding is that it is an "oh, I am so bored with life" kind of a thing. [She provides this meaning because *ennui* was not the target word.]
Student: Oh, like an apathy type of thing. [Rereads target phrase.] OK. So she is not a stock-optioned sybarite achy with ennui. So sybarite has to have something to do with the ennui, obviously. So you would need to have those two pieces. Stock-optioned would mean that she is someone who has a fair amount. She may have ennui because she doesn't have to worry about money, so she isn't in a mode where she is working necessarily because she has this overwhelming need to provide for her survival. [Laughs and reads the rest of the paragraph again under her breath.] The rest of the paragraph tells us that she is not staying at home and working yuppie-style, but she is trying to secure her pregnancy and make sure that it goes well. [Pauses.] Hmm.

Teacher: Does it say she *isn't* a sybarite?

Student: She is not just *another.*

Teacher: Oh, another. I see.

Student: Another is interesting. Umm. She's pregnant. So in other words, maybe there is a sense that if she *were* a "stock-optioned sybarite achy with ennui," it would be someone who stays at home with this "I'm bored because I don't have purpose in my life" type of a thing. But that's *not* why she's working from home. She's there because she *has* to be. So that's the "not just *another* stock-optioned

(Figure continues on next page)

Figure 7.6 *(continued)*

sybarite." So Hoy is someone who would be characterized as different from what's typical of that group of individuals, but it must also mean that she is something that she *could* just be at home, working. Someone who is an -ite is a member of something. So a member of a syber-. [Laughs.] What's a member of a syber-? A member of some type of group. . . . [Student and teacher muse about the possible meanings of that apparently Greek root, which neither knows.]

Teacher: I wonder if it could reference some Greek mythological character.

Student: Right. Or it could be . . . it's obviously somebody who has risen to a particular status. A sybarite has to be somebody who is part of a very privileged group. You make that assumption because of the other words. People with ennui obviously don't have a lot of other cares. They've sort of gotten to a point that the other things in their lives aren't as pressing. The pressing needs that most of us have for taking care of ourselves, they don't have. So "stock-optioned sybarite" might mean somebody who has enough money to throw around in stocks. So she may be a member of the affluent, upper class. She doesn't necessarily have to be working. The stock options are there because she has money.

Teacher: I am smiling and nodding because I am agreeing with everything you say. But that is not a word that I really know. So it's funny, because those are all my theories, too.

Student: So a sybarite is obviously somebody who has affluence of some sort, but we don't know what the source of their affluence is.

Teacher: Right. I am presuming that you have determined a part of speech for sybarite.

Student: It's obviously a noun.

Teacher: Do you want to look it up in the dictionary? [They use the dictionary on the teacher's laptop. The first entry does define Sybarite as a figure in Greek mythology]. "Somebody devoted to luxury and sensual desires."

Student: We got the luxury part, but the sensual desires we didn't pick up on.

Teacher: Well, maybe the lying around.

Student: [Overlapping.] The lounging, the pampering, the grapes, the oils, and the massage.

Teacher: [Overlapping.] Being catered to. I guess that makes sense given this second context, "utilitarian to sybarite." [Looking up *ennui* to make sure they've understood it properly.] The dictionary defines ennui as "weariness and dissatisfaction with life that results from a loss of interest or sense of excitement," which is congruent with the sense we made of that word, also.

Source: M. Kibby, W. Rapaport, K. Wieland, and D. Dechert, 2007, University of Buffalo, Buffalo, NY. Reprinted with permission.

Figure 7.7   CSI Sample Target Words

Potential Target Words Students Might Select from "The Lottery Ticket"

lot	provinces	despondently	detestable
lapsed	villa	dreary	slander
consented	saunters	dismay	impartially
mockery	leisure	farthing	repulsive
skepticism	opaque	parcels	malignantly
douche	flit	begrudge	rubles
hollow	evident	saturated	other people's expense
senseless	soused	grudge	wearisome
torment	leisurely	wretched	husks
tantalize	waistcoat	fawning	damnation
bewildered	fowls	hypocritical	

Source: M. Kibby, W. Rapaport, K. Wieland, and D. Dechert, 2007, University of Buffalo, Buffalo, NY. Reprinted with permission.

Day 2

1. Distribute four copies of the CSI Case File (Figure 7.4) to every student.

2. Ask students what hard words they found. Tell students to keep quiet about meanings they know, so their classmates can figure them out on their own. Once a student suggests a word, take a hand count of how many others found the same word difficult. For a list of possible target words from the Chekhov story, see Figure 7.7.

3. Put up the CSI Case File (Figure 7.4) transparency again and model strategies using a word from the beginning of the story that most students were stumped by. However, this time, elicit help from students. ("I do, you help.")

4. Do a think-aloud (see Figure 7.8 for a sample think-aloud protocol for "The Lottery") and fill in information in the transparency of Figure 7.4 as you speak. Students complete their own copies of Figure 7.4 along with the teacher.

5. Ask for a student volunteer to think-aloud about the meaning of another unknown word. The teacher and the other students can offer suggestions. Again, the teacher models the procedure

---

Figure 7.8   CSI Think-Aloud

An Example of the Teacher Think-Aloud Recommended for Day 2

Teacher: Ivan Dmitritch was very well satisfied with his lot. It says he lives with his family on an income of twelve hundred a year, and he was very well satisfied. Well, we know the expression "to have a lot" means to have a sufficient amount of something. So if he is satisfied with his amount—his amount of money, because he is middle class. Maybe he is satisfied with his family, um, satisfied with his situation. He feels "comfortable," so that means satisfied. Maybe that means happy or content. So my guess about the word "lot" is that "lot" means his situation, his allotment of worldly, spiritual, and relationship goods that he has. It's a noun. . . .

Source: M. Kibby, W. Rapaport, K. Wieland, and D. Dechert, 2007, University of Buffalo, Buffalo, NY. Reprinted with permission.

by completing the transparency of Figure 7.4; students fill out another Figure 7.4 as the student thinks aloud.

6. Once students understand the process, place students into groups of two to four. Assign one unknown word for each group to work on. Students work collaboratively and record their processes and hypotheses on Figure 7.4.

Day 3

1. A spokesperson from each group reports back to the whole class, explaining the thinking that group members did and the hypothesis they came up with from their group activity on Day 2. The whole class discusses the target word, the cues, and the thinking process of the group.

2. Ask each group to pick another hard word from the text and work on that word. The teacher circulates around the room, taking notes, but does not help. ("You do, I watch.")

3. For homework, ask students to find additional occurrences of the target words they have worked on so far. This will allow them to either confirm their initial hypotheses or revise them based on new evidence. Encourage students to take notes about the new contexts where the word was found and update their hypotheses on Figure 7.4.

Extension Activities

1. As a variation of the think-aloud procedure, ask students to write out their reasoning about unknown words in context (write-aloud).

2. Ask students to author a passage for one of their hard words, using sufficient cues for their fellow students to derive a sense of the word. The writer cannot provide a direct definition in the passage.

3. Ask students to turn their work into a narrative of what they did as word detectives. They could write up a report to the police chief of linguistics, putting all the clues together into an original story.

NCTE/IRA Standards: 1, 2, 3, 4, 5, 6, 7, 8, 9, 10, 11, 12

Source: M. Kibby, W. Rapaport, K. Wieland, and D. Dechert, University of Buffalo, Buffalo, NY. Reprinted with permission.

APPENDIX

Standards for the
English Language Arts ▪ ▪ ▪

The following standards are sponsored by the National Council of Teachers of English and the International Reading Association:

1. Students read a wide range of print and nonprint texts to build an understanding of texts, of themselves, and of the cultures of the United States and the world; to acquire new information; to respond to the needs and demands of society and the workplace; and for personal fulfillment. Among these texts are fiction and nonfiction, classic and contemporary works.

2. Students read a wide range of literature from many periods in many genres to build an understanding of the many dimensions (e.g., philosophical, ethical, aesthetic) of human experience.

3. Students apply a wide range of strategies to comprehend, interpret, evaluate, and appreciate texts. They draw on their prior experience, their interactions with other readers and writers, their knowledge of word meaning and of other texts, their word identification strategies, and their understanding of textual features (e.g., sound-letter correspondence, sentence structure, context, graphics).

4. Students adjust their use of spoken, written, and visual language (e.g., conventions, style, vocabulary) to communicate effectively with a variety of audiences and for different purposes.

5. Students employ a wide range of strategies as they write and use different writing process elements appropriately to communicate with different audiences for a variety of purposes.

6. Students apply knowledge of language structure, language conventions (e.g., spelling and punctuation), media techniques, figurative language, and genre to create, critique, and discuss print and nonprint texts.

7. Students conduct research on issues and interests by generating ideas and questions, and by posing problems. They gather, evaluate, and synthesize data from a variety of sources (e.g., print and nonprint texts, artifacts, people) to communicate their discoveries in ways that suit their purpose and audience.

8. Students use a variety of technological and information resources (e.g., libraries, databases, computer networks, video) to gather and synthesize information and to create and communicate knowledge.

9. Students develop an understanding of and respect for diversity in language use, patterns, and dialects across cultures, ethnic groups, geographic regions, and social roles.

10. Students whose first language is not English make use of their first language to develop competency in the English language arts and to develop understanding of content across the curriculum.

11. Students participate as knowledgeable, reflective, creative, and critical members of a variety of literacy communities.

12. Students use spoken, written, and visual language to accomplish their own purposes (e.g., for learning, enjoyment, persuasion, and the exchange of information).

Source: *Standards for the English Language Arts,* by the International Reading Association and the National Council of Teachers of English, Copyright 1996 by the International Reading Association and the National Council of Teachers of English. Reprinted with permission.

B

Candy Freak
Sensory Words ■ ■ ■

Olfactory

acidic	delectable	heady	offensive
acrid	delicate	healthy	oily
alkaline	delicious	hearty	overripe
appetizing	disagreeable	hot	palatable
aroma	disgusting	inedible	peppery
aromatic	dry	insipid	perfumed
bad	earthy	juicy	piney
balmy	essence	luscious	plain
bitter	exquisite	malodorous	pleasant
bittersweet	fishy	medicinal	poisonous
bland	flat	mellow	pungent
bouquet	flavorless	metallic	putrid
briny	flavorsome	mild	rancid
burnt	floral	mildewed	rank
buttery	foul	mint	rare
cheesy	fragrant	moldy	raw
citrus	fresh	musty	reeking
cool	fruity	nasty	rich
creamy	gamy	nice	ripe
crisp	gaseous	noxious	rotten
damp	gingery	nutty	salty
dank	greasy	odorous	savory

177

scented	stagnant	tainted	unripe
scentless	stale	tangy	vile
sharp	stinky	tart	vinegary
sickly	strong	tasteless	warm
smoky	subtle	tasty	watery
sour	succulent	unappetizing	weak
spicy	sugary	unpalatable	whiff
spoiled	sweet	unpleasant	zesty

Touch

abrasive	foamy	mushy	soapy
biting	fragile	musty	soft
boiling	freezing	numbing	soggy
brittle	frosty	oily	sopping
bubbly	furry	open	soupy
bulky	fuzzy	piercing	spongy
bumpy	glassy	plastic	springy
burning	gluey	pocked	squelchy
bushy	gooey	pointed	steamy
clammy	grainy	powdery	steely
close	granular	prickly	sticky
coarse	greasy	perforated	stiff
cold	gritty	pristine	stifled
cool	gushy	pulpy	stinging
cottony	hairy	rigid	stodgy
crisp	hard	rocky	stony
cuddly	heavy	rubbery	stretchy
cushiony	hot	sandy	stubby
damp	humid	satiny	tacky
downy	icy	scalding	tangled
drenched	invigorating	scorching	tender
dry	juicy	scratchy	tepid
dull	knobbed	scummy	thick
elastic	lacy	shaggy	thin
feathery	leathery	sharp	tickling
fine	light	short	tough
firm	limp	silky	untainted
flabby	lukewarm	slimy	velvety
flaky	matted	slippery	warm
fleshy	metallic	sloppy	waxy
flexible	moist	smooth	wet
fluffy	morbidezza	smothering	woolly

Sounds

bang	bedlam	boom	bray
bark	blaring	booming	buzz
bawling	bleat	brawl	chattering

chime
chirp
clamor
clang
clap
clicking
clink
coo
cough
crackle
crackling
crash
croak
crunching
cry
deafening
discord
disorderly
dripping
earsplitting
exploding
faint
fizz
gag
gasp
giggle
grating

groan
growl
grunting
guffaw
gurgle
harmony
hiss
honk
hum
hush
inaudible
jangling
laugh
melody
moaning
mooing
mumbling
murmur
musical
mute
mutter
muttering
noisy
pandemonium
patter
peep
piercing

ping
plop
pop
quack
quiet
racket
rap
raspy
rattling
resonance
ringing
rowdy
rumbling
rustling
scratching
scream
screech
shout
sigh
silent
sing
slam
smash
snap
snarl
snore
speak

speechless
splash
squawk
stammer
stamp
stomp
stutter
swish
tap
tearing
thud
thump
thunder
ticking
tinkling
tumult
twitter
warbling
wheeze
whimper
whine
whisper
whizzing
whoop
yell
zing

Colors

almond
amber
antique brass
apple
apricot
aqua
aquamarine
ashen
asparagus
atomic tangerine
azure
banana mania
beige
bittersweet
black
blizzard blue
blue
blue bell

blue gray
blue green
blue violet
blush
brick
bronze
brown
buff
burgundy
burnt orange
burnt sienna
butter
buttercup
butterscotch
cadet blue
canary
cardinal
Caribbean green

carnation pink
celery
cerise
cerulean
chartreuse
cherry
chocolate
chrome
cinnamon
cobalt
coffee
colorless
copper
coral
cornflower
cotton candy
cream
crimson

dandelion
denim
desert sand
dove
ebony
eggplant
electric lime
emerald
fern
flesh
forest green
fuchsia
fuzzy wuzzy
   brown
garnet
ginger
gold
goldenrod

Granny Smith
  apple
gray
green
green blue
green yellow
hazel
hot magenta
ivory
jazzberry jam
jet
jungle green
khaki
laser lemon
lavender
lemon
licorice
lilac
lime
macaroni and
  cheese
magenta
magic mint
mahogany
maize
manatee
mango tango
marble
maroon
mauve
mauvelous
melon
metallic
milky
mint

mottled
mountain
  meadow
mulberry
mustard
navy
neon carrot
nutmeg
ochre
olive
orange
orange red
orange yellow
orchid
outer space
outrageous
  orange
oyster
pacific blue
peach
peacock
pearl
periwinkle
persimmon
piggy pink
pine green
pink
pink flamingo
pink sherbet
pistachio
platinum
plum
porcelain
Prussian blue
purple

purple heart
purple mountain's
  majesty
purple pizzazz
radical red
rainbow
raspberry
raw sienna
raw umber
razzle dazzle rose
razzmatazz
red
red orange
red violet
robin's egg blue
rose
royal
royal purple
ruby
rust
salmon
sandy
sapphire
screamin' green
sea green
sepia
shadow
shamrock
shocking pink
silver
sky
snow
spotted
spring green
steel

strawberry
sulphur
sunglow
sunset orange
tan
tangerine
tawny
teal blue
thistle
tickle me pink
timber wolf
topaz
torch red
tropical rain
  forest
tumbleweed
turquoise
ultra
unmellow yellow
vermilion
violet
violet red
vivid
walnut
white
wild blue yonder
wild strawberry
wild watermelon
wine
wisteria
yellow
yellow green

Sight

agile
angular
bending
bent
blinding
blotched
blurred
bolting
bouncing

branching
bright
brilliant
broken
burnt
careening
chubby
clear
cloudy

clustered
color
colorless
conical
contoured
crawling
creep
creeping
crimped

crinkled
crisp
crumbly
crystalline
cuboid
curved
cylindrical
dark
darting

dim	gloomy	padded	streaked
dingy	glossy	patterned	stringy
dismal	glowing	pendulous	striped
domed	graceful	plodding	sudsy
dotted	grimy	plummeting	sunset
drab	hard	polka-dotted	swaying
dragging	hazy	portly	swollen
drifting	heaving	proportional	swooping
droopy	heavy	ramming	tarnished
dry	hexagonal	rectangular	tidy
dull	hollow	ripping	tiny
edging	hurl	rotted	top-heavy
emerald	hurling	rotund	torch
faded	immense	round	tottering
faint	iridescent	ruffled	trample
fast	irregular	russet	translucent
fat	ivory	sauntering	transparent
firm	jutting	scalloped	triangular
fizzy	long	shabby	tubular
flaky	loping	shadow	tufted
flared	lovely	shallow	turquoise
flashy	lumbering	sheer	twinkling
flat	luminous	shimmering	untidy
flick	lumpy	shiny	used
flowery	massive	slim	variegation
fluffy	minute	slinking	waddling
fluid	misty	slouching	wavy
foggy	mottled	smashed	weepy
fragile	mountainous	smeared	wet
freckled	muddy	smooth	whisk
frilled	mumble	smudged	winged
gallop	murmur	soaring	wiry
glassy	narrow	sparkling	wispy
glazed	neglected	spinning	worn
gleaming	obese	spotted	wrinkled
glistening	old	square	young
glittering	opaque	staggering	zippy
globular	oval	stalking	

C

Color Plates

Color Plate 1.1   Collaborative Quick Paint

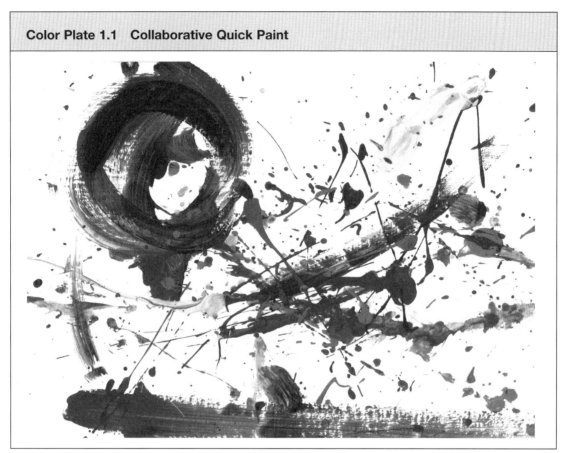

Source: M. Angelotti, 2005, Norman, OK. Reprinted with permission.

Color Plate 1.2   Abstraction with Class

Something messy this way comes

Abstract art makes my head numb

A head peeking over the horizon; shy, afraid of the water

I am an individual, an important part of a collective whole.

And then the sky bled pouring colors from the sun

Blue begins the symphony, orange speaks to blue

as piccolos to the string basics on the canvas of the mind.

Orbs of arcs, a crane with dinner

Splattered swooping in colors of a prism after the rain and after sinking in the bathtub

The blue spider colored like midnight proudly displays his scar.

It's not an actual object, just a collection of colors and random splashes of paint.

Blue clouds shade it from the point the sky breaks

That's the wrapping paper torn to shreds after the fury of opening presents on
Christmas morning

Somewhere over the rainbow red drops fly and mother tells a comfortable colorful
lullaby.

Source: From students of M. Angelotti, 2007, Norman, OK. Reprinted with permission.

Color Plate 1.3   Tranquility

tranquil passing waters
inbetween
mountain peaks of white and violet
on through the rocks
terrestrial waters create
high mountains with low valleys
yearning for the pink blossoms of spring

Color Plate 1.4   Paint Nothing

And the Teacher Said, "Paint Nothing."

So I painted a white moon. And from across the room came, "And he said he couldn't paint—he made a perfect circle freehand." And I swirled in thick paint crater things on it and swabbed black all around to the ends of the paper and daubed in asteroid-planet things not round but like roundish rock chunks in turquoise and mauve and mint-green in different sizes to make depth. And still it was an empty place, so I blasted a red orange and lavender comet across the big white moon through the right page edge—and from across the room came, "And that came from last night?" And I said, "Yes, from the walk in the boneyard past Kit Carson's grave when the moon was full embraced by white night clouds smoke shifting shapes in the dark wind. But I can't paint clouds yet."

— Mike Angelotti, March 2005

Source: M. Angelotti, 2005, Norman, OK. Reprinted with permission.

Color Plate 1.5 *Miners' Wives* by Ben Shahn

Source: Art © Estate of Ben Shahn/Licensed by VAGA, New York, NY.

Color Plate 1.6   Love and Life

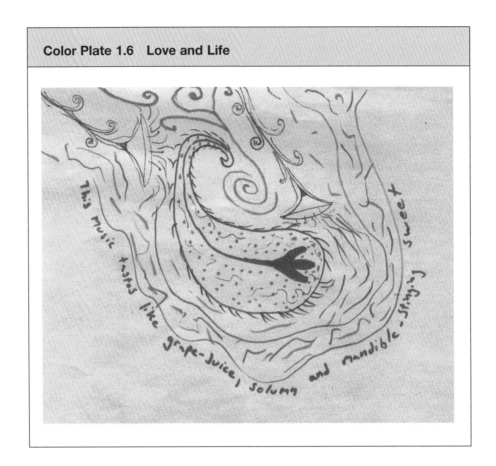

References ■ ■ ■

Abbott, S., & Berninger, V. (1999). It's never too late to remediate. *Annals of Dyslexia, 69,* 223–250.

Achieve. (2005, February 26). National education summit on high schools convenes in Washington. [Press release]. Retrieved April 2, 2008, from www.achieve.org/node93

ACT. (2006). *Reading between the lines.* Iowa City, IA: Author.

Ames, W. S. (1966). The development of a classification scheme of contextual aids. *Reading Research Quarterly, 2*(1), 57–82.

Applebee, A., Langer, J., Nystrand, M., & Gamoran, A. (2003). Discussion-based approaches to developing understanding. *American Educational Research Journal, 40*(3), 685–730.

Apter, N. (2003, March). The human being: J. L. Moreno's vision in psychodrama. *International Journal of Psychotherapy, 8*(1), 31–36.

Aristotle. (1976). *The ethics of Aristotle: The Nicomachean ethics* (J. Thomson, Trans.). New York: Penguin.

Arnheim, R. (1997). *Visual thinking.* Berkeley, CA: University of California Press.

Arnold, P. (1988). *Education, schooling, and the concept of movement.* New York: The Falmer Press.

Artley, A. (1943). Teaching word meaning through context. *Elementary English Review, 20,* 68–71.

Ayto, J. (1990). *Dictionary of word origins.* London: Richard Clay.

Bach-y-Rita, P., Kaczmarek, K., Tyler, M., Garcia-Lara, J. (1998). From perception with a 49-point electrotactile stimulus array on the tongue: A technical note. *Journal of Rehabilitation Research and Development, 35*(4), 427–430.

Baddeley, A. (2004). *Your memory: A user's guide.* Buffalo, NY: Firefly.

Badia, P., Wesensten, W., Lammers, J., Culpepper, J., & Harsh, J. (1990). Responsiveness to olfactory stimuli present in sleep. *Physiology and Behavior, 48,* 87–90.

Baines, L. A. (2001, September). Out of the box. *Voices from the Middle,* 12–20.

Baines, L. A. (2008a). An irrecusable offer: Film in the K–12 classroom. In N. Frey & D. Fisher (Eds.), *Teaching visual literacy: Using comic books, graphic novels, anime, cartoons, and more to develop comprehension and thinking skills* (pp. 149–168). Thousand Oaks, CA: Corwin.

Baines, L. A. (2008b). Film, literature, and language. In J. Flood, S. Heath, & D. Lapp (Eds.), *Handbook of research on teaching literacy through the communicative and visual arts* (pp. 503–512). New York: Taylor & Francis.

Baines, L. A., & Kunkel, A. (2003). *Teaching adolescents to write: The unsubtle art of naked teaching.* New York: Allyn and Bacon.

Baines, L. A., & Stanley, G. K. (2003). Disengagement and loathing in high school. *Educational Horizons, 81*(4), 165–168.

Baker, D., & LeTendre, G. (2005). *National differences, global similarities.* Stanford, CA: Stanford University Press.

Barksdale, A. (2003). *Music therapy and leisure for persons with disabilities.* Champaign, IL: Sagamore.

Barnes, P., Powell-Griner, E., McFann, K., & Nahin, R. (2004, May 27). *Complementary and alternative medicine use among adults: United States 2002. CDC advance data from vital and health statistics #343.* Hyattsville, MD: U.S. Department of Health and Human Services, Centers for Disease Control and Prevention, National Center for Health Statistics.

Baron, R., & Thomley, J. (1994). A whiff of reality: Positive affect as a potential mediator of the effects of pleasant fragrances on task performance and helping. *Environment and Behavior, 26*(6), 766–784.

Bauerlein, M. (2005, February 2). Reading at risk, culture at risk. *Teachers College Record.* Retrieved March 3, 2005, from http://www.tcrecord.org

Bell, T. (1971). *Hard, Seguin, and Kephart: Sensory education—A learning interpretation.* Columbus, OH: Charles E. Merrill.

Blachowicz, C., & Zabroske, B. (1990). Context instruction: A metacognitive approach for at-risk readers. *Journal of Reading, 33*(7), 504–508.

Black, J. (2004). Assessing learning preferences. *Plastic Surgical Nursing, 24*(2), 68–69.

Blackhawk, T. (2002). Ekphrastic poetry: Entering and giving voice to works of art. In T. Foster & K. Prevallet (Eds.), *Third mind: Creative writing through visual art* (pp. 1–14). New York: Teachers & Writers Collaborative.

Bloom, M. (2005). Origins of healing. *Families, Systems, & Health, 23*(3), 251–260.

Bonner, L., & Burton, A. (2003). Getting to know you: How we learn new faces. *Visual Cognition, 10*(5), 527–536.

Boxill, E. (1985). *Music therapy for the developmentally disabled.* Austin, TX: PRO-ED.

Boyd, M. P., & Rubin, D. L. (2002). Elaborated student talk in an elementary classroom. *Research in the Teaching of English, 36*, 495–530.

Bracey, G. (2000). *High stakes testing.* Milwaukee, WI: Center for Education Research, Analysis, and Innovation.

Brinnin, J. M. (1997). Symbolism, imagism, and beyond. In *Elements of literature: Fifth course* (pp. 771–772). Austin, TX: Holt, Rinehart, and Winston.

Brown, J. (1958). Some tests of the decay theory of immediate memory. *Quarterly Journal of Experimental Psychology, 10*, 10–21.

Brownell, M. (2002). Musically adapted social stories to modify behaviors in students with autism: Four case studies. *Journal of Music Therapy, 39*(2), 117–144.

Bruner, J. (1966). *Toward a theory of instruction.* Cambridge, MA: Harvard University.

Bunt, L. (1994). *Music therapy.* New York: Routledge.

Burgeson, C., Wechsler, H., Brener, N., Young, J., & Spain, C. (2001). Physical education and activity: Results from the school health policies and programs study 2000. *Journal of School Health, 71*, 279–293.

California Historical Society & Inada, L. F. (2000). *Only what we could carry: The Japanese American internment experience.* Berkeley, CA: Heyday Books.

Carnine, D., Kame'enui, E. J. & Coyle, G. (1984). Utilization of contextual information in determining the meaning of unfamiliar words. *Reading Research Quarterly, 19*(2), 188–204.

Cazden, C. (1995). New ideas for research on classroom discourse. *TESOL Quarterly, 29*, 384–387.

Cennamo, K. (1993). Learning from video: Factors influencing learners' preconceptions and invested mental effort. *Educational Technology Research and Development, 41*(3), 33–45.

Chaddock, G. (2005, February 25). Governors take aim at high school. *Christian Science Monitor*, p.1.

Civil Society Institute. (2005, August 17). *NCLB left behind: Report finds 47 of 50 states in "some stage of rebellion" against controversial law.* Washington, DC: Civil Society Institute.

Clarke, D. F., & Nation, I. S. P. (1980). Guessing the meanings of words from context: Strategy and techniques. *System, 8,* 211–220.

Coleman, J. (1965). *Adolescents and the schools.* New York: Basic Books.

College Board. (2006a). *College Board standards for college success: English language arts.* New York: Author.

College Board. (2006b). *College Board standards for college success: Mathematics and statistics.* New York: Author.

College Board. (2006c). *The College Board science framework.* Retrieved February 14, 2007, from http://www.collegeboard.com/prod_downloads/about/association/academic/science-framework_06.pdf

College Board. (2006d). *The College Board world languages framework.* Retrieved February 15, 2007, from http://www.collegeboard.com/prod_downloads/about/association/academic/world-languages-framework_06.pdf

Cook, C. (1917). *The play way.* Portsmouth, NH: Heinemann.

Cossou, M. (2001). *Point zero: Creativity without limits.* New York: Tarcher/Putnam.

Courtney-Smith, K., & Angelotti, M. (2005). To search for enlightenment: Responding to *Siddhartha* through paint and poetry. *English Journal, 94*(6), 56–62.

Cox, J. (1975). *Odor control and olfaction.* New York: Pollution Sciences Publishing.

Csikszentmihalyi, M. (1991). *Flow.* New York: Harper Perennial.

Cutler, W., Preti, G., Krieger, A., Huggins, G., Garcia, C., & Lawley, R. (1986). Human auxiliary secretions influence women's menstrual cycles: The role of donor extract from men. *Hormones and Behavior, 20,* 474–482.

Daitz, B. (2003, December 16). Doctors promote healing with the zing of the string of a harp. *New York Times.* Retrieved April 4, 2008, from http://query.nytimes.com/gst/fullpage.html?res=9D07EFD7103CF935A25751C1A9659C8B63

Dale, E. (1969). *Audiovisual methods in teaching.* New York: Dryden Press.

Daly, J. (2004). George Lucas: Life on the screen. *Edutopia, 1*(1), 36–40.

Deighton, L. C. (1959). *Vocabulary development in the classroom.* New York: Teachers College Press.

Dekker, R., & Elshout-Mohr, M. (1998). A process model for interaction and mathematical level raising. *Educational Studies in Mathematics, 36,* 303–314.

Diamond, M. (1988). *Enriching heredity: The impact of the environment on the anatomy of the brain.* New York: Free Press.

Diamond, M., & Hopson, J. (1998). *Magic trees of the mind.* New York: Dutton.

Douglas, G., Brigg, J., Langsford, S., Powell, L., West, J., Chapman, A., et al. (1998). An empirical evaluation of an interactive multi-sensory environment for children with disability. *Journal of Intellectual & Developmental Disability, 23*(4), 267–279.

Dulin, K. L. (1970). Using context clues in word recognition and comprehension. *The Reading Teacher, 23*(5), 440–469.

Dunn, C. (1995). *Conversations in paint: A notebook of fundamentals.* New York: Workman Publishing Group.

Dunn, R. (1984). Learning style: State of the scene. *Theory into Practice, 23,* 10–19.

Dunn, R., & Dunn, K. (1989). *Learning style inventory.* Lawrence, KS: Price Systems.

Dunn, R., & Dunn, K. (1993). *Teaching secondary students through their individual learning styles: Practical approaches for grades 7–12.* New York: Allyn and Bacon.

Dunn, R., Griggs, S. A., Olson, J., Beasley, M., & Gorman, B. S. (1995). A meta-analytical valida-tion of the Dunn and Dunn model of learning-style preferences. *Journal of Educational Research, 88*, 353–362.

Dunning, S. (1974, November 18). *NCTE presidential address*, New Orleans, LA.

Eaves, N. (2005). A Bohemian Rhapsody: Using music technology to fulfill aspirations of teen-age lads with muscular dystrophy. In M. Pavlicivic (Ed.), *Music therapy in children's hos-pices* (pp. 95–109). London: Jessica Kingsley Publishers.

Ehrlich, K. (1995). *Automatic vocabulary expansion through narrative context.* (Technical Report 95-09). Buffalo, NY: University at Buffalo Department of Computer Science.

Ehrlichman, H. (1995). Influence of odors on mood-related behavior. In A. Gilbert (Ed.), *Explorations in aroma-chology: Investigating the sense of smell and human response to odors* (pp. 91–96). Dubuque, IA: Kendall/Hunt.

Elkort, M. (1991). *The secret life of food.* Los Angeles: Jeremy P. Tarcher.

Emerson, R. (1994). *Nature.* Boston: Shambhala.

Entertainment Software Association. (2005). *Essential facts about the computer and video game industry.* Washington, DC: Author.

Ericsson, K. A., & Simon, H. A. (1993). *Protocol analysis: Verbal reports as data* (Rev. ed.). Cam-bridge, MA: MIT Press.

Fanslow, C. (1990). *Touch and the elderly.* In K. Bernard & T. Brazelton (Eds.), *Touch: The founda-tion of experience.* Madison, WI: International Universities Press.

Fernald, G. (1987). *Remedial techniques in basic school subjects.* Austin, TX: McGraw-Hill.

Fernandez, M. (2006, October 29). A study links trucks' exhaust to Bronx schoolchildren's asthma. *New York Times.* Retrieved April 4, 2008, from www.nytimes.com/2006/10/29/nyregion/29asthma.html

Field, T. (2001). *Touch.* Cambridge, MA: MIT Press.

Foster, T., & Prevallet, K. (2002). *Third mind: Creative writing through visual art.* New York: Teach-ers & Writers Collaborative.

Fountain, H. (2004, June 22). The early days of hearing. *New York Times.* Retrieved April 4, 2008, from http://query.nytimes.com/gst/fullpage.html?res=9500EFD61239F931A15755C0A9629C8B63

Frankel, F. (2005). Translating science into pictures: A powerful learning tool. In S. Cunningham (Ed.), *Invention and impact: Building excellence in undergraduate science, technology, engi-neering, and mathematics (STEM) education* (pp. 155–158). Washington, DC: American Association for the Advancement of Science.

Fraser, J., & Kerr, J. (1993). Psychophysiological effects of back massage on elderly institution-alized patients. *Journal of Advanced Nursing, 18,* 238–245.

Gabriel, A. (1999, May–June). Brain-based learning: The scent of the trail. *The Clearing House, 72*(5), 288–290.

Gardner, H. (1999). *Intelligence reframed.* New York: Basic Books.

Gaudiosi, J. (2003, December 10). Games, movies tie the knot. *Wired.* Retrieved March 18, 2005, from http://www.wired.com/gaming/gamingreviews/news/2003/12/61358

Gazzaniga, M. (1995). *The social brain: Discovering the networks of the mind.* New York: Basic Books.

Gensemer, R. (1979). *Movement education.* Washington, DC: National Education Association.

Gershman, K. (2004). *They always test us on things we haven't read.* Lanham, MD: Hamilton.

Gibson, E. (1988). Exploratory behavior in the development of perceiving, activating, and acquiring of knowledge. *Annual Review of Psychology, 39,* 1–41.

Gillingham, A., & Stillman, B. W. (1997). *The Gillingham manual: Remedial training for children with specific disability in reading, spelling, and penmanship.* Cambridge, MA: Educators Publishing Service.

Godfrey B., Newell, B., & Kephart, C. (1969). *Movement patterns and motor education.* New York: Appleton-Century-Crofts.

Goldberg, N. (1985). *Writing down the bones: Freeing the writer within.* Boston: Shambhala.

Gompel, M., Van Bon, W., & Schreuder, R. (2004, December). Word reading and processing of the identity and order of letters by children with low vision and sighted children. *Journal of Visual Impairment & Blindness, 98*(12), 757–772.

Grandin, T. (1998, October). *Consciousness in animals and people with autism.* Retrieved November 5, 2005, from http://www.grandin.com/references/animal.consciousness.html

Grandin, T. (2006a). *Thinking in pictures.* New York: Vintage.

Grandin, T. (2006b). Perspectives on education from a person on the autism spectrum. *Educational Horizons, 84*(4), 229–234.

Graves, M. F. (Ed.). (2000). *A vocabulary program to complement and bolster a middle-grade comprehension program.* New York: Teachers College Press.

Green, J. (2002). *The green book of songs by subject: The thematic guide to popular music.* Nashville, TN: Professional Desk References.

Green, P. (2006, October 12). Accessorizing the air. *New York Times*, pp. D1, D9.

Greiper, S., & Sauter, M. (2005). *The business of connecting dots: The $1 billion intelligence and security informatics/analytics market.* New York: C. E. Unterberg, Towbin/Chesapeake Innovation Center.

Gross, E. (2004, December). Adolescent Internet use: What we expect, what teens report. *Journal of Applied Developmental Psychology, 25,* 633–649.

Guinness World Records. (2008). *Guinness World Records: Gamers edition 2008.* London: Author.

H'Doubler, M. (2002). Education through dance. In A. Mertz (Ed.), *The body can speak* (pp. 10–14). Carbondale, IL: Southern Illinois University Press.

Hair, E., & Graziano, W. (2003). Self-esteem, personality, and achievement in high school: A prospective longitudinal study in Texas. *Journal of Personality, 71*(5), 971–994.

Hansen, C. (2004). Teacher talk: Literacy development through response to story. *Journal of Research in Childhood Education, 19*(2), 115–129.

Harmon, J. S. (1998). Constructing word meanings: Strategies and perceptions of four middle school learners. *Journal of Literacy Research, 30*(4), 561–599.

Harmon, J. S. (1999). Initial encounters with unfamiliar words in independent reading. *Research in the Teaching of English, 33*, 304–339.

Harmon, J. S. (2000). Assessing and supporting independent word learning strategies of middle school students. *Journal of Adolescent and Adult Literacy, 43*(6), 518–527.

Hashimoto, S., Yamaguchi, N., & Kawasaki, M. (1988). Experimental research on the aromatherapeutic effect of fragrances in living environments. *Summaries of technical papers of the annual meeting of the Architectural Institute of Japan*, 1201–1204.

Henry, M. (1998). Structured, sequential, multisensory teaching: The Orton legacy. *Annals of Dyslexia, 48*, 3–26.

Herz, R., Beland, S., & Hellerstein, M. (2004). Changing odor hedonic perception through emotional associations in humans. *International Journal of Comparative Psychology, 17*(4), 315–338.

Herz, R. S., Schankler, C., & Beland, S. (2004). Olfaction, emotion and associative learning: Effects on motivated behavior. *Motivation and Emotion, 28*, 363–383.

Higgins, E. L., & Rashkind, M. H. (2000). Speaking to read: The effects of continuous vs. discrete speech recognition systems on the reading and spelling of children with learning disabilities. *Journal of Special Education Technology, 15* (1), 19–30.

Higgins, E., & Rashkind, M. (2004). Speech recognition–based and automaticity programs to help students with severe reading and spelling problems. *Annals of Dyslexia, 54*(2), 365–392.

High School Survey of Student Engagement. (2005). *Voices of students on engagement.* Bloomington, IN: Center for Evaluation and Education Policy.

Hill, K. K. (2000). *Topaz moon: Chiura Obata's art of the internment.* Berkeley, CA: Heyday Books.

Hillocks, G. (1999). *Ways of thinking, ways of teaching.* New York: Teachers College Press.

Hirsch, A. (1995). Effects of ambient odors on slot-machine usage in a Las Vegas casino. *Psychology and Marketing, 12*(7), 2–3.

Hoetker, J. (1975). *Theater games: One way into drama*. Urbana, IL: National Council of Teachers of English.

Hoffman, D. (1998). *Visual intelligence*. New York: W. W. Norton.

Hope, K. (1997). Using multisensory environments with older people with dementia. *Journal of Advanced Nursing, 25*, 780–785.

Horgan, H. (2004, December 19). Patient, heal thyself. *New York Times*. Retrieved April 8, 2008, from www.nytimes.com/2004/12/19/weekinreview/19horg.html

Hutchinson, R., & Kewin, J. (Eds.). (1994). *Sensations and disability*. Exeter, England: Rompa.

Hutton, D., & Lescohier, J. (1983). Seeing to learn. In M. Fleming & D. Hutton (Eds.), *Mental imagery and learning* (pp. 113–132). Englewood Cliffs, NJ: Educational Technology Publications.

Huxley, A. (1931). *Music at night*. London: Chatto & Windus.

Infoplease. (2008). Best-selling children's books, 2004, paperback. [Online article]. Retrieved April 3, 2008, from www.infoplease.com/ipea/A0933506.html

International Dyslexia Association. (2006). Frequently asked questions about dyslexia. Retrieved April 8, 2008, from http://www.interdys.org/FAQ.htm

Johnson, L., & O'Neill, C. (1984). *Dorothy Heathcote: Collected writings on education and drama*. London: Hutchinson.

Joshi, R., Dahlgren, M., & Boulware-Gooden, R. (2002). Teaching reading in an inner city school through a multisensory teaching approach. *Annals of Dyslexia, 52*, 229–242.

Kaiser Family Foundation. (1999). *Kids & media @ the new millennium*. Washington, DC: Author.

Kaiser Family Foundation. (2005). *Generation M: Media in the lives of 8–18-year-olds*. Washington, DC: Author.

Keller, H. (1980). *The story of my life*. Mahwah, NJ: Watermill.

Kelley, T. (2006, August 28). Now in the recovery room, music for hearts to heal by. *New York Times*, p. A14.

Kephart, H. (1971). *The slow learner in the classroom*. Columbus, OH: Merrill.

Kibby, M. W. (1995). The organization and teaching of things and the words that signify them. *Journal of Adolescent & Adult Literacy, 39*(3), 208–223.

Kibby, M. W., Rapaport, W. J., & Wieland, K. M. (2004). *Contextual vocabulary acquisition: From algorithm to curriculum*. Paper presented at the International Reading Association, Reno, NV. Retrieved January 5, 2006, from http://www.cse.buffalo.edu/~rapaport/CVA/cvaslides.html

King, N. (1993). *Storymaking and drama*. Portsmouth, NH: Heinemann.

King, N. (2008). Entering a novel through the eyes of a doll: Creative responses to an African text. Retrieved April 4, 2008, from http://www.secondaryenglish.com/enteringanovel througheyesofdoll.html

Klein, S. (2006). *The science of happiness*. New York: Marlow.

Knasko, S. (1992). Ambient odors' effect on creativity, mood, and perceived health. *Chemical Senses, 17*, 27–35.

Knasko, S. (1995). Pleasant odors and congruency: Effects on approach behavior. *Chemical Senses, 20*(5), 479–487.

Knight, J. (1997). *Adults with dyslexia*. Baltimore: International Dyslexia Association.

Korsmeyer, C. (1999). *Making sense of taste*. Ithaca, NY: Cornell University Press.

Krendl, K. (1986, September). Media influence on learning. *Educational Communications Technology Journal, 34*, 223–234.

Kutner, M., Greenberg, E., Jin, Y., Boyle, B., Hsu, Y., & Dunleavey, E. (2007). *Literacy in everyday life*. Washington, DC: U.S. Department of Education.

Lacerda, F. (2003). Phonology: An emergent consequence of memory constraints and sensory input. *Reading and Writing: An Interdisciplinary Journal, 16*, 41–59.

Langer, S. (1942). *Philosophy in a new key*. Cambridge, MA: Harvard University Press.

Leavin, J. (1973). Inducing comprehension in poor readers. *Journal of Educational Psychology, 65*(1), 19–24.

Lehrner, J., Eckersberger, C., Walla, P., Potsch, G., & Deecke, L. (2000). Ambient odor of orange in a dental office reduces anxiety and improves mood in female patients. *Physiological Behavior, 71*, 83–86.

Lenay, C., Canu, S., & Villon, P. (1997). Technology and perception: The contribution of sensory substitution systems. In *Proceedings of the Second International Conference on Cognitive Technology* (pp. 44–53). Aizu, Japan and Los Alamitos, NM: IEEE Computer Society.

Levine, R. (2006, February 6). Wave of video game fatigue afflicts sales, not thumbs. *New York Times*. Retrieved February 28, 2008, from http://www.nytimes.com/2006/02/06/technology/06game.html

Lewalter, D. (2003). Cognitive strategies for learning from static and dynamic visuals. *Learning and Instruction, 13*, 177–189.

Lindstrom, M. (2005, Fall). Designing ambiance. *Create Magazine*, 54–61.

Loomis, S., & Bourque, M. (Eds.). (2001). *National Assessment of Educational Progress achievement levels 1992–1998 for writing*. Washington, DC: U.S. Department of Education.

Lord, T., & Kasprzak, M. (1989). Identification of self through olfaction. *Perceptual and Motor Skills, 69*, 219–224.

Martins, Y., Preti, G., Crabtree, C., Runyan, T., Vainius, A., & Wysocki, C. (2005). Preference for human body odors is influenced by gender and sexual orientation. *Psychological Science, 16*(9), 694–701.

Mayer, R., & Massa, L. (2003). Three facets of visual and verbal learners: Cognitive ability, cognitive style, and learning preference. *Journal of Educational Psychology, 95*(4), 833–846.

McCullough, C. M. (1952). Word analysis in the high school program. *The English Journal, 41*(1), 15–23.

McGrath, A. (2005, February 20). A new read on teen literacy. *U.S. News and World Report*. Retrieved February 23, 2008, from http://www.usnews.com/usnews/culture/articles/050228/28literacy.htm

McGrath, M. B., & Brown, J. R. (2005). Visual learning for science and engineering. *IEEE Computer Society Graphics and Applications*, 56–63.

McKeown, M. G. (1985). The acquisition of word meanings from context by children of high and low ability. *Reading Research Quarterly, 20*, 482–496.

Miller, A. (2006, January 31). A genius finds inspiration in the music of another. *New York Times*, p. D3.

Milner, M. (2004). *Freaks, geeks, and cool kids*. New York: Routledge.

Mitchell, J., & Van der Gaag, A. (2002). Through the eye of the cyclops. *British Journal of Learning Disabilities, 30*, 159–165.

Moffett, J., & Wagner, B. (1991). *Student-centered language arts*. Boston: Houghton Mifflin.

Moje, E. B. (1995). Talking about science: An interpretation of the effects of teacher talk in a high school classroom. *Journal of Research in Science Teaching, 32*, 349–371.

Morris, E. (2005). *Beethoven*. New York: HarperCollins.

Naisbitt, J. (1982). *Megatrends*. New York: Warner Books.

National Assessment of Adult Literacy. (2005). *A first look at America's adults in the 21st century*. Washington, DC: U.S. Department of Education.

National Assessment of Educational Progress. (2003). *The nation's report card: Writing 2002*. Washington, DC: U.S. Department of Education.

National Center for Education Statistics. (2005). *A profile of the American high school sophomore in 2002*. Washington, DC: U.S. Department of Education.

National Commission on Writing. (2003). *The neglected R*. New York: College Board.

National Commission on Writing. (2004). *Writing: A ticket to work*. New York: College Board.

National Commission on Writing. (2005). *Writing: A powerful message from state governments*. New York: College Board.

National Committee on Science Education Standards. (1996). *National science education standards*. Washington, DC: National Academies Press.

National Council for the Social Studies. (1994). *Expectations for excellence.* Waldorf, MD: Author.

National Council of Teachers of English. (1996). *Standards for the English language arts.* Newark, DE: International Reading Association.

National Council of Teachers of Mathematics. (2000). *Principals and standards for school mathematics.* Reston, VA: Author.

National Endowment for the Arts. (2004a). *How the United States funds the arts.* Washington, DC: Author.

National Endowment for the Arts. (2004b). *Reading at risk: A survey of literary reading in America.* Washington, DC: Author.

National Reading Research Panel. (1999). *National Reading Research Panel progress report to the National Institute for Children's Health and Development.* Washington, DC: National Institute for Children's Health and Development.

Nielsen, G. (2005, January 31). *Usability of websites for teenagers.* Retrieved February 27, 2008, from http://www.useit.com/alertbox/teenagers.html

Nielsen Media Research. (2004). *2003 television audience report.* New York: Nielsen Media Research.

Nussbaum, J. F. (1992). Effective teacher behavior. *Communication Education, 41,* 167–180.

Nye, N. S. (1994). *Words under the words: Selected poems from Naomi Shihab Nye.* Portland, OR: Eighth Mountain Press.

O'Connor, A. (2004, September 14). The right ear is from Mars. *New York Times.* Retrieved April 5, 2008, from www.nytimes.com/2004/09/14/science/14ear.html

Odell, L. (1981). Defining and assessing competence in writing. In C. Cooper (Ed.), *The nature and measurement of competency in English* (pp. 95-138). Urbana, IL: National Council of Teachers of English.

Odell, L. (2006). Interview. Retrieved March 10, 2006, from http://www.wow-schools.net/interview-odell.htm

Ogden, C., Flegal, K., Carroll, M., & Johnson, C. (2002). Prevalence and trends in overweight among U.S. children and adolescents 1999–2000. *JAMA, 288,* 1728–1732.

Olson, L. (2005, March 9). Summit fuels push to improve high schools. *Education Week, 24* (26), 1.

Oppenheim, J. (1984). *Kids and play.* New York: Ballantine.

Pace, B. (1898). The physiologic psychology of smelling. *Journal of the American Medical Association, 30,* 99–100.

Pagliano, P. (1999). *Multisensory environments.* London: David Fulton.

Paige, G. (2003). News briefs. Retrieved March 8, 2006, from http://www.sciencedaily.com/releases/2003/04/030407075732.htm

Panati, C. (1987). *Extraordinary origins of everyday things.* New York: Harper & Row.

Partnership for 21st Century Skills. (2004). *Learning skills for information and communication.* Tucson, AZ.

Partnership for 21st Century Skills. (2006). *Results that matter.* Washington, DC: U.S. Department of Education.

Percoco, J. (1998). *A passion for the past: Creative teaching of U.S. history.* Portsmouth, NH: Heinemann.

Peters, C. (1974–75). A comparison between the Frayer model of concept attainment and the textbook approach to concept attainment. (Abstract). *Reading Research Quarterly, 10*(2), 252–254.

Petrini, C., & Watson, B. (Eds.) (2001). *Slow food: Collected thoughts on taste, tradition, and the honest pleasures of food.* White River Junction, VT: Chelsea Green Publishing.

Piaget, J. (1953). *The origins of intelligence in children.* London: Routledge.

Pinker, S. (1997). *How the mind works.* New York: Penguin.

Pintrich, P., & Schunk, D. (2002). *Motivation in education.* Upper Saddle River, NJ: Merrill.

Plato. (1977). *Phaedo.* New York: Oxford University Press.

Plomp, R. (2002). *The intelligent ear.* Mahwah, NJ: Lawrence Erlbaum.

Porter, R., Cernoch, J., & McLaughlin, F. (1983). Maternal recognition of neonates through olfactory cues. *Physiology and Behavior, 30,* 151–154.

Preparing America's Future High School Initiative. (2003). Retrieved April 3, 2008, from www.ed.gov/about/offices/list/ovae/pi/hsinit/index.html

Pressley, M. (1979). *The mind's eye.* Escondido, CA: Escondido Union School District.

Pressley, M., & Afflerbach, P. (1995). *Verbal protocols of reading: The nature of constructively responsive reading.* Hillsdale, NJ: Erlbaum.

Prevention. (2006, January). Set-it-yourself success. *Prevention, 58*(1), 34.

Prusak, K. A., Pangrazi, R. P., & Vincent, S. D. (2005). Teacher talk. *Journal of Physical Education, Recreation and Dance, 76*(5), 21–25.

Rainie, L., & Horrigan, J. (2005). *A decade of adoption: How the Internet has woven itself into American life.* Washington, DC: Pew Internet & American Life Project.

Rapaport, W. J. (2003). What is the "context" for contextual vocabulary acquisition? In P. Slezak (Ed.), *Proceedings of the 4th International Conference on Cognitive Science/7th Australasian Society for Cognitive Science Conference* (ICCS/ASCS-2003), (Vol. 2, pp. 547–552). Sydney, Australia: University of New South Wales.

Rapaport, W. J. (2005). In defense of contextual vocabulary acquisition: How to do things with words in context. In A. Dey et al. (Eds.), *Proceedings of the 5th International and Interdisciplinary Conference on Modeling and Using Context* (Context-05i) (pp. 396–409). Berlin, Germany: Springer-Verlag Lecture Notes in Artificial Intelligence 3554.

Rapaport, W. J., & Ehrlich, K. (2000). A computational theory of vocabulary acquisition. In M. Lucja, M. Iwanska, & S. Shapiro (Eds.), *Natural language processing and knowledge representation: Language for knowledge and knowledge for language* (pp. 347–375). Menlo Park, CA/Cambridge, MA: AAAI Press/MIT Press.

Rapaport, W., & Kibby, M. (2002). Contextual vocabulary acquisition: A computational theory and educational curriculum. In N. Callaos, A. Breda, Y. Ma, & J. Fernandez (Eds.), *Proceedings of the 6th World Multiconference on Systemics, Cybernetics and Informatics* (SCI 2002; Orlando, FL). Vol. II: Concepts and Applications of Systemics, Cybernetics, and Informatics I (pp. 261–266). Orlando, FL: International Institute of Informatics and Systemics.

Rashkind, M. H., & Higgins, E. L. (1999). Speaking to read: The effects of speech recognition technology on the reading and spelling performance of children with learning disabilities. *Annals of Dyslexia, 49,* 251–281.

Rawson, M. (1987). The Orton trail: 1896–1986. *Annals of Dyslexia, 37,* 36–48.

Reiff, J. (1992). *Learning styles.* Washington, DC: National Education Association.

Richards, R. (1993). *Learn: Playful techniques to accelerate learning.* Tucson, AZ: Zephyr Press.

Ririe, S. (2002). Spontaneous creation. In A. Mertz (Ed.), *The body can speak* (pp. 58–64). Carbondale, IL: Southern Illinois University Press.

Roach, M. (1999). *Sniff me hard, babe.* Retrieved March 7, 2006, from http://www.salon.com/health/col/roac/1999/08/27/pheromones

Romano, T. (1995). *Writing with passion: Life stories, multiple genres.* Portsmouth, NH: Boynton/Cook Heinemann.

Rose, J. (2006). *Independent review of the teaching of early reading.* Nottingham, England: DfES Publications.

Rosoff, M. (2004). *How I live now.* New York: Wendy Lamb Books.

Russ, S. (2004). *Play in child development and psychotherapy: Toward empirically supported practice.* Mahwah, NJ: Lawrence Erlbaum.

Sadowski, M. (2003). *Adolescents at school.* Cambridge, MA: Harvard Education Press.

Schleidt, M., Neumann, P., & Morishita, H. (1988). Pleasure and disgust: Memories and associations of pleasant and unpleasant odors in Germany and Japan. *Chemical Senses, 13,* 279–293.

Schwartz, R. (1988). Learning to learn vocabulary in content area textbooks. *Journal of Reading, 32,* 108–118.

Schwartz, R., & Raphael, T. E. (1985). Concept of definition: A key to improving students' vocabulary. *The Reading Teacher, 39*, 198–205.

Shaller, J., & Smith, R. (2002, October–December). Music therapy with adolescents experiencing loss. *The Forum, 28*(5), 1, 2–4.

Sherry, J. (2004). Flow and media enjoyment. *Communication Theory, 14*(4), 328–347.

Shimuzu, Ltd. (1990). *Aromanity: Creating a pleasant environment with fragrances* [Brochure]. Tokyo, Japan: Author.

Shiner, R., Masten, A., & Roberts, J. (2003). Childhood personality foreshadows adult personality and life outcomes two decades later. *Journal of Personality, 71*(6), 1145–1170.

Silverman, L. (2002). *Upside-down brilliance: The visual-spatial learner.* Denver, CO: DeLeon Publishing.

Slingerland, B. (1977). *A multi-sensory approach to language arts for specific language disability children.* Cambridge, MA: Educators Publishing Services.

Smith, A. (2006, October 8). Middle school improves learning by design. *Dallas News*, p. 14B.

Smith, M., & Wilhelm, J. (2002). *Reading don't fix no Chevys.* Portmouth, NH: Heinemann.

Smith, S. L. (2002). *Lucy the giant.* New York: Delacorte Books for Young Readers.

Society for Neuroscience. (2005). *Brain facts.* Washington, DC: Author.

Spangenberg, E., Crowley, A., & Henderson, P. (1996). Improving the store environment: Do olfactory cues affect evaluations and behaviors? *Journal of Marketing, 60*(2), 67–80.

Spencer, H. (1891). *Essays: Scientific, political, and speculative* (Library ed., vol. 2). London: Williams and Norgate.

Spencer, H. (2002). Literary style and music. In M. Mark (Ed.), *Music education: Source readings from Ancient Greece to today* (pp.47–48). New York: Routledge.

Steiner, G. (1971). *In Bluebeard's castle.* New Haven, CT: Yale University Press.

Steiner, G. (1990). Struck dumb. In C. Fadiman (Ed.), *Living philosophies* (pp. 213–222). New York: Doubleday.

Sternberg, R. J. (1987). Most vocabulary is learned in context. In M. McKeown & M. Curtis (Eds.), *The nature of vocabulary acquisition* (pp. 89–105). Hillsdale, NJ: Lawrence Erlbaum.

Sternberg, R. J., & Powell, J. S. (1983). Comprehending verbal comprehension. *American Psychologist, 38*, 878–893.

Strain, G. (2006). How well do dogs and other animals hear? Retrieved March 21, 2006, from http://www.lsu.edu/deafness/HearingRange.html

Strauss, V. (2006, October 24). Getting an earful during reading time. *Washington Post*, p. A10.

Striedter, G. (2006). Précis of principles of brain evolution. *Behavioral and Brain Sciences, 29*(1), 1–12.

Sweeney-Brown, C. (2005). Music and medicine. In M. Pavlicivic (Ed.), *Music therapy in children's hospices* (pp. 48-61). London: Jessica Kingsley Publishers.

Taylor, A., Wise, B., & Wise, J. (1990, May–June). The Head Start classroom of the future. *Children Today, 19*, 38–40.

Telfer, E. (1996). *Food for thought.* New York: Routledge.

Trehub, S. E. (2003). The developmental origins of musicality. *Nature Neuroscience, 6*(7), 669–673.

Trindade, J., Fiolhais, C., & Almeida, L. (2002). Science learning in virtual environments. *British Journal of Educational Technology, 33*(4), 471–488.

Turin, L. (2006). *The secret of scent.* New York: HarperCollins.

Tyrangiel, J. (2005). Why you can't ignore Kanye. *Time, 166*(9), 54–61.

U.S. Bureau of Labor Statistics. (2008). *Time-use survey.* Retrieved April 13, 2008, from http://www.bls.gov/news.release/atust11.htm

U.S. Census Bureau. (2005). *Statistical abstract of the United States: 2004–2005.* Washington, DC: U.S. Government Printing Office.

U.S. Department of Health and Human Services, Centers for Disease Control and Prevention, Division of Adolescent and School Health. (2004). *United States all years: Percentage of students who participated in no vigorous physical activity.* [Online report]. Retrieved April 5, 2008, from www.cdc.gov/mmwhtml/ss5302al.htm

Van Daalen-Kapteijns, M., & Elshout-Mohr, M. (1981). The acquisition of word meanings as a cognitive learning process. *Journal of Verbal Learning and Verbal Behavior, 20,* 386–399.

Van Daalen-Kapteijns, M., Elshout-Mohr, M., & de Glopper, K. (2001). Deriving the meaning of unknown words from multiple contexts. *Language Learning, 51*(1), 145–181.

Veronis Suhler Stevenson Communications Group. (2005). *2004 communications industry forecast and report.* New York: Author.

Veronis Suhler Stevenson Communications Group. (2006). *Industry spending projectors 2006–2010.* New York: Author.

Vroon, P. (1994). *Smell: The secret seducer.* New York: Farrar, Straus, and Giroux.

Wadlington, E., & Wadlington, P. (2005). What educators really believe about dyslexia. *Reading Improvement, 42*(1), 16–33.

Wallin, N., Merker, B., & Brown, S. (Eds.) (1999). *The origins of music.* Cambridge, MA: MIT Press.

Werner, H., & Kaplan, E. (1950). The acquisition of word meanings: A developmental study. *Monographs of the Society for Research in Child Development, 15*(51), i–119.

West, T. (1997). *In the mind's eye: Visual thinkers, gifted people with dyslexia and other learning difficulties, computer images and the ironies of creativity.* Amherst, NY: Prometheus Books.

Wieland, K. M. (2005). *The contextual vocabulary acquisition strategies of adolescent readers: An analysis of think-aloud protocol.* Buffalo, NY: University at Buffalo, Graduate School of Education, Department of Learning and Instruction.

Wilhelm, J. D. (2001). *Improving comprehension with think-aloud strategies: Modeling what good readers do.* New York: Scholastic Professional Books.

Wilhelm, J. D., Baker, T. N., & Dube, J. (2001). Strategic reading: Guiding students to lifelong literacy, 6–12. Portsmouth, NH: Heinemann.

Williams, L. (1983). *Teaching for the two-sided mind.* New York: Touchstone.

Zander, M. J. (2003). Talking, thinking, responding and creating: A survey of literature on talk in art education. *Studies in Art Education, 44*(2), 117–134.

Zigler, E., Singer, D., & Bishop-Josef, S. (Eds.). (2004). *Children's play: The roots of reading.* Washington, DC: Zero to Three.

Zwiers, M., Van Opstal, A., & Paige, G. (2003). Plasticity in human sound localization induced by compressed spatial vision. *Nature Neuroscience, 6*(2), 175–182.

Index ■ ■ ■

Note: Page numbers followed by *f* indicate illustrations.

About the Author ■ ■ ■

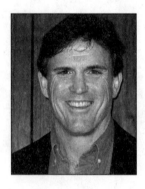

Lawrence Baines is a professor of English education at the University of Toledo. He is the author or editor of three books on literacy, two books of short biographies, and many articles and essays. Baines may be contacted at lawrencebaines@gmail.com.

TCM 2762

Dr. Fry's

Phonics Charts

A
Complete
Phonics
Curriculum
on 99 Charts

by Edward Fry, Ph.D.

Teacher Created Materials, Inc.
6421 Industry Way
Westminster, CA 92683
www.teachercreated.com

ISBN-1-57690-762-7

©1997 by Edward Fry
Laguna Beach Educational Books

Reprinted, 2000
Made in U.S.A.

Y0-BZU-505

TABLE OF CONTENTS

What Can You Do With These Charts?

• **Hang one up**

Teach from it emphasizing the phoneme sound in the words.

Display it for awhile.

Refer back to it when that sound comes up in other lessons.

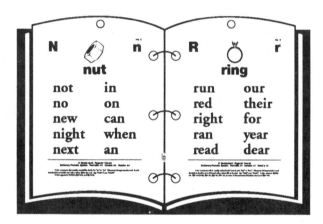

• **Use it in a book**

Turn to specific pages as needed for tutoring and small group instruction.

• **Photocopy a chart**

Let your student(s) take it home.

Cut out the words for a word wall or pocket chart.

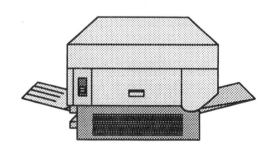

INTRODUCTION

Here is a complete phonics curriculum in just one book. This book contains all or more of the phonics taught in most basal readers or other complete phonics programs. Teaching phonics can be done in many ways. These charts are but one way. They are a "teaching tool." See the suggestions on pages 3 and 5 for using them.

These charts are efficient because using one chart a day (the Sound-of-the-Day plan) covers a complete course of phonics in 99 days, or about 20 weeks of the 35 weeks in a typical school year. Tutoring or other special education situations may take more or less time. Often a teacher may cover one section of the charts in this book, and then, at a later time or other grade level, do a more advanced section.

The charts can be used as early as <u>kindergarten</u> to teach Phonemic Awareness. Real reading should not be expected, but the students will be made aware of the different phonemes in English and of the idea that each phoneme can be represented by letters.

The charts can be used in the <u>primary grades</u> (1–4) for real phonics instruction where reading some of the example words is expected and the students are exposed to all of the phoneme-grapheme (sound-letter) correspondences. They can also be used in upper grades in <u>remedial reading</u>, ESL classes, or for <u>Adult Basic Education</u>.

These charts are presented in a suggested teaching order. This teaching order is based on frequency counts of phoneme-grapheme occurrences in the English language. In other words, easy consonants occur more frequently than short vowels; and short vowels occur more frequently than long vowels. Furthermore, the consonant T in Chart 1 occurs more frequently than the consonant N in Chart 2. Saying the same thing in another way, students are apt to need to know how to sound out the letter T before they need to sound out the letter N. Actually, this fine grading is not too important. More important is that students should learn the easy consonants and short vowels before they learn less common consonants like Q or Z. However, the teacher can select any teaching order, perhaps tying the chart use into other lessons where appropriate.

TEACHING SUGGESTIONS

1. Sound-of-the-Day   Present one chart each day at the beginning of your reading or writing lesson. Discuss the sound; then discuss each example word. Ask your students for other words which use this sound. Have them say some of the words and emphasize the sound as they do so. Have them say the sound in isolation (see author's comments on the charts). Take the chart out of the book or copy it and hang it up in your classroom for the day.

2. Student Activities   Collect old magazines; have students find and cut out pictures of things which use the sound being studied. Have one student be in charge of each sound. Let him or her color the chart and mount it on a large piece of posterboard with the other students' cut out pictures. Label the pictures (write the word).

3. Phonemic Awareness   For younger students and ESL or special education students, point out the sound similarity in the different words. Show that the words are composed of different sounds and that each letter or pair of letters makes a sound. In going through these charts almost all of the sounds of English will be covered together with their common spelling (phoneme-grapheme correspondence). While developing phonemic awareness, it is not necessary that the student be able to read all, or even any, of the words; the student must, however, get the idea that English words are composed of a limited number of sounds (about 40 phonemes) and that these sounds can be represented by letters.

4. Games   There are many commercial and teacher-made games available. Using the phonemes in the first 10 to 20 of these charts, you can make bingo cards, a rummy card game, word cards, and many other game-like devices to help students learn the sounds of letters.

5. Review   Go back over charts at the end of the week and the end of the month. Review really helps learning. For an interesting application of phonemes, see TCM 2761, Phonics Patterns, listed inside the back cover.

6. Writing and Spelling   Phonics can be taught in writing and spelling lessons just as well as in reading lessons. These charts can supplement the phonics section of the lessons in Dr. Fry's Spelling Book (see inside back cover).

7. Caution   Phonics teaching can be deadly boring. Keep your phonics lessons lively and short. Leave plenty of time for story reading and story writing. But phonics lessons can help many students learn to read and write better.

PHONICS DISCUSSION

Teaching phonics helps children and adults who cannot read or write well. It helps them because phonics is built into our system of writing. We write with an alphabet and, theoretically, an alphabet is a set of written symbols that stand for speech sounds. Linguists call this a *phoneme-grapheme correspondence*. A phoneme is a speech sound like the /s/ sound at the beginning of "sat," and the written letter S is the grapheme. Teachers usually call the learning of the relationship between phonemes and graphemes "phonics." Viewed one way, learning to look at the letter and say the sound is part of reading or word recognition and, viewed the other way, writing the letter that represents a sound is spelling. There is much more to learning to read or spell than phonics, but it is a good start. Phonics teaching should even be at least a small part of advanced reading lessons.

The 99 phoneme-grapheme correspondences on these charts cover much of, and sometimes more, phonics than is taught in most elementary reading and spelling programs. There are, of course, many more details, or "exceptions," than are covered on these charts, but we are trying to develop beginning readers and writers, not university-trained phonologists. In fact, use only as many of the charts as you feel are suitable for your students.

On the charts we use the terms "digraph" and "diphthong," so we will explain them. A digraph is simply two letters written together which represent one phoneme. An example of a consonant digraph is SH as in "shoe," and a vowel digraph would be the EA in "bread." A diphthong is a sound, not a written letter. A diphthong is a sort of vowel blend which is technically a vowel plus a semi-vowel. Diphthongs are treated as single sounds (single phonemes) like the OU in "out."

Phonics teachers often like to teach that there is a Long U (see chart 27), but dictionaries do not recognize such a sound. They say it is simply a Long OO sound as is heard in "student," which is the same sound as heard in "moon." The U sound in "music" is really /yoo/. However, for teaching a beginning reader, this is getting a little too technical, so we have not differentiated these sounds.

Some phonics teachers like to have students pronounce phonemes in *isolation* (not in a word). If you do this, try to do so without emphasizing a *schwa* (short U sound) at the end, or even omit the schwa sound if possible. The comments on each chart will help you with this. Or, you can just point out the sound in the example words (no isolation of sound).

At the bottom of each chart we have given the Dictionary Phonetic Symbol for the sound (phoneme) taught on the chart. You can further note that dictionaries do not always agree. They do agree on consonants and long and short vowels, but there is less agreement on Schwa-Short U, Broad O, Short OO-One Dot U, and a few more. You can ignore this controversy and teach just the symbol for the dictionary you use. Children frequently do not learn dictionary phonetic symbols; they are more often taught to adults or ESL students. However, phonetic symbols help anyone using a dictionary to look up and learn to pronounce new words.

T   t

top

to	not
two	at
take	it
tell	out
too	get

T Consonant: Regular Sound
Dictionary Phonetic Symbol: Thorndike /t/   Random /t/   Webster /t/

    T is a consonant which almost always makes the /t/ sound, as in "top" or "sat". This sound can be made without using the vocal cords or the schwa /ə/ sound at the end.

    T does not make this sound when it is part of the digraph TH, as in "the" and "thin", taught in #37 and #38.

    T is also found in the #75-TR, #81-ST and #94-TW.

N

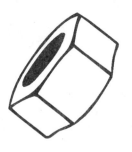

n

nut

not	in
no	on
new	can
night	when
next	an

N Consonant: Regular Sound
Dictionary Phonetic Symbol: Thorndike /n/   Random /n/   Webster /n/

N is a consonant that usually sounds like the /n/ in "no" or "in". This sound always uses the vocal chords but should not be followed with a schwa /ə/ at the end. Say "NNN", not "NUH".

N also appears in #87-SN, #96-KN, and #98-NG.

R

r

ring

run	our
red	their
right	for
ran	year
read	dear

R Consonant: Regular Sound
Dictionary Phonetic Symbol: Thorndike /r/   Random /r/   Webster /r/

R is a consonant which usually makes the /r/ sound, as in "red" or "our". This sound always uses the vocal chords but should not be followed with a schwa /ə/ at the end. Say "RRR", not "RUH". R also occurs in #56-AR. #57-AR (AIR), #58-ER, #59-IR, #60-UR, in some of the consonant blends in Set F, and #97-WR.

M

m

man

me	from
my	them
make	am
much	seem
many	warm

M Consonant: Regular Sound

Dictionary Phonetic Symbol: Thorndike /m/   Random /m/   Webster /m/

M is a consonant which usually makes the /m/ sound, as in "man" or "them". This sound always uses the vocal chords but should not be followed with a schwa /ə/ at the end. Say "MMM", not "MUH." M is also found in #87-SM.

D

d

dog

do	and
day	good
did	had
dear	said
down	red

D Consonant: Regular Sound
Dictionary Phonetic Symbol: Thorndike /d/   Random /d/   Webster /d/

D is a consonant that almost always has the sound /d/, as in "dog" or "had". This sound uses the vocal chords and the schwa /∂/, but don't overemphasize the schwa.

D also appears in #79-DR.

S

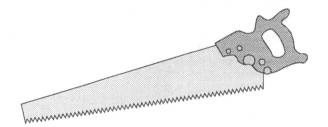

s

saw

some	**this**
so	**us**
see	**likes**
said	**makes**
soon	**yes**

S Consonant: Regular Sound
Dictionary Phonetic Symbol: Thorndike /s/   Random /s/   Webster /s/

S is one of the few consonants that has two sounds. The sound of /s/, as in "saw," is the most common. S almost always makes this sound at the beginning of a word. This sound can be made without using the vocal cords or the schwa /ə/ sound at the end. Say "SSS," not "SUH." S does not make this sound when it is part of the digraph SH (#40), as in "shoes," nor when it is at the end of some words, such as "has" (#43), where it makes the sound of Z. S is also found in consonant blends, #81-ST, #82-SP, #83-SC, #84-SW, #87-SN, and #92-SL.

L l

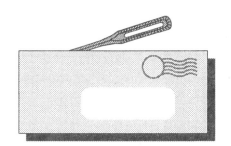

letter

little	will
like	all
long	girl
look	school
live	shall

L Consonant: Regular Sound
Dictionary Phonetic Symbol: Thorndike /l/   Random /l/   Webster /l/

L is a consonant that usually makes the /l/ sound, as in "look" or "girl." This sound always uses the vocal cords but should not be followed with a schwa /ə/ at the end. Say "LLL," not "LUH." L is also found in #62-AL and in the consonant blends #88-PL, #89-CL, #90-BL, #91-FL, #92- SL, and #93-GL. Note: At the end of a word the L sound is often made by a double L (ll).

C  c

cat

can	back
come	rock
came	sick
camp	lock
color	kick

C Consonant: Regular K Sound
Dictionary Phonetic Symbol: Thorndike /k/   Random /k/   Webster /k/

C usually has the sound of /k/. For example, the C in the word "cat" has the sound of /k/. This sound can be made without using the vocal cords or the schwa /ə/ sound at the end. C usually makes the /k/ sound before A, O, and U. The sound of C before I, E, and Y, as in "city" is in #42. Note that CH is a digraph. It is taught in #39. At the end of a word, this K sound is usually made by CK, as in "back".

C also occurs in #78-CR, #83-SC, and #89-CL.

P p

pencil

put	up
people	sleep
play	jump
pair	help
part	stop

P Consonant: Regular Sound
Dictionary Phonetic Symbol: Thorndike /p/   Random /p/   Webster /p/

P is a consonant that usually has the sound of /p/ as in "pig" or "up". This sound can be made without using the vocal cords or the schwa /ə/ sound at the end. Say "PPP", not "PUH".

P is also found in #74-PR, #88-PL, and in #95-PH.

B

b

book

be	tub
by	cab
boy	rob
been	cub
box	rib

B Consonant: Regular Sound
Dictionary Phonetic Symbol: Thorndike /b/   Random /b/   Webster /b/

B is a consonant that makes the sound of /b/, as in "boy" or "bib". This sound uses the vocal chords and the schwa /ə/, but don't overemphasize the schwa. However, remember that you are trying to teach B. Say "BBB", not "BUH".

B is also found in consonant blends #77-BR and #90-BL.

F   f

fish

for   if

first   half

find   myself

four   off

funny   leaf

F Consonant: Regular Sound
Dictionary Phonetic Symbol: Thorndike / f /   Random / f /   Webster / f /

F is a consonant that almost always makes the sound /f/, as in "fish" or "off". This sound can be made without using the vocal cords or the schwa /ə/ sound at the end. Say "FFF", not "FUH".

F also occurs in consonant blends #80-FR and #91-FL.

V

V

valentine

very	five
visit	give
voice	gave
vote	twelve
view	love

V Consonant: Regular Sound
Dictionary Phonetic Symbol: Thorndike /v/   Random /v/   Webster /v/

V is a consonant that usually has the sound /v/ as in "very". This sound always uses the vocal chords but should not be followed with a schwa /ə/ at the end. Say "VVV", not "VUH".

At the end of a word, V is usually followed by a silent E.

I  **i**

Indian

in	with
is	did
if	this
into	little
inch	which

I Vowel: Short I Sound
Dictionary Phonetic Symbol: Thorndike /i/   Random /i/   Webster /i/

   I is a vowel that has several sounds. The short sound of I, as in "is", should be taught first, because it is the most common.

   Other sounds of I are taught in #21-I "Long Final E Rule" and in #25-I "Long Open Syllable Rule". Y sometimes makes the long I sound (#45). I also occurs in #51-AI, #59-IR, and #67-OI.

E

e

elephant

end	when
egg	get
every	then
extra	left
enemy	let

E Vowel: Short E Sound

Dictionary Phonetic Symbol: Thorndike /e/   Random /e/   Webster /e/

E is a vowel that has several sounds. The short sound of E, as in "end", should be taught first, because it is the most common. The short sound of E is sometimes made by EA (#73). E is usually silent at the end of a word, taught in #19. The E "Long Open Syllable Rule" is in #24. The long sound of E is also made by EE (#50), and sometimes by EA (#49) and Y (#18). The schwa sound of E is in #47. E is also found in #58-ER.

A

a

apple

and	**that**
at	**can**
as	**had**
after	**back**
an	**last**

A Vowel: Short A Sound
Dictionary Phonetic Symbol: Thorndike /a/   Random /a/   Webster /a/

A is a vowel that has several sounds. The short sound of A, as in "as", is the most common and should be taught first. Other sounds of A are: "Long Final E Rule" (#20), and "Long Open Syllable Rule" (#23). The long A sound is also made by AI (#51) and AY (#52). The schwa is in #46. A also occurs in #49-EA, #53-OA, #56-AR, #57-AR (AIR), #62-AL, #63-AW, #64-AU, and in #73-EA.

O O

box

not	fox
box	drop
hot	pop
stop	pot
body	clock

O Vowel: Short O Sound
Dictionary Phonetic Symbol: Thorndike /o/   Random /o/   Webster /ă/

O is a vowel that has several sounds. The short sound of O, as in "on", is the most common and should be taught first. Other sounds of O are: "Long Final E Rule" (#22), and "Long Open Syllable Rule" (#26). The long O sound is also made by OA (#53), and is sometimes made by OW (#54).. The schwa is in #48 and the Broad O in #61. AL (#62), AW (#63), and AU (#64) also make the broad O sound. O also occurs in #55-OR, #65-OU, #66-OW, #67-OI, #68-OY, #69-OO (long), and #70-OO (short).

22

U u

umbrella

up   run

us   much

under   just

until   cut

but   funny

U Vowel: Short U Sound
Dictionary Phonetic Symbol: Thorndike /u/ Random /u/ Webster /ə/

    U is a vowel that has several sounds. The short sound of U, as in "up", is the most common and should be taught first. Other sounds of U are: "Long Open Syllable Rule" (#27), the "2-Dot" U (#71), and the "1-Dot" U (#72). OO sometimes makes the "2-Dot" U sound (#69), and sometimes makes the "1-Dot" U sound (#70). U also appears in #60-UR, #64-AU, and #65-OU.

Y y

baby

very	funny
any	happy
many	lady
pretty	story
only	family

Y Vowel: Long E Sound
Dictionary Phonetic Symbol: Thorndike /ē/ Random /ē/ Webster /ē/

Y is most frequently a vowel which has the long E sound, as in "very". This is true when Y is at the end of a word that contains another vowel.

The consonant sound of Y at the beginning of a word, such as in "yes", is taught in #36. The long I sound of Y, as in "my", is taught in #45. When Y follows A in the digraph AY, as in "day", it is not part of the above rules. The AY sound is taught in #52. Y is also found in #68-OY.

24

whale

are	like
one	were
there	before
come	here
little	came

E Vowel: Silent E

Dictionary Phonetic Symbol: Thorndike / / Random / / Webster / /

E at the end of a word that contains another vowel sound is usually silent. This rule is more useful and consistent that the "Final E Rule", which will be taught in #20-A, #21-I, and #22-O.

The short sound of E is in #14. EA (#73) sometimes makes the short E sound. The "Long Open Syllable Rule" is in #24. EE (#50) also makes the long E sound. Y (#18) and EA (#49) sometimes make the long E sound. The schwa E is in #47. E will also be found in #58-ER.

A_e  a_e

cake

make	**came**
made	**state**
face	**able**
ate	**late**
same	**tale**

A Vowel: Long A Sound – Final E Rule
Dictionary Phonetic Symbol: Thorndike /ā/   Random /ā/   Webster /ā/

The second most common sound of A is the long sound, as in "take". The long A sound is frequently made by placing a silent E at the end of the word or syllable. Note the difference between "mad" and "made". A seldom makes this sound when it is the beginning of a word. The long A sound is also made by the "Long Open Syllable Rule" (#23) and AI (#51) and AY (#52). Other sounds of A are: short (#15) and schwa (#46).

A is also found in #49-EA, #53-OA, #56-AR, #57-AR (AIR), #62-AL, #63-AW, #64-AU, and #73-EA.

I_e   i_e

ice cream

five	write
white	life
ride	side
time	nine
fire	bite

I Vowel: Long I Sound – Final E Rule
Dictionary Phonetic Symbol: Thorndike / ī /   Random / ī /   Webster / ī /

The second most common sound of I is the long sound, as in "like". The long I sound is frequently made by placing a silent E at the end of the word. Note the difference between "rid" and "ride". I seldom makes this sound at the beginning of a word.

The long sound of I is also made by the "Long Open Syllable Rule" (#25) and sometimes by Y (#45). The short sound of I was taught in #13. I also appears in #51-AI, #59-IR, and in #60-OI.

O_e O_e

globe

home	alone
those	rode
hope	nose
rope	stone
note	joke

O Vowel: Long O Sound – Final E Rule
Dictionary Phonetic Symbol: Thorndike /ō/   Random /ō/   Webster /ō/

The second most common sound of O, the long sound, as in "home", is frequently made by placing a silent E at the end of the word or syllable, as in "not" and "note". O seldom makes this sound at the beginning of a word. The long O sound is also made by the "Long Open Syllable Rule" (#26), by OA (#53), and sometimes by OW (#54). Other sounds of O are: short (#16), schwa (#48), and broad (#61-O, #62-AL, #63-AW, and #64-AU). O also appears in #55-OR, #65-OU, #66-OW, #67-OI, #68-OY, #69-OO (long), and #70-OO (short).

A a

table

paper   labor

lady   lazy

baby   flavor

radio   tomato

crazy   navy

A Vowel: Long A Sound – Open Syllable Rule
Dictionary Phonetic Symbol: Thorndike /ā/ Random /ā/ Webster /ā/

The long sound of A is sometimes made by the "Open Syllable Rule", which holds that when a syllable ends in a vowel that the vowel is pronounced with the long sound, as in "paper". At the end of a word, the long A sound is usually made by the digraph AY, which is taught in #52. The long sound of A is also made by the "Long Final E Rule" (#20) and by AI (#51), and AY (#52). Other sounds of A are: short (#15) and schwa (#46). A will also be found in #49-EA, #53-OA, #56-AR, #57-AR (AIR), #62-AL, #63-AW, #64-AU, and #73-EA.

E = e

equal

me	before
he	even
she	because
we	secret
be	equator

E Vowel: Long E Sound – Open Syllable Rule
Dictionary Phonetic Symbol: Thorndike /ē/ Random /ē/ Webster /ē/

The long sound of E is sometimes made by the "Open Syllable Rule", which holds that when a syllable ends in a vowel that the vowel is pronounced with the long sound, as in "me".

The long sound of E is also made by EE (#50), and sometimes by Y (#45), and EA (#49).

The short sound of E is taught in #14. EA sometimes makes the short sound of E (#73).

The silent E is taught in #19, and the schwa in #47. E also appears in #58-ER.

30   ©*Teacher Created Materials, Inc.*

I  **i**

iron

I	bicycle
idea	tiny
I'll	silent
iron	rifle
I'm	pilot

I Vowel: Long I Sound – Open Syllable Rule
Dictionary Phonetic Symbol: Thorndike /ī/   Random /ī/   Webster /ī/

The long sound of I is sometimes made by the "Open Syllable Rule", which holds that when a syllable ends in a vowel that the vowel is pronounced with the long sound, as in "tiger". Words on one syllable which make the long I sound at the end usually end in Y (#45).

The long sound of I is also made by the "Long Final E Rule" (#21) and sometimes by Y (#45). The short sound of I is taught in #13. I also occurs in 351-AI, #59-IR, and #67-OI.

O   O

radio

go	hello
no	also
so	ago
open	auto
over	zero

O Vowel: Long O Sound – Open Syllable Rule
Dictionary Phonetic Symbol: Thorndike / ō /   Random / ō /   Webster / ō /

The long sound of O is sometimes made by the "Open Syllable Rule", which holds that when a syllable ends in a vowel that the vowel is pronounced with the long sound, as in "go".

The long sound of O is also made by the "Long Final E Rule" (#22), by OA (#53), and sometimes by OW (#54). Other sounds of O are: short (#16), schwa (#48), and broad (#61-O, #62-AL, #63-AW, and #64-AU). O is also found in #55-OR, #65-OU, #66-OW, #67-OI, #68-OY, #69-OO (long), and #70-OO (short).

U u

music

student	humor
music	January
unit	popular
united	universe
human	rumor

U Vowel: Long U Sound – Open Syllable Rule
Dictionary Phonetic Symbol: Thorndike /yü/ Random /yo͞o/ Webster /yü/

The long sound of U is sometimes made by the "Open Syllable Rule", which holds that when a syllable ends in a vowel that the vowel is pronounced with the long sound, as in "human".

Other sounds of U are: short (#17), "2-Dot" (#71) and "1-Dot" (#72). OO can make either the "2-Dot" U sound (#69), or the "1-Dot" U sound (#71). U also appears in #60-UR, #64-AU, and #65-OU.

G

g

gate

go	dog
good	again
got	big
gave	ago
girl	egg

G Consonant: Regular Sound
Dictionary Phonetic Symbol: Thorndike /g/   Random /g/   Webster /g/

The consonant G has two sounds. The most common is the /g/ sound, as in "good" and "big". It frequently makes this sound before A, O, and U, and when it is the last letter in a word. This sound uses the vocal chords and the schwa /ə/, but don't overemphasize the schwa. G is usually silent when it is part of the so-called silent blend, GH as in "right" (#99). The second sound of G, before I, E, or Y as in "gem", is taught in #44. G also occurs in #75-GR, #93-GL, and #98-NG.

H

h

hand

he   how

had   help

have   here

her   happy

him   home

H Consonant: Regular Sound
Dictionary Phonetic Symbol: Thorndike / h /   Random / h /   Webster / h /

H is a consonant that usually makes the / h / sound, as in "hat". This sound can be made without using the vocal cords or the schwa /∂/ sound at the end. Say "HHH", not "HUH".

H does not make this sound when it is part of a digraph. See #37-TH (voiced), #38-TH (voiceless), #39-CH, #40-SH, and #41-WH. H is usually silent when it is part of the so-called silent blend, GH as in "right" (#99). H also occurs in #95-PH.

K

k

kite

kind	like
key	make
kill	book
king	look
keep	cake

K Consonant: Regular Sound
Dictionary Phonetic Symbol: Thorndike /k/   Random /k/   Webster /k/

K is a consonant that usually makes the /k/ sound, as in "kind". This sound can be made without using the vocal cords or the schwa /ə/ sound at the end. Say "KKK", not "KUH".

K is often silent before N, as in "know" (#96-KN).

The letter C frequently makes the sound of K (#8-C). K also appears in #84-SK.

W

window

we	away
with	reward
will	forward
was	want
work	sandwich

W Consonant: Regular Sound
Dictionary Phonetic Symbol: Thorndike /w/   Random /w/   Webster /w/

W is a consonant that usually makes the /w/ sound, as in "we". This sound uses the vocal chords and the schwa /ə/, but don't overemphasize the schwa. Say "WWW", not "WUH". W does not make this sound when it is part of the digraph WH, as in "white" which is taught in #41.

W is also found in #54-OW, #63-AW, #66-OW, #85-SW, #94-TW, and #97-WR.

J j

jar

jar	object
jump	enjoy
June	subject
jaw	major
July	banjo

J Consonant: Regular Sound
Dictionary Phonetic Symbol: Thorndike /j/   Random /j/   Webster /j/

J is a consonant that usually makes the /j/ sound, as in "just". This sound uses the vocal chords and the schwa /∂/, but don't overemphasize the schwa.

The letter G sometimes makes the /j/ sound (#44).

X   **X**

box

fox	fix
ax	relax
six	next
tax	extra
ox	excuse

X Consonant: Regular KS Sound
Dictionary Phonetic Symbol: Thorndike /ks/   Random /ks/   Webster /ks/

The letter X does not have a sound of its own. X usually sounds like /ks/, as in "box". This sound can be made without using the vocal cords or the schwa /ə/ sound at the end.

X is usually found only at the end of a word or syllable.

Q

q

queen

quart	**square**
quite	**equal**
quail	**squirrel**
quick	**frequent**
quit	**require**

Q Consonant: Regular KW Sound
Dictionary Phonetic Symbol: Thorndike /kw/ Random /kw/ Webster /kw/

Q is a consonant of relatively low frequency. It always appears with a U and the combination QU makes the /kw/ sound, as in "queen". This sound uses the vocal chords and the schwa /ə/, but don't overemphasize the schwa.

z

z

zebra

zero	puzzle
zoo	dozen
lazy	freeze
size	quiz
crazy	prize

Z Consonant: Regular Sound

Dictionary Phonetic Symbol: Thorndike /z/ Random /z/ Webster /z/

Z is a consonant that usually makes the /z/ sound, as in "zoo". This sound always uses the vocal chords but should not be followed with a schwa /ə/ at the end. Say "ZZZ", not "ZUH".

The letter S sometimes makes the /z/ sound (#43).

Y
y

yarn

you	young
year	youth
yellow	yawn
yes	lawyer
yell	canyon

Y Consonant: Regular Y Sound
Dictionary Phonetic Symbol: Thorndike /y/ Random /y/ Webster /y/

When Y is at the beginning of a word it makes the /y/ sound, as in "yes". This sound uses the vocal chords and the schwa /ə/, but don't overemphasize the schwa. Say "YYY", not "YUH".

Other sounds of Y are: long E (#18), and long I (#45).

Y also occurs in #52-AY, and #68-OY.

TH

th

feather

the	mother
that	other
them	brother
they	smooth
this	father

TH Consonant Digraph: Voiced TH Sound
Dictionary Phonetic Symbol: Thorndike /TH/ Random /t͟h/ Webster /th/

TH is a consonant digraph which has two sounds, neither of which is a blend of T and H. This sound most frequently found in words commonly taught to beginning readers is the voiced TH, as seen in the word "the". Voiced means that the vocal cords are used is making the TH sound. It can be made without the schwa /ə/ sound at the end. The other sound of TH is taught in #38-TH (voiceless).

TH 3 th

three

thank	with
think	both
thing	fourth
third	ninth
thirty	worth

TH Consonant Digraph: Voiceless TH Sound
Dictionary Phonetic Symbol: Thorndike / th /   Random / th̪ /   Webster / th /

The voiceless TH, as in the word "thin", does not use the vocal cords. It can be made without the schwa /ə/ sound at the end.

The other sound of TH is taught in #37-TH (voiced).

CH

ch

chair

child	which
church	each
change	much
chance	such
cheer	teach

CH Consonant Digraph: CH Sound
Dictionary Phonetic Symbol: Thorndike /ch/   Random /ch/   Webster /ch/

The digraph CH makes the sound heard at the beginning of the word "child". It is not a blend of C and H, but is a unique sound. This sound is voiceless and can be made without the schwa /ə/ sound at the end.

SH

shoe

S

she	wish
shall	wash
show	fish
ship	push
short	cash

SH Consonant Digraph: SH Sound
Dictionary Phonetic Symbol: Thorndike / sh /   Random / s̱h /   Webster / sh /

The digraph SH makes the sound heard at the beginning of the word "she". It is not a blend of S and H, but is a unique sound. This sound is voiceless and can be made without the schwa /ə/ sound at the end.

WH   wh

wheel

when	white
what	while
which	why
white	wheat
where	awhile

WH Consonant Digraph: HW Blend Sound
Dictionary Phonetic Symbol: Thorndike / hw/   Random / hw/   Webster / hw/

The digraph WH makes the sound heard at the beginning of the word "when". It is not a traditional blend of W and H. It is a unique sound, usually called a consonant digraph, but sometimes referred to as the sound of H and W blended. This sound is voiceless and can be made without the schwa /ə/ sound at the end.

c

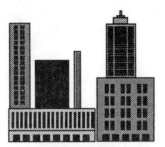

city

C

cent	**face**
circle	**since**
cycle	**pencil**
circus	**fancy**
center	**ice**

C Consonant: S Sound
Dictionary Phonetic Symbol: Thorndike /s/ Random /s/ Webster /s/

The second sound of C is the /s/ sound, as in "city". C frequently makes this sound before I, E, and Y. This sound can be made without using the vocal cords or the schwa /ə/ sound at the end. The first sound of C, /k/, as in "cat", was taught in #8.

C also appears in #39-CH, #83-SC, and #89-CL.

S ^ ^ S

eyes

is   music

as   cheese

was   wise

his   easy

please these

S Consonant: Z Sound

Dictionary Phonetic Symbol: Thorndike /z/ Random /z/ Webster /z/

The second sound of S is the /z/ sound, as in "has". This sound always uses the vocal chords but should not be followed with a schwa /ə/ at the end. S tends to make the /z/ sound when it is the final sound in a word or syllable if it is preceded by a voiced sound. S makes the /z/ sound in words much more frequently than Z itself does. Therefore, the most common way to spell the /z/ sound is with S. The letter S at the beginning of a word almost always makes the /s/ sound, as in "say". This was in #6-S (Regular). S also occurs in #40-SH, #81-ST, #82-SP, #83-SC, #84-SK, #85-SW, #86-SM, #87-SN, and #92-SL.

G   g

gem

gem	change
giant	large
germ	bridge
giant	age
generous	page

G Consonant: J Sound

Dictionary Phonetic Symbol: Thorndike /j/   Random /j/   Webster /j/

The second sound of G is the /j/ sound, as in "general". This /j/ sound of G is often made when G is followed by I, E, or Y. This sound uses the vocal chords and the schwa /ə/, but don't overemphasize the schwa.

The first sound of G, /g/, as in "gate", was taught in #28.

The sound of J was taught in 0#32.

Y   y

fly

my	**sky**
by	**myself**
why	**nylon**
buy	**July**
cry	**fry**

Y Vowel: Long I Sound

Dictionary Phonetic Symbol: Thorndike / ī /   Random / ī /   Webster / ī /

Y sometimes sounds like long I, as in "my". This is usually when it is at the end of a word that contains no other vowel or when Y appears in the middle of a word, as in "cyclone".

The long I sound is also made by the "Long Final E Rule" (#21), and the "Long Open Syllable Rule" (#25). Other sounds of Y are: Long E (#18), and consonant (#36). Y is also found in #52-AY, and #68-OY.

A      a

announcer

about	several
above	national
ago	senator
alone	final
again	casual

A Vowel: Schwa Sound
Dictionary Phonetic Symbol: Thorndike /ə/   Random /ə/   Webster /ə/

The schwa sound is the unaccented vowel sound like A in "ago". It is the same sound whether it is made by A in "ago", E is "enough", of O in "of". Some dictionaries (i.e. Webster) say that the schwa sound and the short U sound are the same. The schwa sound has a fairly high frequency, and is important for anyone using phonics.

Other sounds of A are: short (#15), "Long Final E Rule" (#20), and "Long Open Syllable Rule" (#23). A also appears in #49-EA, #53-OA, #56-AR, #57-AR (AIR), #62-AL, #63-AW, #64-AU, and #73-EA.

E e

11

eleven

happen	calendar
item	scientist
united	problem
silent	hundred
quiet	children

E Vowel: Schwa Sound

Dictionary Phonetic Symbol: Thorndike /ə/ **Random** /ə/ **Webster** /ə/

The schwa sound is the unaccented vowel sound like E in "enough". It is the same sound whether it is made by A in "ago", E in "enough", or O in "of". The schwa sound has a fairly high frequency, and is important for anyone using phonics. Other sounds of E are: short (#14). EA may make the short E sound (#73). Long E is made by the "Long Open Syllable Rule" (#24), by EE (#50), and sometimes by Y (#18), and EA (#49). Silent E is in #19. E also occurs in the #58-ER.

O   o

violin

original   some

other   mother

of   money

official   love

observe   second

O Vowel: Schwa Sound
Dictionary Phonetic Symbol: Thorndike /ə/ or /u/   Random /ə/ or /u/   Webster /ə/

The schwa sound is the unaccented vowel or short u like O in "come". It is the same sound whether it is made by A in "ago", E in "enough", or O in "of". The schwa sound has a fairly high frequency, and is important for anyone using phonics. The short sound of O is in #16. The long O sound is made by the "Long Final E Rule" (#22), the "Long Open Syllable Rule" (#26), by OA (#53), and sometimes by OW (#54). The broad O sound is in #61-O, #62-AL, #63-AW, and #64-AU. O also appears in #55-OR, #65-OR, #66-OW, #67-OI, #68-OY, #69-OO (long) and #70-OO (short).

EA

ear

ea

eat   sea

each   tea

east   dear

easy   read

eagle   hear

EA Vowel Digraph: Long E Sound
Dictionary Phonetic Symbol: Thorndike /ē/   Random /ē/   Webster /ē/

The long E sound is sometimes made by the two letter combination (digraph) EA, as in "eat". This is sometimes referred to as the double vowel rule, but there are so many double vowels which do not make a long vowel sound, that it is preferable to pick out only those which do, and call them long vowel digraphs.

The long E sound is also found in #50-EE, and in #24-E ("Long Open Syllable Rule"). Y (#18) sometimes makes the long E sound. The short E sound of EA is taught in #73.

EE

ee

deer

see
three
tree
sleep
green

keep
street
feet
wheel
feel

EE Vowel Digraph: Long E Sound

Dictionary Phonetic Symbol: Thorndike /ē/ Random /ē/ Webster /ē/

The long E sound is sometimes made by the two letter combination (digraph) EE, as in "three". This is sometimes referred to as the double vowel rule, but there are so many double vowels which do not make a long vowel sound, that it is preferable to pick out only those which do, and call them long vowel digraphs.

The long E sound is also made by #24-E ("Long Open Syllable Rule"), and is sometimes made by Y (#18) and EA (#49).

AI

ai

nail

rain	jail
train	mail
wait	pain
tail	sail
chain	strait

AI Vowel Digraph: Long A Sound

Dictionary Phonetic Symbol: Thorndike /ā/   Random /ā/   Webster /ā/

The long A sound is sometimes made by the two letter combination (digraph) AI, as in "rain". This is sometimes referred to as the double vowel rule, but there are so many double vowels which do not make a long vowel sound, that it is preferable to pick out only those which do, and call them long vowel digraphs.

Other long A sounds are #20-A ("Long Final E Rule"), #23-A (Long Open Syllable Rule"), and #52-AY.

AY

ay

hay

day	today
say	always
away	pay
play	mayor
may	gray

AY Vowel Digraph: Long A Sound

Dictionary Phonetic Symbol: Thorndike /ā/   Random /ā/   Webster /ā/

The long A sound is sometimes made by the two letter combination (digraph) AY, as in "day". This is sometimes referred to as the double vowel rule, but there are so many double vowels which do not make a long vowel sound, that it is preferable to pick out only those which do, and call them long vowel digraphs.

Other long A sounds are #20-A ("Long Final E Rule"), #23-A (Long Open Syllable Rule"), and #51-AI.

OA

oa

boat

coat   toast

soap   loan

road   goat

coast   goal

load   oak

OA Vowel Digraph: Long O Sound
Dictionary Phonetic Symbol: Thorndike /ō/   Random /ō/   Webster /ō/

The long O sound is sometimes made by the two letter combination (digraph) OA, as in "coat". This is sometimes referred to as the double vowel rule, but there are so many double vowels which do not make a long vowel sound, that it is preferable to pick out only those which do, and call them long vowel digraphs.

Other long O sounds are #22-O ("Long Final E Rule"), and #26-O (Long Open Syllable Rule"). OW (#54) sometimes makes the long O sound.

OW  ow

window

show	**yellow**
low	**follow**
slow	**grown**
snow	**throw**
row	**bowl**

OW Vowel Digraph: Long O Sound
Dictionary Phonetic Symbol: Thorndike /ō/ Random /ō/ Webster /ō/

The long O sound is sometimes made by the two letter combination (digraph) OW, as in "show". This is sometimes referred to as the double vowel rule, but there are so many double vowels which do not make a long vowel sound, that it is preferable to pick out only those which do, and call them long vowel digraphs. OW also has a second sound, as in "how", which will be taught in #66. Other long O sounds are #22-O ("Long Final E Rule"), #26-O (Long Open Syllable Rule"), and #53-OA.

OR

or

fork

or	horn
for	fork
more	forget
order	born
short	cord

OR Vowel Combination: Broad O + R Sound

Dictionary Phonetic Symbol: Thorndike /ôr/   Random /ôr/   Webster /ȯr/

The letter combination OR makes the sound heard in "or" or "for".
This is sometimes called the Broad O (plus R) sound.

AR

star

ar

are	car
arm	card
army	March
art	farm
artist	hard

AR Vowel Combination: Broad A + R Sound
Dictionary Phonetic Symbol: Thorndike /är/ Random /är/ Webster /är/

The letter combination AR makes two sounds. The first sound is like AR in "far".
    This A is sometimes called the Broad A sound.
The second sound of AR is taught in #57-AR (AIR).

AR

library

ar

care   January
rare   Mary

aware   vary

share   primary

spare   secretary

AR Vowel Combination: Short E + R Sound
Dictionary Phonetic Symbol: Thorndike /er/   Random /er/   Webster /er/

The letter combination AR makes two sounds. The AR as in "care" is the second sound and is really a combination of short E /e/, plus R /r/.

The other sound of AR was taught in #56-AR.

ER

er

letter

her	**better**
mother	**sister**
over	**under**
other	**after**
were	**water**

ER Vowel Combination: Short U + R Sound
Dictionary Phonetic Symbol: Thorndike /ur/   Random /ur/   Webster /ər/

The letter combination ER makes the sound made by the ER in "her". It is a combination of short U /u/, plus R /r/.

This is the same sound as that made by IR in "sir" (#59), and UR in "turn" (#60).

IR

ir

girl

girl	fir
first	sir
third	skirt
shirt	birth
dirt	thirsty

IR Vowel Combination: Short U + R Sound
Dictionary Phonetic Symbol: Thorndike /ur/   Random /ur/   Webster /∂r/

The letter combination IR makes the sound made by the IR in "girl". It is a combination of short U /u/, plus R /r/.

This is the same sound as that made by ER in "her" (#58), and UR in "turn" (#60).

UR

ur

church

turn

curb

burn

purse

fur

purple

hurry

hurt

curl

turkey

UR Vowel Combination: Short U + R Sound
Dictionary Phonetic Symbol: Thorndike /ur/   Random /ur/   Webster /ər/

The letter combination UR makes the sound made by the UR in "turn". It is a combination of short U /u/, plus R /r/.

This is the same sound as that made by ER in "her" (#58), and IR in "girl" (#59).

O   o

dog

off	soft
office	log
officer	long
often	along
on	cost

O Vowel: Broad: O Sound

Dictionary Phonetic Symbol: Thorndike /ô/   Random /ô/   Webster /ȯ/

The broad O sound, as in "off", is frequently made by the letter O. It is also often made by A in combination with L, U, or W. Examples are: #62-AL (as in "all"), #63-AW (as in "awful"), and #64-AU (as in "auto"). The short sound of O was taught in #16. The long O sound is in #22-O (Long Final E Rule), #26-O (Long Open Syllable Rule), and #53-OA. OW (#54) sometimes makes the long O sound. The schwa is in #48.

AL

al

ball

all	call
always	tall
also	talk
already	walk
almost	fall

AL Vowel Combination: Broad O + L Sound
Dictionary Phonetic Symbol: Thorndike /ôl/ Random /ôl/ Webster /ȯl/

The broad O sound is frequently made by A followed by L or LL as in "call."
It is also made by O as in "off" (#61), by AW as in "awful" (#63), and by AU as in "auto" (#64).

AW  aw

saw

awful	lawn
awkward	dawn
law	lawyer
jaw	straw
straw	drawn

AW Vowel Digraph: Broad O Sound
Dictionary Phonetic Symbol: Thorndike /ô/ Random /ô/ Webster /ȯ/

The broad O sound is frequently made by AW, as in "awful".

It is also made by O, as in "off" (#61), by AL as in "all" (#62), and by AU, as in "auto" (#64).

AU

auto

au

August **because**

author **caught**

audio **haul**

haunt **laundry**

autumn **fault**

AU Vowel Digraph: Broad O Sound
Dictionary Phonetic Symbol: Thorndike /ô/ Random /ô/ Webster /ȯ/

The broad O sound is frequently made by AU, as in "auto".
It is also made by O, as in "off" (#61), by AL as in "all" (#62), and by AW, as in "awful" (#63).

OU

ou

house

out	about
our	round
ounce	around
hour	scout
sound	amount

OU Vowel Digraph: OU Diphthong Sound
Dictionary Phonetic Symbol: Thorndike /ou/   Random /ou/   Webster /aů/

The diphthong sound OU is usually made by the letters OU, as in "out".
The diphthong sound of /ou/ may also be made by OW (#66).

OW

owl

OW

how	down
now	town
cow	brown
plow	flower
allow	crowd

OW Vowel Digraph: OW Diphthong Sound

Dictionary Phonetic Symbol: Thorndike /ou/   Random /ou/   Webster /aủ/

The diphthong sound /ou/, as in "out", is also made by OW as in "cow".

You will recall that this is the second sound for OW. The primary sound of OW as in "know", has already been taught in #54.

The diphthong sound /ou/ was also taught in #65-OU.

oi

oil

join	noise
point	boil
voice	spoil
coin	avoid
choice	poison

OI Vowel Digraph: OI Diphthong Sound
Dictionary Phonetic Symbol: Thorndike /oi/ Random /oi/ Webster /ȯi/

The diphthong sound /oi/ is usually made by the letters OI, as in "oil", but it is also made by OY, as in "boy" (#68).

Generally, the OI is used to make the sound in the middle of a syllable and OY is used when the same sound is desired at the end of a word or syllable ("joy" – "rejoice").

OY

boy

oy

toy	royal
joy	voyage
enjoy	coy
employ	loyal
destroy	cowboy

OY Vowel Digraph: OI Diphthong Sound
Dictionary Phonetic Symbol: Thorndike /oi/ Random /oi/ Webster /òi/

The diphthong sound /oi/ is usually made by the letters OI, as in "oil" (#67), but it is also made by OY, as in "boy".

Generally, the OI is used to make the sound in the middle of a syllable and OY is used when the same sound is desired at the end of a word or syllable ("joy" – "rejoice").

oo   oo

moon

too	shoot
soon	pool
school	smooth
room	tooth
food	zoo

OO Vowel Digraph: Long OO Sound
Dictionary Phonetic Symbol: Thorndike /ü/   Random /o͞o/   Webster /ü/

The letter combination OO has two sounds, as seen in the words "moon" and "book". The so-called long sound, or 2-dot U sound, as in "moon", is the most common.

This sound is also made by U, as in "ruler" (#71).

The other sound of OO, as in "book", is taught in #70.

OO
oo

book

look	stood
good	shook
took	goodby
wood	brook
foot	wool

OO Vowel Digraph: Short OO Sound
Dictionary Phonetic Symbol: Thorndike /u̇/ Random /o͝o/ Webster /u̇/

The second sound of the letter combination OO is the so-called Short OO or 1-dot U sound, as in the word "look".

This sound is also made by U, as in "put" (#72).

The other sound of OO, as in "moon", was taught in #69.

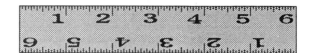

U   u

ruler

June	crude
July	flute
truth	prune
junior	cruel
rule	Ruth

U Vowel: Long OO Sound
Dictionary Phonetic Symbol: Thorndike / ü /   Random / o͞o /   Webster / ü /

The sound of U, as in "rule", is sometimes called the Long OO or 2-dot U sound, and is the same sound made by "moon" (#69). This sound is similar to the long sound of U, as in "use (#27), but most dictionaries and linguists classify it as a different sound. Another sound of U was taught in #17 (U–short). The sound of U, sometimes called the short OO sound, is taught in #72.

U

u

bull

bullet	bush
full	bushel
pull	sugar
push	jury
put	butcher

U Vowel: Short OO Sound
Dictionary Phonetic Symbol: Thorndike /ủ/   Random /o͝o/   Webster /u̇/

The sound of U, as in "put", is sometimes called the Short OO or 1-dot U sound, and is the same sound made by OO in "look".

Other sounds of U are: short (#17), the "Long Open Syllable Rule" (#27), and the Long OO (#71).

EA

ea

bread

head	dead
heavy	breath
ready	deaf
thread	ahead
steady	bear

EA Vowel Digraph: Short E Sound
Dictionary Phonetic Symbol: Thorndike /e/   Random /e/   Webster /e/

The Short E sound is sometimes made by the letter combination EA, as in "head".
The Short E sound is also made by E (#14).
The Long E /e/ sound of EA, as in "ear", was taught in #49.

PR

pr

propeller

pretty	president
price	prince
press	program
prize	surprise
print	April

TR

tr

truck

track	try
tractor	trick
truck	extra
trade	electric
truly	central

GR

gr

grapes

grade	gray
great	grand
grow	angry
grew	hungry
grass	congress

BR

br

broom

bread	brown
break	bring
brick	breath
broad	library
brother	umbrella

CR

cr

crab

cry	crew
crack	crazy
crowd	across
crash	secret
cream	increase

DR

dr

drum

dry	dress
draw	dream
drug	address
drove	hundred
drop	children

FR

fr

frog

free	fry
from	frost
front	frank
friend	freshman
Friday	afraid

ST

st

stamp

stop	store
step	story
stay	street
state	instead
still	destroy

SP

sp

spoon

sports	special
space	speed
speak	spell
spring	inspect
spread	respect

SC

sc

scale

scale	scar
school	scatter
screen	scholar
scratch	describe
scarf	telescope

SK

sk

skate

sky	skip
skin	skull
skill	skeleton
skate	skid
skirt	sketch

SW

sw

switch

swim	sweep
swell	swing
swept	swung
sweat	swam
sweater	swallow

SM

sm

smoke

smile	smother
smooth	smash
smell	smear
small	smith
smart	smolder

SN

sn

snake

snow	snug
snowball	snuggle
snare	snip
sneeze	snarl
snore	snap

PL

pl

plate

play   plus
plant   place
plain   multiply
please   supply
plow   employ

CL

cl

clock

clean   clear
cloth   class
clay   enclose
claim   include
club   cyclone

BL

bl

block

black	blame
blue	bloom
bleed	blossom
blood	blond
blind	oblige

FL

fl

flag

flower	float
flat	floor
flight	flavor
flew	flood
fly	flute

SL

sl

sled

slow	slap
sleep	slave
slept	slide
slip	sleeve
slid	asleep

GL

gl

glass

glad	glisten
globe	gloom
glow	glue
glory	glum
glove	glamour

TW

tw

twins

twelve	twine
twenty	tweed
twice	twinkle
twig	twilight
twirl	between

PH

ph

phone

photo	alphabet
phonics	orphan
phrase	nephew
physical	trophy
physician	sulphur

KN  **kn**

knife

knee	knelt
knew	knit
know	knock
knowledge	knight
knot	knuckle

WR  **wr**

wrench

write	wrap
writing	wrestle
written	wrist
wrote	wreath
wrong	wring

NG

ng

king

sing	long
bring	song
thing	hang
going	gang
swing	young

G̷H̷

g̷h̷

eight

high	fought
light	bought
right	daughter
sight	caught
tight	taught

PHONICS SURVEY DIRECTIONS

Phonics is an important and useful skill associated with reading. Poor ability in phonics does not always mean poor reading ability, but if reading ability is poor, it can often be aided by having part of the instruction include phonics lessons.

How to Test. Using the survey test sheet on the next page, ask the student to read the nonsense words aloud. Tell him that these are not real words. If he makes an error, allow him a second chance (but not a third).

How to Score. Using a copy of the survey, mark each letter read incorrectly. At the right-hand margin, note if the student was "Perfect", "Knew Some", or "Knew None" for each of the following skills: Consonants, Short Vowels, Long Vowels, Difficult Vowels. This information will be very useful in selection material for phonics instruction.

Repeated Use. This survey may be repeated at a later date after more phonics instruction, or the teacher can make up nonsense words for testing and instruction.

PHONICS SURVEY
Based on the Phonics Charts by Edward Fry

Name _____

Examiner _____ Date _____

Student reads nonsense words using phonics rules. Teacher checks box to right of line according to amount known.

	Perfect	Knew Some	Knew None

Easy Consonants and Short Vowels
Charts 1 – 17

			Perfect	Knew Some	Knew None
TIF	**NEL**	**ROM**	❑	❑	❑
DUP	**CAV**	**SEB**	❑	❑	❑

Harder Consonants and Long Vowels (Final E & Long Open Syllable Rule)
Charts 18 – 36

					Perfect	Knew Some	Knew None
KO	**HOAB**	**WAJE**	**KE**	**YATE**	❑	❑	❑
ZEEX	**QUIDE**	**YAIG**	**ZAY**	**SUDE**	❑	❑	❑

Consonant Digraphs and Vowel Digraphs
Charts 37 – 73

				Perfect	Knew Some	Knew None
WHAW	**THOIM**	**PHER**	**KOYCH**	❑	❑	❑
OUSH	**CHAU**	**EANG**	**HOON**	❑	❑	❑

CONSONANT SOUNDS

Single Consonants

b	h	n	v
c	j	p	w
d	k	r	y
f	l	s	z
g	m	t	

Important Exceptions

qu = / kw / blend as in "quick"
(the letter "q" is never used without "u")
ph = / f / sound as in "phone"
c = / s / before i, e, or y, as in "city"
c = / k / before a, o, or u, as in "cat"
g = / j / before i, e, or y, as in "gem"
g = / g / before a, o, or u, as in "good"
x = / ks / blend as in "fox"
s = / z / sound at the end of some words as in "is"
ng = / ng / unique phoneme, as in "sing"
ck = / k / often at end of word as in "back"

Consonant Digraphs

ch as in "church"
sh as in "shoe"
th (voiced) as in "thin"
th (voiceless) as in "this"
wh (hw blend) as in "which"

Rare Exceptions

ch = / k / as in "character"
ch = / sh / as in "chef"
ti = / sh / as in "attention"
s = / sh / as in "sure"
x = / gz / as in "exact"
s = / zh / as in "measure"
si = / zh / as in "vision"

Silent Consonants

gn = / n / as in gnat"
kn = / n /as in "knife"
wr = / r / as in "write"
gh = / - / as in "right"
mb = / m / as in "lamb"
lf = / f / as in "calf"
lk = / k / as in "walk"
tle = / l / as in "castle"

Beginning Consonant Blends

(r family)	(l family)	(s letter)	(s family)	(no family)
br	bl	sc	scr	dw
cr	cl	sk	squ	tw
dr	fl	sm	str	thr
fr	gl	sn	spr	
gr	pl	sp	spl	
pr	sl	st	shr	
tr		sw	sch	
wr				

Final Consonant Blends

Note: These are usually best learned as part of rhymes.

ct - act	mp - jump	nt - ant	rk - dark
ft - lift	nc(e) - since	pt - kept	rt - art
ld - old	nd - and	rd - hard	st - least
lt - salt	nk - ink		sk - risk

VOWEL SOUNDS

Short Vowels

a - at　　　/ă/
e - end　　/ĕ/
i - is　　　/ĭ/
o - hot　　/ŏ/
u - up　　　/ŭ/

Long Vowel
Digraphs

ai - aid　　/ā/
ay - say　　/ā/
ea - eat　　/ē/
ee - see　　/ē/
oa - oat　　/ō/
ow - own　　/ō/

Dipthongs

oi - oil　　/oi/
oy - boy　　/oi/
ou - out　　/ou/
ow - how　　/ou/

Long Vowels
Open Syllable Rule

a - baby　　/ā/
e - we　　　/ē/
i - idea　　/ī/
o - so　　　/ō/

Schwa

a - ago　　/ə/
e - happen　/ə/
o - other　/ə/

Vowel Y

y - try, cycle　/ī/
y - funny　　　/ē/

Double O

oo - soon　/ōō/
oo - good　/ŏŏ/
u - truth　/ōō/
u - put　　/ŏŏ/

Long Vowels
Final E Rule

a - make　　/ā/
e - here　　/ē/
i - five　　/ī/
o - home　　/ō/
u - use　　　/ū/ or /yōō/

Vowel Plus R

er - her　　/ər/
ir - sir　　/ər/
ur - fur　　/ər/
ar - far　　/är/
ar - vary　/ār/
or - for　　/ôr/

Broad O

o - long　　/ô/
a (l) - also　/ô/
a (w) - saw　/ô/
a (u) - auto　/ô/

Vowel Exceptions

ea - bread　/ĕ/ or /ē/ seat　　"ea" makes both a long and a short E sound.

e (silent) - come, make　　E at the end of a word is usually silent and sometimes makes the preceding vowel long.

y - yes　　/y/　　y is a consonant at the beginning of a word. (yes)
　　　　　　　　　y is long I in a one syllable word or middle. (cycle) (by)
　　　　　　　　　y is long E at the end of a polysyllable word. (funny)

le - candle　/əl/　　final LE makes a schwa plus L sound.
al - pedal　/əl/　　final AL makes a schwa plus L sound also.
ul - awful　/əl/　　final UL makes a schwa plus L sound also.